THE

FIRST-TIME
MANAGER

LEADING THROUGH

CRISIS

THE

FIRST-TIME
MANAGER

LEADING THROUGH
CRISIS

PAUL FALCONE

HarperCollins
LEADERSHIP

An Imprint of HarperCollins

Published by HarperCollins Leadership, an imprint of HarperCollins Focus LLC.

Any internet addresses, phone numbers, or company or product information printed in this book are offered as a resource and are not intended in any way to be or to imply an endorsement by HarperCollins Leadership, nor does HarperCollins Leadership vouch for the existence, content, or services of these sites, phone numbers, companies, or products beyond the life of this book.

ISBN 978-1-4002-4231-3 (eBook)
ISBN 978-1-4002-4230-6 (TP)

Library of Congress Control Number: 2023931384

Printed in the United States of America
23 24 25 26 27 LBC 5 4 3 2 1

CONTENTS

PART TWO

Departmental/Team Crises 91

PERMISSIONS

The following materials were taken from articles written by Paul Falcone:

Question 35: From "How to Handle Overtime, Meal Break and Other Wage and Hour Crises." SHRM.org, February 15, 2023. Copyright ©2023 by the Society for Human Resource Management. Used by permission of the publisher. All rights reserved.

Question 37: From "An Ethical Filter for Addressing Questionable Situations in the Workplace." SHRM.org, February 6, 2023. Copyright ©2023 by the Society for Human Resource Management. Used by permission of the publisher. All rights reserved.

Question 39: From "Creating and Sustaining High-Performing Teams in a Remote Work Environment." SHRM.org, November 21, 2022. Copyright ©2022 by the Society for Human Resource Management. Used by permission of the publisher. All rights reserved.

INTRODUCTION
Workplace Crisis Management, Conflict Resolution, and Navigating Extreme Change

When *The First-Time Manager* was originally published in 1981, it immediately began its rise to the rank of bestsellers because it taught more than knowledge and how-tos—it actually taught wisdom, which is knowledge applied. It was in that spirit of timeless sharing that the book has continued to be reprinted for decades, now on its seventh updated edition, bringing its spirit of uniqueness and commonsense applications to new generations of managers the world over.

Most people would agree, however, that the world has changed significantly from those earlier days of the book's origin. Management and leadership are consumed with unforeseen challenges that seem to come at increasingly alarming frequency, with more dire consequences. Changes in technology and globalization are exponential in nature, and today in the new millennium, we face evolutionary change at revolutionary speed. Crises seem to abound all around us, and business cycles are shortening to the degree that we often experience whiplash from the extremes of, for example, severe talent shortages followed quickly by layoffs because of falling demand and excessive head count, only to be met with the challenges of new talent shortages in specialty areas that didn't even exist several years prior.

In short, it's time to dedicate a special edition of *The First-Time Manager* series to dealing with the difficult situations managers face in the workplace. As you'll see by quickly glancing at the table of contents, conflict, crises, and disruption abound at the individual, team, and company levels. Changes in the stock market, world economic conditions, labor markets, and technology are making "business as usual" a thing of the past for most organizations. Not surprisingly, a 2022 IBM study of more than fifteen hundred executives showed that managing disruption ranked among CEOs' top concerns. In addition, demographics are destiny, and the number of Gen Y millennials and Gen Z zoomers are growing exponentially in the workplace, systemically replacing the Traditionalist Generation, baby boomers, and Gen Xers and bringing with them new ideas of an organization's role in terms of corporate social responsibility, environmentalism, diversity of people, voices, and ideas, and work-life-family balance, control, and equilibrium. For the first time, we're experiencing five generations in the workplace simultaneously. Unions are aggressively attempting to make a comeback, women-in-leadership initiatives are a core focus of many organizations' strategic workforce planning efforts, and DEI&B (diversity, equity, inclusion, and belonging) initiatives are meeting the challenges of labor force scarcity while ensuring that everyone has a voice as well as a seat at the proverbial table.

WHERE THIS BOOK COMES IN

Leadership in the trenches is not something commonly taught in business schools or even in the corporate classroom. Yes, there are a myriad of books that tell you *what* to do but very few that show you *how* to do things. That's where *The First-Time Manager: Leading Through Crisis* steps in to fill the void. You'll benefit most from learning how to hire effectively, manage and motivate your team, act ethically and morally, and communicate, lead, and build teams successfully. But as is so often the case, the rubber meets the road at the point of conflict, confrontation, and crisis. Those are the pain points that new managers need to overcome early on in their careers to avoid the land mines and pitfalls that may await them.

Unfortunately, that's typically where the literature falls short. Managers are left to figure this all out on their own, leaving hard-won experience to be their greatest teacher. If they're wise, however, they'll look to get ahead of the curve by drawing on the wisdom of those who have gone before them. Initially, they'll partner with their bosses and with their HR team to make sure they're not going it alone. Still, the traps can be subtle yet have devastating consequences, so more is needed to educate you and create a greater sense of wisdom and confidence. For example, if we run a simple Google search of *crisis* near the word *workplace*, we'll find an exceptional number of entries:

Crisis dynamics	Crisis escalation
Exacerbating a crisis	Crisis interventions
Isolated versus multiple crises	Crisis response plan
Recurring crises	Crisis management model
Creeping crises, slow-burn crises, and sudden crises	Natural crises, technological crises, confrontation crises, crises of malevolence, crises of organizational misdeeds, crises due to workplace violence
Crisis communications	Crisis avoidance
The crisis management cycle	Crisis preparedness, response, and recovery
Crisis aversion and mitigation	Returning to precrisis levels

Clearly, the list goes on. But wait, there's more. . . . A lot more. Crises of all kinds can come out of nowhere and throw you into a reactive phase. Individual, team, and company crises can be matched and eclipsed by societal crises, including pandemics, recessions, and even war. Unless you understand how to "keep your head," partner with your boss and/or HR department, and exercise the appropriate amount of wisdom, discretion, and judgment, things can go off the rails quickly. As a first-time manager, you play a vital role in helping staff members manage their crises, while minimizing liability to your organization and protecting yourself from personal damages. (Yes, managers can be sued personally for acting outside the course and scope of their responsibilities or otherwise engaging in what are known as *managerial bad acts*, so this book will help protect you and your organization simultaneously.)

In short, *The First-Time Manager: Leading Through Crisis* will teach you how to think of crises as developing events that should be carefully addressed with specific approaches. We'll address approaches for how to get ahead of problems proactively and even prevent them when possible. You'll learn how to effectively intervene when staff members are experiencing a crisis. You'll gain an appreciation for support networks and services that can help you and your team members navigate crises and stress-filled events in real time. Most important, you'll build critical muscle and confidence in an area that finds most managers lacking.

Crises come in all shapes and sizes, large and small, long term and immediate, personal and global. Extreme and sudden change and disruption are the new normal. And you shouldn't have to go it alone. Yes, your management team is there for you but only if you know how to access and leverage them as a true resource. Let *The First-Time Manager: Leading Through Crisis* serve as a guiding hand and a handy guide to raise your awareness about critical issues that may come your way on a moment's notice. Look to this resource as a specialty book to help you navigate some of the most challenging situations that can come your way as a manager—new or seasoned. It will help fine-tune your understanding of the workplace, employment law, and your role as a coach and mentor. It will assist in insulating your organization from unwanted liability in the litigation arena. And most important, it will help raise your awareness of when you need to escalate, how you need to respond, and what your next logical steps should be when faced with a crisis unlike anything you've ever seen before.

We've got your back. You don't have to do this alone. And you can invest in yourself and build critical muscle around such an important and critical skill that builds your confidence and makes you much more effective in your role and more valuable to your company—right from your first formal leadership role. The goal of this book is to provide you with information and resources on how to identify, prevent, and safely intervene during crises of all kinds. Even more important, it will teach you how to think things through, react constructively, and demonstrate wisdom and calmness in even the most challenging and intense workplace situations. It will help you serve as a role model for others and become a stronger developer of people and talent. And it will allow you to stand out as a rarity among your peers because top performance, wisdom, and judgment are needed most when there are no guardrails or precedent to follow. Just like leadership and emotional intelligence can be increased and strengthened over time, so can crisis management and your ability to lead effectively through extreme adversity. I'm happy to accompany you down this path. And I hope that some of the lessons you glean from this book remain with you for the rest of your career.

Paul Falcone
Los Angeles, 2023

PART ONE

INDIVIDUAL CRISES

1

TOUGH CONVERSATIONS SURROUNDING PERFORMANCE AND CONDUCT CHALLENGES

LET'S JUMP IN FEET FIRST. Many organizations suffer from time to time with "rebel" top producers—sales executives, senior leaders, and even family members of the owner who act with impunity, assuming they can't do wrong or be held accountable for their actions. Their logic typically follows a path like this: "I'm consistently the number-one producer in this branch, so they can't touch me." It likewise might sound like this: "I've been here for thirty years, and I have neckties older than many of these employees— they simply have to accommodate my personality and who I am." You might even hear, "My dad is the chief operations officer, so anyone who has a problem with me will likely need to go through him" (or something similar). All these scenarios typically land in HR's lap at some point, leaving HR with conflicts of interest, entitlement mentalities, and bullying behaviors to sort out.

How do you get in front of performers who may indeed function as the "rainmakers" of your organization, feel entitled to their toxic behaviors, or otherwise act with impunity under some sort of protective "blanket"—whether real or perceived—to get them back on track? The key lies in holding them accountable in a special way that appeals to their career interests and doesn't leave you in a "bad guy" position with your neck sticking out. Taking the example of a top sales producer, for instance, we can build a three-part strategy for addressing the problematic conduct in a way that serves the individual's as well as the organization's interests as follows.

PERFORMANCE-CONDUCT CIRCLE

Top sales producers that demonstrate toxic behaviors may sometimes hold a sales branch hostage by "eating their young," ensuring turnover of new hires, and basically allowing branch sales not to exceed their monthly production results. "Rebel sales producers," as they're known, often believe that they cannot be touched because without them, the branch sales numbers would implode. They're often correct: if they bring in 80 percent of the branch's revenue month after month, there's a chance that the branch will close without them. But if the organization truly wants to grow sales and treat its people well, it will have to address the rebel producer's behavior and conduct head-on. Opening with a simple tool that you could explain on the back of a napkin is a great place to start:

> David, I wanted to meet with you one-on-one to discuss your career progression and professional development. I have some thoughts I'll want to share with you so you can consider them, and I believe they could help tremendously in terms of your longer-term career goals. There are certain issues that may have missed your awareness but that could benefit you and the branch considerably. Sound like a good idea? [*Yes.*]

At that point, you can draw a circle on a piece of paper or on the back of a napkin and place a line through the middle of it, cutting the circle in half. Write the word *Performance* in the top half of the circle and *Conduct* (or *Behavior*) in the bottom half of the circle. Explain to the employee that he, like everyone else, is responsible for both halves. Your conversation might sound like this:

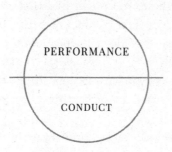

David, all of us—myself included—are responsible for both our performance as well as our behavior. It's two halves of the same whole. In the top half of the circle, you're knocking it out of the park. You consistently pull in 80+ percent of our branch's revenue, and you're one of the top producers in our region, which is very impressive and something I know you want to continue excelling at. But you're likewise responsible for the bottom half of the circle—your conduct or your behavior. That includes creating a friendly and inclusive work environment where others seek out your help and advice and where you serve as a role model leader. That's where you're not meeting expectations in my opinion at this point. Failing half a circle means the whole circle isn't meeting overall expectations. How do you feel you're performing behavior-wise in the bottom half of that circle right now?

Some interesting dialogue may ensue at this point, so simply listen to the individual's self-assessment and level of personal awareness.

PERCEPTION MANAGEMENT

In situations like these, you might find that employees asked to self-assess in terms of their conduct or behavior often go on the offensive rather than play defense, meaning they feel the need to self-justify their behaviors or make excuses based on others' shortcomings. That's where you have an opportunity to step in and help them raise their self-awareness like this:

> David, I hear what you're saying, but allow me to share what things look like from my vantage point from time to time. I sometimes see you appearing to diminish others, making remarks about their lack of productivity, or their leaving you all the "heavy lifting" to make the branch's monthly sales numbers. Can you recall ever making comments along those lines?" [*Yes, but . . .*]
>
> Okay, there's no need to justify anything. I'm just trying to raise your awareness. But here's the catch: I have to hold you accountable for your own perception management just like I do my own and every other member of the branch. That's where there may be a disconnect: what you're telling me doesn't jibe with the perception you're creating in others' eyes. How do you feel you might strengthen that perception relative to your level of leadership, communication style, and willingness to serve as a mentor and coach to foster others' performance and achievement levels?"

Note the use of words and phrases like "sometimes" or "from time to time." You're much better off using that kind of limited language than employing "extreme" adverbs like *always* and *never*, which often are exaggerated and frustrate the recipient of your message and trigger self-defense mechanisms. In any event, you can expect the typical "It's not my job to motivate others" defense response at this point in the conversation.

LONGER-TERM CAREER APPEAL

You then have an opportunity to move into the close of your argument:

> I don't quite see it that way. If you can become as strong in the bottom half of the circle (conduct) as you are in the top half (performance), then the sky's your limit. Yes, you're the top producer in the branch, but that may not be your ultimate goal. For example, I often wonder how I can help you advance to a branch manager role. What about regional or even general manager responsibilities—when working with people with your level of talent, I often ask myself how I can help top producers excel to reach those levels of career progression. You certainly can get there based on your sales numbers, but that's not going to be enough: you also have to be able to build strong teams, turn around flagging units, and build a great reputation as a leader and communicator.
>
> In short, what got you here won't get you there. As you progress throughout your career, you can succeed best and quickest by helping others to succeed. Your success is measured *through* people, not *despite* them. Your skills in the areas of leadership, communication, and team building prepare you to take on greater responsibilities with bigger teams in larger leagues.
>
> I'd like to be the one to get you there. I want to be the career mentor and coach to make it safe for you to learn how to do this the right way, right here and right now, while I'm here to have your back. I'd like to be your sponsor and mentor, but it's going to take a significant turnaround in terms of how you've been approaching others. Are you up for the challenge? Are you ready to reinvent yourself? I'd like you to give that some thought and come back to me over the next week so we can discuss this further.

Appealing to a top producer's career interests and personal growth strategy is likely to yield the greatest results, because once the recipient of your message can funnel your communication through his or her personal interests, the acceptance of your message skyrockets. Likewise, you'll have made an excellent record in terms of inviting the employee to turn around problematic and toxic behavior: if you move later to progressive disciplinary action, you can document the date and time of this meeting as your initial attempt at notifying the individual of the problematic conduct. And voilà—a win-win situation where the employee is encouraged to turn around toxic behavior for personal benefit while minimizing liability to your organization, potentially via progressive discipline. Maximize the chances of engagement and turnaround by convincing employees that you're the right coach at the right time in their career to help them scale their achievements according to their own self-interests.

2

WHY CAN'T I
FIRE ANYONE "AT WILL"?
When HR Appears to Be a Roadblock

"I HONESTLY DON'T GET IT. We make new hires sign all this documentation acknowledging that they're employed at will and can be terminated at any time, with or without cause or notice. But I'm never allowed to terminate anyone 'at will.' HR makes me jump through hoops by issuing progressive discipline first. What gives: is the person employed at will or not? And how come HR won't fix my crisis by allowing me to terminate a substandard performer, someone with a terrible attitude, or someone who can't get to work on time?" All valid questions and points, but there's a deeper understanding that you may be missing if you make this argument about being able to "terminate at whim" just because someone is employed "at will."

If HR professionals had a nickel for every time they were blindsided by a manager who wanted an employee fired because of their "at-will status," HR would be the best-compensated discipline in corporate America. Unfortunately, managers often avoid HR at all costs and come to visit the folks in "Personnel" only when a crisis is unfolding. Of course, the crisis could likely have been avoided in the first place had the manager partnered with HR earlier in the process. As you might imagine, there's a lot that goes into terminating employees for cause, and when your HR department is blindsided by such "requests in a vacuum," it can place HR at odds with line management. Ideally, HR should be in a situation to aid frontline operational managers (that is, their internal clients) when substandard job performers get in the way of maximizing a department's productivity.

But alas, that's only management theory in many cases. More often than not, HR has to attempt to "build a paper case" to justify the termination during a crisis, and there's little if any documentation on file to justify the separation of employment. Whose fault is that? You guessed it—the frontline operational manager. So here's what you need to know to avoid the "crisis" of not being able to terminate at whim using what's known as the "employment-at-will affirmative defense." Your HR department will love you if you understand how this works!

First, employees can leave the company any time they want, with or without cause or notice. Why can't employers do the same? The short answer is because companies are considered "corporate citizens," and because of their power, they shouldn't appear to terminate workers without at least giving them a fighting chance to save their jobs. This is also underscored in employment law history. When the nation was founded in the eighteenth century, American colonists borrowed from British law what is known as the job as property doctrine. It basically posited that the right to work is so fundamental to US citizens that it shouldn't be arbitrarily taken away without due process under the law (as later codified under the Fourteenth Amendment).

The job as property doctrine remained the law of the land until the Great Depression in the 1930s. Congress enacted a series of laws in light of the Great Depression in an attempt—quite literally—to save capitalism. Employment at will became the law of the land. The "property right" that workers historically possessed was transferred to companies, who could now terminate at whim to remain afloat. Most of us have seen movies of what this mayhem looked like at the time: long lines of workers standing outside of factories waiting for a turn to be employed. If someone was killed, maimed, or injured, out they went and a new worker from the line was brought in to pick up with production. It was brutal, no doubt, but allowed companies to continue operations without having to wait to "provide due process" to workers. The problem was that World War II broke out soon thereafter, and no one bothered to eliminate employment at will. It still remains in effect today, causing all sorts of confusion out there.

If the job as property doctrine in the eighteenth century is step 1, and the employment-at-will theory of the 1930s is step 2, then we have to look to a California court in 1980 for the third and final step that leads to today's current status of employment and termination rights for employers and workers (at least until something new comes along in the future). In Tameny v. Atlantic Richfield Co. (June 2, 1980), the California Supreme Court ruled that there can be exceptions to employment at will. Gordon Tameny was a fifteen-year retail sales representative for Arco whose responsibilities included the management of relations between Arco and the various independent service station dealers (franchisees) in his assigned territory of Bakersfield, California.

Tameny attended a meeting with independent service station owners and felt pressured by the parent company to set the price of retail gasoline "for the purpose of reducing, controlling, stabilizing, fixing, and pegging the retail gasoline prices of Arco service station franchisees" (which is as an unlawful antitrust violation and falls under "price fixing"). The lawsuit asserted that Arco pressured Tameny to "threaten [and] cajole . . . the so-called 'independent' service station dealers in [his] territory to cut their gasoline prices to a point at or below a designated level specified by Arco." When Tameny refused to yield to his employer's pressure to engage in such tactics, his supervisor told him that his discharge was imminent, and soon thereafter he was fired, effective March 25, 1975.

The employer, Arco Oil, argued that Tameny was employed at will and was terminated for unsatisfactory performance and incompetence and shouldn't be permitted to bring suit against the company for wrongful discharge, among other things. The California Supreme Court saw this as retaliation for Tameny's good acts. Justice Rose Bird famously said, "We won't countenance firing a long-term employee, even if at will, for reasons that violate public policy." As such, the public policy exception was born. Tort law became part of the legal landscape from that point forward. Other conditions where employment at will could no longer serve as a "blanket" property right to terminate workers included:

1. on account of the employee's age, race, sex, sexual orientation, gender, or other protected class,
2. in retaliation for an employee exercising certain statutory rights, including filing a worker's compensation claim, engaging in whistleblowing activities, opposing discrimination, or complaining about illegal or perceived illegal activity, or
3. in retaliation for an employee taking a protected leave of absence, including medical or family leave.

Moreover, workers who are employed pursuant to an express employment contract for a set term that includes non–at will termination events or who are employed pursuant to implied contracts also may not be able to be terminated at the will of the employer. Rather, the employer would have to have good cause or reason to terminate the worker or potentially face claims for breach of contract and/or breach of the implied covenant of good faith and fair dealing.

In addition to the many exceptions to the at-will doctrine, the mechanics behind how lawsuits work play a significant role. An employee suing an employer for discrimination or retaliation must demonstrate that the employer took an adverse employment action against them and that the employee is in a protected class or they engaged in a protected activity. Once the employee has satisfied their initial burden, the burden shifts to the employer to justify its reason for taking the adverse employment action.

An employer can do this by demonstrating that its adverse employment action was made for a legitimate nondiscriminatory or nonretaliatory reason, including that the employer exercised its rights to terminate the employee at will. Assuming the employer meets its burden, the employee must then establish that the employer's reasoning was "pretextual" or a cover-up for the real discriminatory and/or retaliatory reason. If the employer relies on only the at-will doctrine as its defense, and does not put forward any legitimate reason for the termination (including documentation supporting it), the employer will not prevail on summary judgment (a mechanism by which an employer can move the court to dismiss an employment lawsuit before trial).

Instead, think of it this way: it's not *either-or*, it's *both*. Yes, you should always maintain, document, and reiterate the employment-at-will relationship with your employees (by including language in your employment application, offer letters, and employee handbooks, for example). But since most of the cases will not be dismissed based on only the at-will employment defense, you also should be prepared to demonstrate that you had good cause to terminate your employee. And your documentation leading up to the termination is critical. After all, most employees will claim, "If it wasn't written down, it never happened." So your documentation becomes your primary defense lever during any employment discrimination or retaliation litigation. Without it, you'll have a very thin defense. Rather than risk losing at trial, you will likely have to settle "out of court," which, too, can be exceptionally costly if the employer cannot point to any documentation supporting the termination decision. Phew—now you know why documentation is so important!

Note: Most states, but not all, allow at-will employment relationships. For example, the state of Montana has enacted a statute that completely abrogates employment at will. As a result, Montana employers are prohibited from discharging employees without good cause.

3

ISSUING PROGRESSIVE DISCIPLINARY ACTIONS AND CREATING THE RIGHT WRITTEN RECORD

I KNOW, I KNOW ... you don't want to take the time to issue progressive discipline. It takes too long. It's confrontational in nature. The employee could double down on bad behavior, making the continuing employment relationship a nightmare, right? Well, as much as issuing progressive discipline might sound like a *crisis* in and of itself, it's usually the right thing to do, both for the worker's benefit and to protect your organization in the litigation arena if you're later sued.

First things first. While you should create a written record demonstrating why an employee is terminated, you don't always have to issue progressive discipline before you fire someone. For example, if an employee engages in egregious acts of misconduct by committing theft, fraud, embezzlement, or forgery, immediate dismissal may be appropriate. These are known as "summary offenses" because one such infraction typically justifies immediate termination of employment, no matter how much tenure the employee has or any other considerations. Likewise, new hires in their initial ninety-day "probationary" (a.k.a. introductory or training) periods are not necessarily due "workplace due process" in the form of progressive discipline. Each case is different but be careful: companies can be sued for terminating (nonunion) new hires in their first ninety days, so don't assume that you can terminate at whim in such circumstances. Each case should be reviewed on its own merits with management and preferably qualified legal counsel.

A record of progressive discipline can serve as a strong defense to a discrimination claim as well. An employee may allege that some illegal motive, such as age discrimination, was the basis for a termination decision. To counter that allegation, a company could produce a clear record of progressive discipline and an opportunity to demonstrate adequate performance or proper conduct. That being said, let's discuss how to document performance, conduct, attendance, or other problems to ensure that your organization is being fair to the employee and upholding its general practice of providing "workplace due process" so that workers have a chance to improve the situation and remain employed.

The traditional three-tier paradigm used by most companies helps to prove, via documentation, that you made a good-faith effort to lead the employee down the right path. Your affirmative efforts to help your employees improve performance must have been willfully rebuffed despite repeated warnings so that you, as a reasonable employer, were left with no choice other than termination. Keep in mind that you may be required to demonstrate that the discipline was meted out in a fair manner that was consistent with your own policies and practices so that any worker could reasonably expect to be terminated under similar circumstances.

THE THREE-STRIKES-BEFORE-YOU'RE-OUT MODEL

Summary dismissals aside, it's a very "American" and fair concept to give workers three bites at the apple before terminating for cause. Companies sometimes use different terms, but the three-step progressive disciplinary process often looks like this:

	WHAT IT'S OFTEN CALLED	WHAT IT'S ALSO KNOWN AS . . .
STEP 1	Verbal Warning	First Written Warning
STEP 2	Written Warning	Second Written Warning
STEP 3	Final Written Warning	Performance Improvement Plan
STEP 4	Termination	Termination

Again, this basic structure has multiple applications. An employee with three months of service may be treated differently than someone with thirty years' tenure. Likewise, some organizations apply disciplinary "suspensions" (that is, time off without pay) before terminating. Since each company handles matters differently, and dismissal decisions are unique and turn on specific facts, be sure to check with your own manager and with your organizations' HR department before recommending or communicating termination to anyone.

REPEATED VIOLATIONS TRIGGER DISCIPLINARY PROGRESSION

But how exactly does progressive discipline progress? Usually, the impetus that moves the process from one stage to the next is a repeated violation of the same rule or type of rule (for example, repeated tardiness or unexcused absence). In essence, there ought to be a link or nexus between events to move to the next stage. Without an interrelationship between and among events, you could end up with a series of independent verbal warnings rather than a progression from a verbal to a written to a final written warning.

For example, an employee who violates your organization's attendance policy and one week later fails to meet a deadline may receive two separate verbal warnings for independent and unrelated transgressions. On the other hand, an employee who violates your company's attendance policy and then develops a tardiness problem will indeed progress through the discipline system because both transgressions are intrinsically connected: unauthorized absence and tardiness both have a negative effect on the workflow of your office.

It is by no means uncommon to have an employee on separate paths of discipline. A shipping clerk who is already on final written warning for insubordination shouldn't necessarily be terminated if a tardiness problem begins. Tardiness, an event unrelated to insubordination, would not typically be used as the proverbial "straw that breaks the camel's back" to justify termination. That's because there is no nexus or interrelationship between the events: tardiness interferes with workflow, whereas insubordination relates to individual behavior and conduct—a separate business issue altogether.

On the other hand, because insubordination is a conduct infraction, any other behavior or conduct infractions during the active period of the write-up may indeed result in dismissal. For example, if this shipping clerk on final written warning for insubordination suddenly engages in antagonistic behavior toward his coworkers, insults a customer, or refuses to follow a supervisor's instructions, then a discharge determination could be warranted (barring any significant mitigating circumstances, of course).

Finally, understand that companies have the right to "bundle" offenses. This means that companies may interpret infractions of any sort more broadly, progressing through the progressive disciplinary system for any and all transgressions, no matter whether they're based on performance, conduct, or attendance. In short, some companies take a much more aggressive stance when it comes to worker misconduct and substandard job performance, and you won't know until you ask. In all cases, therefore, you must check with your manager and/or HR department for guidance. Be careful, though, as your manager may not realize how HR handles such matters either. The best resource will be HR, if your organization is large enough to have an HR department. When it comes to rules regarding disciplinary documentation, how to structure the template, and how to address problematic specific performance challenges in writing, please see my book *101 Sample Write-Ups for Documenting Employee Performance Problems: A Guide to Progressive Discipline and Termination.*

4

LETTERS OF CLARIFICATION
Alternatives to Formal Progressive Discipline

OKAY, HERE'S A MINI CRISIS THAT could turn into a major headache if not handled well: Let's say you have an employee who keeps making the same types of errors, but they're all fairly minor and "fall under the radar," so to speak. If you issue formal disciplinary action, it may feel heavy handed and like overkill.

"But she's just not hearing my words: no matter how many times I tell her something, she says she'll fix it and then makes the same errors repeatedly. She may not care anymore and just be apathetic about her job. But disciplining her for fairly minor incidents doesn't feel right to me either. What's a poor manager to do?"

Practically every manager faces issues that, at best, are an irritation and, at worst, require a formal written management response in the form of progressive discipline. Still, documenting discipline is often a confrontational experience for managers and a disappointing experience for staff. Since the path of least resistance is avoidance, it's not hard to see why many managers avoid addressing minor problems until they become major impediments. Life doesn't have to be that frustrating, though. A simple tool called a letter of clarification or letter of confirmation will give you, the manager, a significant advantage in dealing with minor employee infractions that don't rise to the level of formal discipline. Let's look at an example.

Janet is a hospital orderly who's responsible for pulling patients' charts and transporting patients in wheelchairs. Let's assume that Janet has been with your hospital for five years and has a fairly clean employment record: all performance evaluations show that she meets company expectations, and you've never had a need to formally document disciplinary infractions. Lately, however, you sense that she's having issues outside of work that may be spilling over into the workplace. She seems more apathetic about the quality of her work, and in general, she seems not to care anymore about her patients or coworkers. What are your options?

Step 1, of course, is to meet with Janet in private and explain your concerns. You share with her that she may be developing a "PR problem"—in other words, she may be giving off an impression to others that she's not aware of. Explaining that perception is reality until proven otherwise, you sensitize Janet to your concerns and tell her that you're holding her accountable for reinventing her relationship to the department and her coworkers. We'll assume she agrees, and off you go: a proactive management intervention designed to sustain the individual's dignity and self-respect. Bravo—you've done well!

Several weeks later, however, you notice the same apathetic behaviors setting in: Janet's not returning medical files, she's not using the department's magnetic scoreboard to show when she's out of the office, and recently a patient complained about Janet sitting her in a wheelchair wet from the rain and covered in pine needles from a nearby tree. A letter of clarification might be just the right tool to impress upon Janet the seriousness of her infractions. On one hand, letters of clarification are presented to the employee in written format and require the employee's signature. Logically, when things are written down, they are perceived more seriously.

In addition, when employees sign their names to documents related to their performance or conduct, they develop a healthy sense of paranoia that those documents may be used later down the line to establish some pattern of past history in their actions.

That's what progressive discipline and workplace due process are all about:

- showing employees what is wrong with their performance or conduct
- telling them what they need to do to fix the problem at hand
- giving them a reasonable amount of time to fix the problem
- clearly documenting the consequences of failing to meet your expectations

The letter of clarification will accomplish the first three (positive) goals of progressive discipline without having the sting of the fourth criterion regarding consequences—language along the lines of "further disciplinary action up to and including termination."

In fact, letters of clarification should specifically state that they are not disciplinary documents. As such, they don't carry the heavy stigma of "being written up." Here's what Janet's letter of confirmation might look like:

Janet, over the past three weeks, I've shared with you my concerns regarding your performance and conduct. Specifically, I've shared with you that you are not handling patients' files correctly because items are being misfiled and files are being left in patient rooms without being returned to the central filing area. In addition, a patient complained that you delivered to the patient pick-up area a wheelchair that was still wet from the rain and covered in pine needles. Finally, you have failed on several occasions to use the magnetic location board indicator to show when you were on break or lunch. As a result, the schedulers were not able to locate you in a timely fashion.

This isn't a disciplinary document, Janet. It will not be placed in your formal personnel file and will not be shared with other members of management at this time. But I have put my concerns in writing to impress upon you the seriousness of these multiple, smaller errors. My greatest concern lies in that you sometimes appear less focused on your work now than at any time in the past five years. You also appear at times to be apathetic about the outcome of your assignments, and several of your coworkers have asked me if you're doing okay because they too noticed a change in your work.

I want you to know that I'm here to help you in any way I can. On the other hand, I am holding you fully accountable for meeting all hospital expectations regarding performance and conduct. I recognize that you may have certain ideas to improve the situation at hand and welcome you to include those ideas in writing as an addendum to this letter of clarification.

Please sign this document to evidence not only that you received it but also that you agree to accept full responsibility for correcting these issues and improving the perception problems that exist. I'm here to support you in any way I can but will rely on you to let me know how I or the organization can best help you. Thank you.

X _____

Employee Signature   Date

Could this document later be used to justify formal disciplinary action if the employee doesn't clean up her act? Absolutely! Indeed, a written warning will make more sense after this informal, written clarification letter is given to the employee. Simply attach this letter to the disciplinary documentation that you issue in the future to demonstrate that you've addressed this before resorting to formal disciplinary action. Just be careful not to make it a practice or habit of issuing "letters of clarification" before issuing formal disciplinary documentation: you don't want to inadvertently turn a three-step process into a four-step process! But used occasionally and under the right circumstances, this tool could help avert an individual employee crisis that might otherwise result in disciplinary action or even outright termination.

By the way, letters of clarification work well with teams and departments too. For example, if you learn that several of your line managers are sharing employment-related references regarding past workers, then a verbal announcement to the staff may not be enough to show how serious you are about fixing the problem. Still, writing everyone up wouldn't make sense since following the "no references" policy hasn't been formally enforced in the past. Your best bet? Try a letter of clarification like this:

To All Engineering Staff:

Company policy strictly prohibits providing prospective employers with reference information on past workers. All requests for references must be forwarded to human resources. Human resources will then provide the former workers' dates of employment and last title held.

Subjective references that reveal information about past workers' performance, character, or work habits—especially if negative—could expose our organization to claims of defamation and other legal remedies. Since any managers who provide such references could be named individually in a lawsuit arising from a claim of defamation, it is critical that you all conform to this existing policy. Thank you.

I agree not to release any reference-checking information to any outside employers, employment agencies, or search firms, and I agree to forward all future reference calls to human resources for appropriate handling.

X _____

    Employee Signature   Date

When issuing such group confirmation letters, always require that employees individually sign separate documents. Advise them that you will keep their signed letters in your department file for future reference. That should cement in their minds the commitment you've made and they've now made to following company procedures and placing a particular rule "back on the front burner." If further violations occur, however, that signed document will also establish clear grounds for further formal disciplinary measures. Letters of clarification, viewed by many employees as precursors to formal discipline, have the same prophylactic effect as formal discipline without the negative trappings. Added to your performance-management toolbox, this alternative could strengthen communications by clarifying your expectations and, more importantly, involving employees in their own rehabilitation by treating them with dignity and respect.

5

DECISION-MAKING LEAVES
Dramatic Turnarounds Without a Lot of Drama

IF LETTERS OF CLARIFICATION ARE an alternative to formal, documented progressive discipline, then decision-making leaves are yet another tool you can apply to avoid a crisis—the "crisis" of terminating someone for cause. First, a definition: a "decision-making leave" or "day of contemplation" is a *paid* day off in which someone causing lots of grief is granted the opportunity to rethink their commitment to working at your company. Unlike a suspension, it isn't a formal step in your company's documented progressive disciplinary process. Also, unlike a traditional suspension, the employee's pay is not docked for the time away from work. The worker gets paid to stay home for a day with pay and think about whether working for your company is the right long-term career move.

If this sounds like too lenient a strategy that lets the worker "benefit from being bad," so to speak, don't be too quick to judge how effective this tool can be in the workplace. Here's why: adult learning theory will tell you that when you treat people like adults, they will typically respond in kind. Unlike formal suspensions, which tend to punish workers formally for substandard job performance or inappropriate workplace conduct, decision-making leaves are much more subtle. More important, they don't negatively impact the worker's take-home pay, so there's no element of resentment toward the employer or embarrassment in front of family members for having to explain why a paycheck is less that particular week.

Decision-making leaves tend to work best in two instances: first, with younger workers, often freshly minted graduates, who may come across as a bit pampered, skeptical, or all too eager to voice their dissatisfaction about workplace matters; second, with longer-term workers who, by their very tenure, are typically accorded extra steps of "workplace due process" before termination occurs.

Let's say, for example, that you've inherited a new employee in your unit who happens to be the CEO's nephew. How's that for a crisis? The upside clearly is that if all goes well between you and the young scion, then your career could skyrocket. The risk of course is that if there's a constant, nagging voice in the uncle's suite about your shortcomings as a manager, then this situation could certainly represent a career-limiting move in terms of your own internal progression. What's for sure, though, is that your style of supervision will be the topic of conversation with your company's CEO outside the workplace.

Now let's assume that this younger worker demonstrates a bit of an entitlement mentality and tends to name drop his relationship to his uncle. At first, it's a bit awkward but then becomes downright uncomfortable. Worse, it's soon followed by excessive tardiness, absenteeism, and substandard work performance. Your first reaction is to speak with your supervisor and to human resources to make sure you're politically not going to commit career suicide by facing this problem head-on. Assuming, though, that you've got a comfortable level of support from senior management to mentor and "redirect" this younger individual, your numerous verbal conversations may require a documented next step.

Clearly, you don't want to formally write up the CEO's nephew if you can avoid it, and truth be told, you don't really feel it's necessary at this point. After all, he may be a bit overindulged and suffer from an entitlement mentality, but he has a number of positive attributes, and you genuinely like him. You just want the behavior to change and the performance to improve, not only for your and for your staff's sake but for the good of the individual as well.

Again, assuming you've got senior management's buy-in to approach and handle this potentially career-damaging predicament, introduce the concept of the decision-making leave before initiating any formal, written warnings like this:

> Sean, we've had a number of conversations and "coaching sessions," if you will, discussing some of the perception problems that might exist in terms of your performance or conduct. We initially addressed your over-mentioning your relationship to our CEO to people you came in contact with, which, as you know now, intimidates some of your coworkers. Then we discussed your tardiness and, following that, your excessive absenteeism. Now I'm noticing that a number of projects are falling through the cracks, and some of my peers are starting to question how reliable you are and whether you could be depended upon.
>
> I don't want to give you a formal written warning because I feel that may only demotivate you. But I am going to place you on what we call a decision-making leave for a day, and I'll explain how it works. First of all, today is Tuesday, and tomorrow I'm going to ask you stay home. I'm paying you for the day tomorrow, so you don't have to worry about your paycheck being affected, and I want you to know that this is a once-in-a-career benefit that you should use to your advantage.
>
> While you're at home, I want you to give some serious thought as to whether you really want to work here. If you come back to work on Thursday morning and tell me that you'd rather resign and look for work elsewhere, I'll be totally supportive of your decision. But if you come back to work on Thursday and tell me that you really want to keep your job, then you'll have one additional assignment while you're away from work tomorrow.

Now, remember that I'm paying you for the day, so here's your homework assignment: if you to return to work on Thursday morning with the intention of keeping your job, you'll need to prepare a letter for me convincing me that you assume full and total responsibility for the perception problem that exists in terms of both your performance and conduct. You'll need to convince me in writing that you recognize why there may be a perception problem and again convince me in writing that the problem will be fixed and that we'll never have to have these discussions again. I'll hold on to that letter—keeping it outside of your personnel file for now—but with a clear understanding that if you violate the terms of your own agreement and commitment, then you may end up firing yourself. I'm considering this a very serious exercise and something that could be an incredibly important turnaround point in your career development. Now tell me what questions, issues, or concerns you have about this decision-making leave that you'll be taking tomorrow.

The value of this paid leave is that it forces the individual to be introspective and to engage in self-critical insight without the traditional trappings of formal progressive discipline. The worker won't walk away thinking, "I can't believe my boss gave me a written warning and is docking my pay. *She's* a terrible supervisor. . . ." It's much more about, "Wow, I guess she's taking this pretty seriously. I know I won't get a written warning or get my pay docked, which is good. I just can't believe that she said that she'd accept my resignation when I'm back on Thursday morning and that she'd be supportive of my leaving the company. Ouch, I guess I'd better be good, and I hope my uncle doesn't find out about this!" It's in shifting the traditional disciplinary paradigm that a day of contemplation provides the most value. When workers are disciplined, they're *angry*, and anger is external, so the problem is someone else's fault. When they're held accountable without formal discipline, they're feeling *guilty*, and guilt is internal. Guilt, in a healthy sense, as well as awareness is always where you want to be when dealing with your subordinates, because once problems are internalized, they are fixed once and for all.

This technique works exceptionally effectively with longer-term employees as well. When you have a thirty-year employee on your hands who has gone through the various steps of verbal, written, and final written warnings, then one final breach of company performance standards may be enough to justify a termination for cause. On the other hand, you may feel uncomfortable pulling the trigger either because of loyalty to the individual or because you fear a lawsuit in light of his decades of continuous service (and acceptable performance appraisals) in comparison to three or six months of recent performance problems.

In such cases, a day of contemplation may also make sense. Think of it this way: you'll have exhausted your traditional means of three-step discipline and want to offer a nonpunitive alternative to ensure that the employee understands that his or her job is now in serious jeopardy. In your meeting with the employee, you might explain the following in addition to the verbiage in the previous example:

> Joe, if you decide to return on Thursday morning and confirm that you want to keep this job, I'm going to ask you to provide a bit more verbiage in the letter that you prepare on Wednesday while you're home. I want you to explicitly write down (1) that you realize that your job is now in serious jeopardy of being lost and that this day of contemplation with pay is our way of telling you that and (2) that we really want you to be successful with us but that we're holding you fully accountable for the outcome here. We want you to succeed, but only you can demonstrate the willingness and the care necessary to get back on track. You don't have to use my exact words, but will you acknowledge that for me in your letter? [Yes.]

The value here clearly lies in the extra due process that you're according this worker due to his long tenure with your company. Hopefully it will turn things around, but if it doesn't and the worker must be terminated nonetheless, you'll demonstrate your reasonableness and caring as an employer. Again, the goal is to shift the paradigm away from "irresponsible company failed to communicate the graveness of the situation and did little to help the employee improve" to "responsible corporate citizen did its duty in every way to help proactively rehabilitate the worker and communicate the severity of the problem, but employee refused to respond." That's how creating an effective written record accords workplace due process to employees.

Decision-making leaves can be a very effective tool but may provide little value when the individual's performance problem has to do with excessive absenteeism. In essence, if the individual is having a difficult time getting to work every day, then giving her more time to spend at home to think about getting to work probably isn't necessary. In addition, if your employees are covered by a union's collective bargaining agreement, then an unpaid "suspension" may be part of the formal progressive disciplinary process, so adding a paid leave to an unpaid leave may not be necessary or make much sense. In any case, don't expect the union or an arbitrator to recognize this day of contemplation as a replacement for any formal step(s) in the disciplinary process outlined in the union contract.

Managing your CEO's family members, younger workers who may not take the position seriously, or longer-term employees whom the law expects to be accorded extra steps of due process in accordance with their tenure, pose some of the trickiest and stickiest problems for managers and supervisors. This decision-making leave strategy is a low-profile, low-drama type of employee intervention that speaks volumes in its subtlety. As a tool in your management toolbox, it may be just what you need to help others see things your way, keep them out of harm's way, and protect your company and your own career interests all at the same time.

6

TERMINATIONS FOR CAUSE
The Ultimate Crisis

DESPITE ANY EMPLOYER'S BEST EFFORTS, terminations for cause will happen from time to time. There are different ways of approaching a topic as broad as this: the mechanics of the written record, communicating your message to the affected worker, and helping the team heal after the fact. We'll focus on the communication to the employee at the time the organization gives notice that it has decided to terminate. We'll cover other aspects of termination elsewhere in the book.

Termination meetings are always challenging. Minutes before you call the employee into your office, your heart pounds; you experience mixed emotions of guilt, fear, and justification; and you mentally rehearse what to say and how to say it. When a breach of progressive disciplinary warnings results in a termination for cause due to poor performance, you have choices: keep the individual at arm's length throughout the discussion; create a threatening and intimidating atmosphere to persuade the individual not to sue you; or extend an olive branch and help the individual come to terms with this new reality, heal the wound, and get on with his or her life. I always recommend this third option and approach.

Let's assume you've provided an employee with verbal, written, and final written warnings as outlined in your company's policies and in accordance with past practices. You've also spoken with outside legal counsel, as needed, to ensure that your termination decision is on solid and legally defensible ground should the individual pursue post-termination litigation, and you've received the appropriate internal approvals to move forward with the termination. What do you say and, more important, how do you say it? Because there have been previous documented warnings of the problems as well as expectations and consequences, the termination decision shouldn't typically come as a surprise, especially if the employee is aware of the error that violated the terms of the final written warning. In such cases, the individual may not be happy with the organization's decision to terminate employment, but it should not blindside the individual who has received multiple prior notices.

Caveat: This scenario assumes you have "proof positive" that the employee violated the terms of the final written warning or that you've already spoken with the individual to learn the other side of the story before finalizing your termination decision.

When starting your conversation, be direct and caring but get to the point right away:

David, we've met several times to discuss your performance, and unfortunately, we need to separate your employment today.

Then, while the initial shock reverberates in the individual's head and emotions start kicking in, it's important that you state your justification in a clear and to-the-point manner. Follow the italicized phrases in the discussion below to see how the justification is delivered:

David, we've gone through a number of interventions with you regarding your overall performance on the job, via a combination of both verbal and documented notices, and I'm afraid that we've made the decision to *go our separate ways.*

I know you've been trying to meet the expectations outlined in the notices you received, and I appreciate that. Please don't think that we

INDIVIDUAL CRISES   . 33 .

see this as a lack of effort on your part. It's just that sometimes we come to the realization that our interventions are not really sustainable in terms of matching a person's efforts with our needs, and it becomes best to separate employment.

I thank you for all you've done for us. I'm sorry it had to come to this, but I hope that as you think about this, you'll realize this was probably the right thing to do for both sides. As a company, we don't want to see someone constantly fighting an uphill battle just because *the job's needs and that individual's strengths really aren't a good match or otherwise in sync.*

Don't underestimate the importance of the words *thank you* and *I'm sorry* in these types of communications. Terminations should never feel personal. Being terminated is one of the most vulnerable experiences that human beings can feel, so it's important that the employer demonstrates a human touch. Cold and distant tones of voice and keeping individuals at arm's length make it difficult for them to look inside, forgive themselves, and focus on their future. In fact, as an HR practitioner with three decades of experience behind me, I've often extended additional support like this. "I'm happy to help you with your unemployment application and walk you through your COBRA application. And to the extent you're comfortable, I'll be happy to review your résumé with you and even do a mock interview so you feel better prepared moving forward. Just let me know however I can help you through this transition."

Yes, you may feel like that's too much, and that's your call. It's what made it easier for me to help people through termination discussions like this, but we all have to work from our own comfort zone. What I would never recommend doing, in comparison, is appearing to be threatening or confrontational with workers during the termination process. One HR practitioner whom I worked with ended his termination meeting notices with the admonition, "And if you're planning on suing us, good luck, because we've got the best outside counsel in Los Angeles to defend us." Ouch. Why would an HR person close a meeting with such a warning? Probably because he was uncomfortable delivering the message and somehow felt he was "protecting the company" with his admonition. In fact, such attacks when people are feeling vulnerable will almost always create perceptions of resentment and anger, and no one should walk away from an experience with your organization feeling demonized or diminished.

In fact, the lawsuit is typically a tool of workplace revenge. Strip people of their dignity and humiliate them when they're most vulnerable, and you'll significantly increase your chances of posttermination litigation. There's simply no need for such aggressive behavior at the finish line. Help people realize the company's decision was not personal, help them hear healing words like "Thank you for all you've done for us—we know you tried," and allow people to move on in their careers without resentment that could lead to lawsuits or potential violence. As a reminder, terminate early in the day and early in the week—not on Friday afternoons at 5:00 p.m. Employees need access to people and information, and "sweeping them out the door" and not being available to them for seventy-two hours (that is, Friday to Monday) could be a recipe for disaster should the individual be mentally unbalanced or set on revenge.

Finally, you have options when discussing the physical separation: permit the employee to pack up and leave now; allow him to return after hours or over the weekend, when fewer people will be around; or assign security to accompany the employee back to his desk and out the door. The options available should be customized to the situation at hand. Whenever possible, though, avoid the "perp walk," where the individual is marched out in shame while accompanied by security. That being said, in cases of theft, fraud, or embezzlement, you may be left with little choice other than to do so.

Barring such extremes, however, allow the individual to have some choice in the matter. Ask if he needs help with packing or moving his belongings to the car. And by all means, ask if that person would like a few minutes to say goodbye to coworkers.

Healing the wound can start right away if the individual feels he's being treated with respect and dignity. Keeping this in mind, your exit conversation may sound like this:

> In addition, David, we want to handle this respectfully and thought-fully. Although we'd like you to leave the premises shortly, will you want boxes to pack up your personal materials? If you're not comfortable doing that now, we can arrange for you to come back and pack up later, or we could simply do that for you and courier your items back to your home later today. Also, would you prefer to leave quietly, or would you like to say goodbye to some of your coworkers before you leave the office?
>
> I know this is a lot of information coming at you at once. Do you have any questions that I can answer for you? [No.] Thanks for everything you've done for us, David. I wish you all the best in your career. How much time do you think you'll need to pack up your desk and say goodbye to your friends? [Twenty minutes.] Okay, then, I'll let our security folks know that you'll be leaving no later than thirty minutes from now.

At this point, the employee should be asked to return his ID badge, cell phone, laptop, office keys, and any other company items. Ask whether the company owes the employee anything in terms of pending expense reimbursements. Likewise, if the employee seems exceptionally upset and you have an EAP (employee assistance program) provider, you likely have the discretion to extend the EAP's services for an additional thirty to ninety days beyond the termination date so the individual has resources available to help with the transition. (Confirm that this service is available from your EAP provider and how much it will cost. Expenses will likely be minimal.) Handled respectfully and communicated thoughtfully, this meeting should leave you feeling good about the way you've managed a particularly difficult situation and will give the employee the chance to focus on the future rather than dwell on the past.

7

LAYOFFS AND POSITION ELIMINATIONS
The *Other* Ultimate Crisis

MUCH LIKE OUR APPROACH TO the previous challenge—terminations for cause—we'll address this very broad topic in terms of how your message affects the employee. There is a lot of background in terms of how layoffs and position eliminations occur in the workplace— the legitimate business need to eliminate a position, the written record of the individual employees with the same or similar titles in the "selection pool," not backfilling the position within a certain period of time (typically one year), and more. But where the rubber meets the road as far as first-time managers goes is in the commu- nication with the employee, who is often shocked to hear the news. Unlike with terminations for cause, in which the individual can often "see it coming," layoffs and reductions in force (RIFs) tend to blindside and paralyze individuals when they first learn of the news. So let's discuss your communication strategy here.

First, a quick differentiation in terms. Typically, a "layoff" is used to describe one or more separations from employment due to a lack of work. But the employer may recall the employee(s) back to work if circumstances change. That's similar to a "furlough," where companies may temporarily lay off employees or reduce their hours due to a lack in production demand with the intention of returning them to work fully at some point. A "reduction in force," in comparison, typically describes a permanent elimination of positions with no intention of refilling them. Employers often use the terms interchangeably, which is understandable, but it's important that you understand the difference. In our example below, we'll assume that a full "reduction in force" is at hand, but know that your workers likely won't know the difference if you use the words interchangeably.

Here's a typical opener of what you might say in the initial employee notice meeting:

> Lauren, in an effort to reduce costs, we're restructuring our business, and that will result in the elimination of a number of positions in our organization. Unfortunately, your position has been selected, and I'm afraid we're going to have to lay you off. Today will be your last day of work with us, and we have information to share with you regarding your severance package, COBRA, and unemployment insurance. I know this is a lot of information coming at you at once, and I'm so sorry to have to relay this message to you because this is primarily about budget issues, not individual performance. I realize it's so difficult to hear these words because your livelihood is being affected and you're being forced to address a challenge you weren't prepared for or expecting. Before I go any further, I want to see how you're doing. Are you okay?
>
> [**Option:** Just so you're aware, several other positions are being eliminated throughout the day. Yours isn't the only one. Out of respect for the other people involved, I would ask that you say as little as possible today. We would prefer to tell the affected employees ourselves; we want to avoid people hearing about this through the grapevine if we can help it.] In addition, I know that some people prefer to leave quietly while others want to say goodbye to a few close friends. We'll respect whatever decision you make. How do you think you would like to handle that?
>
> Finally, I just want to thank you for all your hard work and dedication for the past two years. You have made it a better place

around here, and I'm personally going to miss working with you. Thank you for all you've done for us.

This language can change depending on your practices and your specific situation. If there is only one layoff, not multiple ones, you can amend your talking points accordingly. If people are being notified all at once versus throughout the day, you can likewise eliminate the option of Lauren's speaking with her colleagues to say goodbye. The point is, if you speak softly and with genuine concern and if you soothe your message with empathy, most employees will appreciate your sincere approach. After your opening statement, expect some employees to question the reasoning behind their position elimination. Following are different sample responses that you might expect to hear under the circumstances:

Question: Why was my position chosen for elimination?

Answer: It was a business decision. When a reduction in force occurs, positions are eliminated. The people who are attached to those jobs then get laid off. Selecting positions for elimination is so difficult because you realize that people's lives will be interrupted. *That's why I'm so sorry that this is occurring.* (Note: It's fine to say, "That's why I'm sorry this is happening." But it's not okay to say, "That's why I'm sorry we had to pick you for the elimination." Make no reference to or apologize for the selection procedure involved.)

Question: Who else is being laid off? Am I the only one in our department? Why me?

Answer: Lauren, I can't share specifics about who else is being laid off today at this point. We haven't spoken to the other individual(s) yet, so I would ask that you allow me to hold off on answering that for now. [Or:] Yes, yours is the only position in our department that's being eliminated. Again, please don't feel that you've disappointed anyone. I want you to know that you could be considered for rehire once another similar position to yours is created and if you apply. For now, though, understand that we had to eliminate one position, and purely from a functional standpoint, your position made the most sense.

Question: How can that be? Who's going to do all the work that I do once I'm gone?

Answer: With the elimination of your position, other members of the department will have to take on the job duties that you've handled up to now. That's something we'll simply have to deal with in this new "downsized" mode. Lisa is here with us from human resources to discuss some of the details related to your severance package, COBRA, unemployment insurance, and other important benefits details relating to this layoff.

Question: You can't lay me off and keep the other administrative assistants. I have more seniority than everyone else.

Answer: I recognize your seniority. But I want you to know that we did not base our decision solely on tenure. We looked at skill level, performance, experience, education, and other factors when determining what positions to eliminate and who would be the most qualified to assume the remaining duties after the reduction in force. We determined that, based on all that historical information along with our evaluation of who would work best in the post-layoff environment, your position would be selected for elimination.

Let's discuss with Lisa how your severance package works, along with COBRA and unemployment. It's important at this point that you have a clear understanding of next steps to help prepare for your upcoming transition and job search.

This last section is particularly important. Employees notified that their positions are being eliminated often panic. Questions

pop up in an attempt to understand—out loud—why this is happening to them and what they can do to save their jobs. That's
natural. What you have to understand as a manager notifying
employees of position eliminations is that employees will be on
"pure adrenaline" throughout your discussion. Raw emotion kicks
in, but you can't answer an unlimited number of questions in the
initial notice meeting, especially since the employee isn't really
capable of "hearing" your responses when in panic mode. Instead,
after allowing two or three questions, gently move the conversation in the direction of the individual's severance package,
COBRA, and unemployment filing. This is where their minds will
typically go next, as they worry about the immediate needs of paying bills, what to tell their family members, and how they're going
to make ends meet until they find a new position.

In short, answering several questions makes sense, but pointing affected workers to their next logical area of focus can help
ease the pain of the initial notice meeting. Likewise, treat the
individual with as much dignity and respect as possible. The
employee wasn't a bad person five minutes before you gave them
notice, so permit them to say goodbye to friends and associates, if
possible. Again, avoid the "perp walk" where security walks them
back to their office or desk in front of others to avoid any perception of shame or embarrassment. Layoffs are a function of globalization, technological change, suffering sales, expense budgets,
and more. Help people heal. Thank them for a job well done. Let
them know you'll miss working with them. Most important, let
them know you'll be there to help them any time if they have any
questions or need anything from the organization.

Finally, you'll want to address the remaining employees in your
group about Lauren's sudden departure from your team. Call a
team or department meeting after Lauren has left the campus to
attempt to heal the wound of her departure, as many of the
remaining employees will likely be wondering how she's doing
and if more layoffs are to follow. Your group discussion might
sound like this:

I wanted to call you all into a meeting to follow up regarding a layoff that took place earlier today in our department. As you may have heard, layoffs were announced today in certain departments throughout the organization. Lauren's position was eliminated in our department, and we provided her notice that today would be her last day of employment with us. Lisa from HR provided Lauren with information regarding her severance package, COBRA, and unemployment application and is working with her through this transition. We treated Lauren with respect and dignity, as she deserves, and we'll help her in any way we can through this unexpected transition in her career. (If applicable: She's also going to receive outplacement services, which will help her update her résumé, prepare for interviews, and target companies where she'd be most interested in working.)

Of course, no guarantees of job security can be given, but as far as we understand, there aren't any other planned layoffs in our department at this time. I wanted to let you all know that to allay any fears you might have about your own job security right now. We wish those affected well and thank them for their contributions to our organization over time. I know I can count on your support in doing the same.

I also want to remind you that if you get any reference-checking phone calls from prospective employers or headhunters, those calls are to be referred to me. I will in turn pass them along to human resources as per company policy.

We'll discuss divvying up Lauren's responsibilities among the rest of us, but that discussion can wait until tomorrow. Does anyone have any questions that I can answer? [No.] If there are no other questions, I thank you all for coming. I appreciate your patience and understanding, and I look forward to moving beyond this difficult period.

The goal in any layoff or RIF action is to treat employees with dignity and respect. The best way to achieve that is to communicate openly and honestly with those laid off and with those who survive and assume the remaining job responsibilities. Yes, this is a crisis that cannot be averted. But demonstrating your leadership in the form of heartfelt communication to the affected employee and the rest of the team will be appreciated and allow the team to heal over time.

8

DELIVERING BAD NEWS
TO THE BOSS
Success Lies All in the "How"

CRISES COME IN ALL SHAPES AND SIZES, large and small, urgent and long term, dire and sometimes simply unpleasant. Managing leadership communication in times of crisis requires a steady hand on your part and a willingness to lean in and bring out the best in others, especially during trying times. Delivering bad news likewise works in all directions—up to your boss, sideways to your peers, and downward to your team members. Let's take a look at how to deliver bad news to your boss in as tasteful and strategic a way as possible. First, let's start with a story to bring some perspective to the exercise.

Hollywood lore passes on a story of the fear of bearing bad news: in 1939, subordinates to Adolph Zukor, Paramount Pictures' founder, were terrified of telling their studio boss of the box office success of rival MGM's *Gone with the Wind* for fear of his suffering a heart attack. Maybe that seems a bit exaggerated in today's world of mergers, acquisitions, large-scale restructurings, and the like, but it makes an important point nonetheless: we all walk the delicate line of balancing the delivery of bad news with the fear of being blamed for holding it back. "Don't kill the messenger" is a legitimate concern for many, so let's approach this topic in a transparent yet cautious way.

Giving and receiving bad news is a common part of business. But focusing on *how* to deliver bad news to senior management as well as ensuring that your subordinates are keeping you abreast of unpleasant changes in circumstances is critical in our information-driven work environment. A simple rule to share with your employees is this:

> I don't mind that bad news occasionally hits the fan; I simply need to know which way to duck when it does. You're responsible for communicating any problems with me before I learn about them from anyone else. There can be no exceptions while I'm at the helm. Do I have everyone's commitment to doing so in order to avoid drama or feeling like I'm flying blind? [*Yes.*]

Okay, simple enough. But what about delivering bad news to CEOs, business owners, and other members of senior management who may not take negative news particularly well? Unfortunately, too many managers opt to take the path of least resistance by avoiding unpleasant confrontations with senior managers, even if this is to the detriment of the company. Only you know how *welcome* your comments and suggestions will be to your senior management team. As an officer and manager of your company, you are indeed responsible for the well-being of the organization and the fulfillment of its mission of profitability. Open your message by confirming your commitment to keeping the CEO or business owner informed.

CONFIRM YOUR COMMITMENT TO KEEP
THE ENLIGHTENED CEO INFORMED

Simply stated, every CEO relies on her immediate core of managers to remain abreast of changes in company circumstances and employee attitudes. Here's what a typical conversation might sound like between your head of HR and your company's owner or CEO, for example:

> I've got to share some unpleasant information with you, and I'm not looking forward to this conversation, but that's why you pay me. I figure if I can't bring problematic issues to your attention, then I'm not doing my job. This won't make you particularly happy, but we've got a few options that I'd like to discuss with you to help us through this. Here goes: we're continuing to see an increase in the number of resignations among our top-performing employees. I think you know Kendra Sharp in finance: she just resigned, leaving the accounting team scrambling. If we don't address how much we've fallen behind in market pricing for some of our key positions and likewise don't amend our approach to equity adjustments and promotions over the past year, then I'm afraid that other "keeper" employees may jump ship because they feel like we're being tone deaf to the broader opportunities and challenges in the market.
>
> The bad news is this will cost money. We've crunched the numbers, and if we bring our key contributors to market—the top ten employees we don't want to lose—then we're looking at a total cost of $65–$85,000, depending on the timing of how you want to spread this out. The good news is, if we institute a management training program for all directors and above and also reward a small number of key players with promotions and equity adjustments, then I think we'll have a greater chance of stemming the tide of turnover that's upon us right now and keeping within a reasonable budget.

Notice how the opener addresses the need to share the negative news gently and respectively, introduces the problem, and offers a high-level overview of the solution. You can now continue to discuss details that led to your initial recommendation of the $65–$85,000 variance that will need to be incorporated into the budget. Next, it's time to prepare in advance for the boss's objections and weave them proactively into your follow-up:

I'm sure you're wondering why I'm recommending the change now that we're seeing that much of the Great Resignation has passed us by. Our turnover has been exceptionally low over the past three years. We averaged 16 percent annual turnover over the past two years, but since the market sprang back to life in the first quarter, our overall turnover has crept up to 20 percent, which is high for us but average relative to most surveys that I've researched. We've responded logically to the "whiplash" markets over the last few years by investing in leadership training and professional development, but some of our top performers may feel like they're treading water career-wise and want or need higher base compensation or a title increase. We have less flexibility with title changes and promotions than we do with equity adjustments (that is, raising individual rates to market on a case-by-case basis), but it's time to gear up for change in the recruitment marketplace and reward our top performers before we lose them.

The bottom line is that we've got a lean staff that is very talented and committed, and changes to the lineup at a point when we have little bench strength could be very costly. The general level of burnout is high right now, though, and people are exhausted. Many may be looking to make up for lost time salary-wise. If we don't address wage discrepancies for our top quartile of employees, we may remain vulnerable to losing some of them when we can afford that least. In short, our lack of proactive change at this point could make us appear penny smart and pound-foolish.

With your boss's objections built into your initial argument, you'll hopefully get to that point where she wants to see your spreadsheet with the dollar allocations you're recommending. Once there, your spreadsheet can do the talking by looking at current versus proposed base salary, bonus, or other considerations. Just keep in mind that any "lofty" proposals that haven't been logically thought out or financially justified will seem naive at best and could result in your loss of credibility. Here are some considerations you might include in your closing, including cost savings that your boss might not be thinking about right now:

> We've looked at promoting three key employees and giving equity adjustments to six others, for a total payroll cost of $65,000. If you want to build a little more into their bonus targets, it will bring the number closer to $85,000. We believe we could show a permanent savings offset of $40,000 by cutting certain underused employee programs that don't give us much return on investment, but we'd still end up $25,000 to $45,000 over budget. Still, it's a strategic investment for our key players, and we've looked at external market surveys as well as internal equity, so we believe the fundamentals are in place and the timing is right. I also think we could cover part of that budget shortfall by outsourcing our temp desk, although it would take eighteen months to show those savings. What are your initial thoughts?

Regardless of the senior manager's ultimate decision, you'll have created a compelling presentation with a logical business conclusion. More importantly, you'll have couched the bad news in a contextual framework that forces your boss to consider your proposal on its objective merits, and you'll have fulfilled your responsibility of providing organizational insights that the senior manager may not have focused on—a well-done argument that will hopefully lead to further questions and investigation.

9

EAPS AND DEALING WITH EMPLOYEES IN CRISIS

EMPLOYEE CRISES ARE YOUR CRISES, plain and simple. Knowing how to recognize individuals who may be in crisis is an important starting point for this chapter. Signs of individual crisis escalation often look like this:

1. Early warning signs: mild irritation to increased agitation, trouble with daily tasks, and isolation
2. Sudden extreme changes in mood: irritation develops into anger, accusations, and blaming others
3. Issues multiply: one problem turns into many
4. Generalizations: issues become clouded so that "nothing" is ever right; vocabulary generalizes into "always" and "never" phrasing, as in "This company *never* . . ." or "You *always* . . ."
5. Goals shift: the goal changes from resolving a particular conflict to hurting the enemy and acting "on principle"
6. Taking sides: gossip spreads so that outsiders begin taking sides; this stage feels like war
7. Impasse: refusal to cooperate stems from one or both sides

8. Conflict, confrontation, abusive behavior to self and others (including substance abuse), and even potential violence undermines culture

And as you can see, once you get to the latter stages (items 6, 7, and 8), the individual challenges may escalate into a team or departmental crisis, which we'll address more thoroughly in part 2. But employee disengagement, isolation, and aggression can wreak havoc on your team and overall culture. Left unaddressed, it can wear down even the most positive players on your team and, at worst, result in lawsuits or potential workplace violence.

Preventing violence and enhancing workplace safety is every employer's goal. But instructing managers on how to deal with employee crisis proactively sometimes gets short shrift in the business press. What do you do when you notice employees isolating themselves from the rest of the group? How do you deal with an employee who shares suicidal thoughts? And what if your "suicidal" employee seems to go a step further and becomes potentially "homicidal"? True, these extreme behavioral reactions don't occur every day in the workplace. Still, most human resources practitioners will have seen more than their share of employees in crisis, and there is a definite need to get the word out in advance to line managers that a methodology exists for addressing proactively an employee crisis.

All efforts should begin by inviting the isolated worker back into the fold. Workers vulnerable to crisis themselves typically appear as loners isolated from the rest of the group. These people often develop a "time clock" mentality in which they go through the motions of doing their jobs day in, day out but are otherwise disengaged. Extending a helping hand to those who have extricated themselves from the social group over a number of years is daunting. Many managers will simply take the path of least resistance and avoid the "odd" employee whenever possible, sweeping issues under the rug rather than addressing them.

Left in a vacuum void of information and two-way communication, however, isolated or angry workers may tend to create their own versions of reality. Generally speaking, such individuals may tend to demonstrate an "entitlement mentality with victim syndrome" combination that makes it very hard for them to accept help. As such, to justify their anger, they may attribute negative intentions to others' actions where none are intended. What these loners may need is an opportunity to reconnect to the group and enjoy the social elements of work—recognition and appreciation for a job well done as well as a sense that they belong and can make a positive difference in the workplace.

But what if they don't want to accept your olive branch or otherwise appear to enjoy the drama?

This is no easy task for you if you're the newcomer supervisor. But your lack of history or "emotional baggage" as a new leader may be used to your advantage as you take a fresh look at the situation. For example, let's assume you're a newly hired hospital administrator responsible for overseeing a staff of a half dozen nurses in a particular wing of your hospital. Five of the six nurses get along with one another well: they engage in healthy banter, cover for one another when one goes on break, and answer other patients' call lights should the primary nurse be engaged elsewhere.

One team member, however, holds out stubbornly from engaging with the others. You learn that he's been employed the longest, he used to be known as one of the nicest nurses on staff but who has long since given up on trying to make others like him, and he seems to find fault with most people around him. In fact, when he speaks with you, he seems to use the words *always* and *never* often, attributing blame and fault to others who "*never* want to help" or "*always* look to avoid work." Such generalizations are rarely true. In fact, the other nurses may describe this nurse's behavior in the same way. Five against one seems to be the math driving your unit, and it's visible to other members of management, which doesn't reflect a unified team. Worse, patient care

suffers as patients' call lights go unanswered whenever this particular nurse is on shift.

Your first step will always be to meet with your staff members
one-on-one to learn how they view the situation. Start first with
the natural-born leaders on your team, the ones who seem to drive
much of the employee behavior around them and who seem to
exert the strongest influence on the group overall. Ask questions
like these:

> How would you grade our group in terms of camaraderie and team-
> work? How do staff members get along with one other, and have
> you had any particular problems with other members of the group?
>
> Are you aware of any particular historical problems among the
> team members, and could you tell me how they were or weren't
> resolved? Did anyone "disengage" after any particular incidents or
> otherwise appear to be isolated or abandoned from the group?
>
> What would you recommend we do to better the situation?
>
> I've got to ask a favor of you. If I attempt to bring peace to both
> sides of this rift, would you support me and welcome that particu-
> lar nurse back into the fold?

More likely than not, you'll hear fairly consistent stories and
explanations of the ongoing strife with each employee group, and
you'll probably see both sides of the story objectively and have a
better understanding of how the fallout came to be. With every
individual's commitment to do their part in bettering the situation, it will then be time to hold a group meeting, which might
sound like this:

> Folks, life is short. We spend more time with our coworkers than
> we do with our family members, and there's certainly more than
> enough work to go around. What could make this unbearable for all
> of us, though, is the negative environment that we create because of
> a lack of communication, harbored unresolved resentments, or a
> perceived lack of respect in terms of how we treat one another.

You know that I've met individually with each of you to learn about this historical rift, and I want you to know that I'm holding each of you accountable for creating a work environment where everyone is treated with respect and dignity. I'm also holding you fully responsible for your own "perception management," meaning it's not about right or wrong. It's about ensuring that others understand your good intentions and are made to feel welcome in our department.

I realize that this situation may have taken years to get to this point, and I'm not naive—it may take just as many years to get to a point where there's a natural trust and respect in your interactions. But people tend to respond in kind, and if you treat others respectfully, they'll do the same to you. I'm here to ensure that that's the case, and I'll be here for each of you should you need me. Please understand, though, that I won't stand for missed patient call lights or any attempts at placing blame on others. I also won't have any members of our staff feeling singled out or otherwise isolated from the rest of the team. In short, if the current situation keeps up, then there will be disciplinary consequences. On the other hand, if you support me in making this a more inclusive working environment, then we could all begin to let bygones be bygones and discover new ways of adding value to our hospital's patient care system and feeling better about our team and our work. Can I count on your individual and group support? [*Yes.*]

Allowing people to feel safe about coming out of their foxholes will do more than anything else to avert potential crisis in the workplace. But what if the individual nurse in this case continues to feel even more isolated from the group or to begin demonstrating signs of psychological trauma? What happens, for instance, if this individual reports to your office one morning sharing suicidal thoughts? Employee assistance programs are there to help. Assuming your company offers this benefit, you may simply provide the brochure to an employee and ask that individual to call the EAP when convenient. But that's clearly not enough in this circumstance: with a suicidal threat at hand, contact your manager, human resources, and/or your legal department. Depending on your culture and operating environment, the CEO or business owner will likely want to know of this as well. With HR and/or the legal department's guidance, it may make sense to tell the employee:

> Robin, I want you to wait here with me in my office. Let's call our EAP together, because I'm not your best resource if you're feeling that way, and I know that Marilyn Walters at the EAP would certainly be able to help. Will you wait here with me and let me help by calling Marilyn together?

In addition to an individual talking to a crisis counselor, an EAP can arrange for a licensed counselor to come to your workplace to speak to the employee in the event of a crisis. Both individual and group counseling services may be available for both individual and company-wide crises and are key tools to helping those in need while mitigating organizational risk. Note, however, that crisis assistance and management referrals may not be available in all EAP models. They are standard in full-service EAP models but not necessarily in the free EAPs that are add-ons to another carrier (such as disability, life, or medical carriers that provide an EAP add-on for free or at a very reduced price).

Caution: Making a "formal" referral to an EAP (as opposed to a "voluntary" referral where the employee self-refers) should almost always occur with the employee's consent. But in extreme cases where a formal referral may be warranted, you must ensure that the employee has a job performance problem in addition to appearing to be mentally depressed, suicidal, or potentially hostile. In the case of formal referrals, you would discuss your perceptions of the work performance problems with the intake counselor on the front end (although not necessarily in front of the employee). With a signed release from the employee, the EAP would later be able to provide you with limited feedback about the individual's attendance, compliance, and prognosis.

In certain cases (for example, with potential workplace violence issues), you have the option of not permitting the individual back to work without a fitness-for-duty certificate from a licensed health-care practitioner. Note that such leaves are typically paid through the initial period of evaluation. Beyond that, employees typically use accrued time off to be compensated while receiving further treatment.

One caveat about "formal" EAP referrals: although they may certainly be justified in cases of threats of employee suicide, recent case law shows that formal EAP referrals have created burdens on employers under the Americans with Disabilities Act (ADA). Specifically, plaintiff attorneys have argued, on the basis of a mandatory EAP referral, that the employer did indeed *perceive* that their client was disabled. (The ADA and some state disability discrimination laws protect individuals who either have or *are perceived as* having a disability, including a mental disability.) Such an interpretation could become legally problematic should you then decide to take some adverse action (especially termination) against the employee.

In addition, you should not mandate that an employee attend treatment sessions by threatening termination if they don't, as such a requirement could appear to make an EAP referral an extension of your disciplinary authority and give rise to claims of disability discrimination based on a perceived mental disability, invasion of privacy, or misuse of confidential medical information in certain states. "Formal" EAP referrals, in short, may be fraught with legal challenges, which is why you'll want to involve HR and/or legal right up front.

All else being equal, however, you have to put safety first. After all, an extreme worker reaction might also result in veiled threats of homicide rather than suicide. For example, what if an employee came to your office one morning, placed a live shell of ammunition on your desk, and stated that his coworkers better not bother him today "if they knew what's good for them"? Pretty creepy, to be sure, but veiled threats like these are not uncommon in extreme cases.

Your first reaction would probably be to fire this person and ensure that he has no further access to company property. And that may be the best decision for your organization in the end. Still, it's probably best to make a record that you didn't overreact or jump to unfair conclusions. In such cases, placing the employee on a paid administrative leave might make the most sense. Explain your rationale to the employee this way:

> Roberto, I know you've met with our EAP provider, and they gave us a written release for you to return to work. You also told me that you were feeling much better about work and about your relationship with your peers at that time. But the feelings you're sharing with me right now raise some concern, as I'm sure you can understand. I think it's best to send you home with pay while I check with my superiors in terms of how to best handle this. We'll call it an "administrative leave with pay" and continue to pay you as though you were working full time. I'll call you later tonight at home to follow up.
>
> I've got to ask a favor, though. The way that our company normally handles these things is to ask the employee to go straight home. I can't have the employee here at work while I do my objective fact-finding. Having the employee wait at home is always part of an administrative leave. Do you understand, and will you support my request with that? [*Yes.*]

Gently escort the employee off the premises and alert security or take other reasonable steps to ensure your workers' safety. (Consult your safety or antiviolence policies, which may include items such as disabling security badges, changing access or gate codes, securing doors normally left open, hiring on-site security personnel and alerting law enforcement authorities.) Most employment lawyers will recommend that you share with the potential victims that a threat, whether overt or veiled, was indeed made and the steps the organization is taking to address the situation. As a general rule, however, you should limit disclosure of specifics only to those individuals with a specific need to know in order to protect the problematic individual's privacy and to avoid later claims of defamation.

Bring these newfound threats to the attention of the EAP, and at this point, be sure to seek the advice of qualified legal counsel before moving to terminate. If you then choose to dismiss, do so over the phone within twenty-four to forty-eight hours. Ship home the employee's personal belongings plus final checks via courier. Include a letter that states that the individual may no longer enter company property for any reason without the advance approval of the vice president of human resources. Your attorney should approve the final draft of the letter. Finally, remember that EAPs could also serve as an excellent resource for your remaining employees should they need someone to talk to. Yes, people may freak out if they learn that a peer was threatening violence, but honesty and transparency are critical at a time like this to set everyone's expectations properly and heighten awareness should they see anything questionable or concerning in the future.

PSYCHOLOGICAL SAFETY

The idea of creating psychological safety in the workplace was first introduced in 1999 by Harvard professor Amy Edmondson. Psychological safety in the workplace is defined as a belief that you will not be humiliated or punished for speaking out with your ideas, concerns, questions, or mistakes. As such, it's a critical factor for high-performing teams and fosters a culture based on respect, inclusion, and goodwill. If your team members feel safe psychologically, they will be less afraid of negative consequences from sharing ideas and suggestions, providing constructive (that is, negative) feedback, and taking healthy risks. Overall, psychological safety is about ensuring that your team feels able and capable of performing at the highest level because of your and their peers' ongoing support. It's about making it safe for team members to make themselves *vulnerable* in the healthiest sense, knowing that support for them, their ideas, and suggestions are a given.

The Center for Creative Leadership defines it as follows: "Psychological safety at work doesn't mean that everybody is nice all the time. It means that you embrace the conflict and you speak up, knowing that the team has your back, and you have their backs." Discuss this with your team, grade yourselves on a scale of 1 to 10 on your current state, and build a plan to make psychological safety and selfless leadership something that you work on together purposely and deliberately.

SPECIAL NOTE ABOUT SUICIDE PREVENTION

According to SHRM, the Society for Human Resource Management, if employers strongly feel that a worker is considering suicide, dial 9-8-8. The **988 Suicide & Crisis Lifeline** is the new national suicide prevention network comprising more than 160 crisis centers that provide 24/7 service via a toll-free hotline. The lifeline provides free and confidential support for people in distress as well as crisis resources and best practices for professionals. (See https://988lifeline.org/.)

10

ENCOURAGING EMPLOYEES TO LEAVE WHEN THERE IS NO PROGRESSIVE DISCIPLINARY DOCUMENTATION ON FILE

WANT ANOTHER CRISIS TO REALLY catch your attention as a first-time manager? When dealing with employees who in your opinion should have been terminated years or decades ago, don't go it alone. You need your supervisor, HR, and legal to support you through this. More likely than not, they've seen these types of challenges before and may even be aware of the employee in question. It sometimes becomes necessary from time to time to convince employees to leave your company. Why? Because employees who are experiencing performance and conduct problems will often stay "on principle"—in other words, they'll rationalize that they'll stay until *they're* good and ready to leave. "No one's forcing me out of my job until I'm ready to go—especially not that boss of mine!" goes the skewed logic of the disenfranchised and victimized worker.

Unfortunately, the results can be very problematic: workers' comp stress claims, union organizing attempts, or wrongful termination lawsuits await your company. Months or years of feeling unappreciated and disrespected may await the employee in question. Therefore, your best solution from an employee-relations standpoint may be to broker a peace in which one party may walk out of the working relationship with dignity and respect intact.

A caveat from the outset: meetings such as this require a third-party mediator (like HR). First, if immediate supervisors who are part of the problematic interpersonal relationship with disenfranchised employees attempt to "talk them into" leaving their job, those supervisors' efforts may be seen as insincere or self-serving at best and lead to legal claims of "constructive discharge" (inferring that any reasonable person would have left the company under similar circumstances, tantamount to forcing someone to quit). Second, whatever is shared with the employee in meetings like this may take on a different meaning twelve months down the road when the company is defending itself in a courtroom, so the third-party witness can help significantly in terms of explaining how things actually played out in real time.

To avoid creating a record that could be construed as a manager giving an employee no choice but to resign, the manager can't be the deliverer of this message. Instead, a neutral third party must be used. Human resources or a member of your company's senior management team is the typical mediator in such cases. Here's how these cases typically sounded to me as a human resource practitioner over the decades:

The Manager:
The problematic employee is disrespectful, noncommunicative, and does not hold himself accountable for his own actions. As a result, I delegate as little to him as I can. Instead, I do the work myself or give it to the other members of the team. My other staff members resent that he doesn't do his own share of the work, and they're tired of my cutting a wide swath around him for fear of upsetting him or making matters worse.

The Disenfranchised Employee:
Are you kidding? My boss shows me no respect, she never makes me feel like I'm part of the team, and she constantly holds me to a higher standard than everyone else. I'm never in the communication loop, and I'm never told when I do something right—only when I do something wrong. I'm sick and tired of being worked so hard and being so underappreciated!

Who's right and who's wrong in these situations? Both sides typically. Employees too often take the easy road out and justify their irresponsible behavior by arguing favoritism and blaming their bosses for their own unhappiness. Managers, however, are indeed responsible for creating a working environment where employees can motivate themselves, and if they constantly avoid the individual or sweep issues under the rug, the employee will assume it's personal and intentional. In essence, if the working relationship has gotten to this point, both the manager and worker have failed. Sometimes, however, trying to fix these problems just becomes an ongoing battle of wills in which little good results. That's when it may be time to consider this option of encouraging an employee to leave—even when there's no record of disciplinary action on file.

In steps human resources, legal, or senior management. This third-party mediator needs to attempt to fix the problem with the help of both the affected manager and employee. When progressive discipline or an employee transfer isn't feasible, then the mediator/broker may attempt to gently inject respect, dignity, and professionalism back into the working relationship by allowing the employee an "easy out" exit strategy:

Kyle, you've worked as Sybil's executive assistant for the past two years, and I don't believe that you or Sybil has felt that this working relationship was ever a good fit. In other words, sometimes it's just not the right personality mix or the right timing in people's lives, and the working relationship suffers. Would you agree that it hasn't been ideal for you? [Yes, although it's Sybil's fault, not mine.]

Sybil, you've shared your frustrations about Kyle's substandard job performance and inappropriate workplace conduct with me privately. I've also recommended that you speak with Kyle directly, and you've done that on multiple occasions. So, you're frustrated too, right? [*Yes, although not as often as I could have.*]

Okay, then it's time to lay down our shields and extend the proverbial olive branch. There's enough work around here to sink a battleship. When you add the interpersonal friction that you've been both experiencing for the past year or so, it becomes unbearable. I don't want to minimize the importance of your working relationship together, but with all due respect, it's *only* work. I mean, when you think about families who lose their health or parents who have to see their children through serious illnesses—that's important in life. If we're not suffering from that kind of challenge, we're lucky. So let's keep that in perspective as we look at this workplace issue, okay?

Sometimes it's fair to say that it just isn't a good fit. What's important to me is that both parties feel like they're being supported and treated with dignity and respect. I don't want people feeling like their egos and self-esteem are being trashed. Life is simply too short for that, so laying our proverbial cards on the table is a healthy place to start for this meeting.

Kyle, as an executive assistant, I need to share with you that Sybil isn't going anywhere. She's a senior vice president, she's under contract for several more years, and senior management believes she's doing an excellent job. That's an important factor for you to keep in mind. As an objective third party, it appears to me that you're not happy here. You seem to be disappointed in the management team. You appear not to enjoy your work on occasion. And I'm sure you feel like you're not appreciated or part of the team, at least at certain times. Am I correct? [*Yes.*]

Okay, so tell me your thoughts: Would leaving now on your own accord allow you an honorable exit strategy? Would exploring other opportunities outside the company while you're still employed here make sense for you at this point in your career? We'd be willing to allow you to begin interviewing at other companies as long as you make sure that our work comes first and that we're given at least twenty-four hours' notice of an upcoming interview. I'm only mentioning this because I don't want you to feel like you need to feign illness or conjure up doctors' and dentists' appointments if you've got an interview coming up. I'd rather we all be aboveboard and that you let us help you.

One other thing, Kyle. I want you to know that this is strictly up to you. If you'd like our support to either resign on your own terms now or to begin looking for other work, then we'll help you. If not, that's okay too. We'll do everything we can to help you reinvent your working relationship with Sybil and to feel more appreciated for your efforts. I just want you to feel like you have choices in the matter: stay, leave, or look for something else with our knowledge. We'll help you through this if you agree that it's an important matter in your life. It's better that we discuss these things openly than leave them unsaid. What are your thoughts?

This velvet glove approach typically lowers the tension in the relationship immediately. The logic to this intervention is simply this: it's always better to tell people where they stand. When people are treated professionally and respectfully, they'll respond in kind. Although delivering a message like this can be confrontational, it's therapeutic. After all, you and I would feel better if our managers told us that they'd prefer that we take our marbles and play in somebody else's game, wouldn't we? That's a much better alternative than having to "divine" from our managers' actions that they don't want us around anymore.

Are there downsides to this type of intervention technique? Not really as long as you're careful to ensure that the employees understand that this is *their* decision (thereby avoiding a constructive discharge claim later down the road). People need to hear how others feel about them. Most employees will appreciate the opportunity to hear about problems concerning them in an open and honest forum. Addressing matters proactively in cases like this helps employees take back control of their careers and literally give you your department back without the constant underlying tension from a disgruntled employee. Look to partner with your boss, HR, and even legal to ensure that this is handled correctly by a third-party mediator like HR who can broker a peace between you both and hopefully encourage the employee to consider alternative career options outside your organization.

11

WHISTLEBLOWERS VERSUS CHARACTER ASSASSINS
When You're the Accused

IF YOU'VE EVER HEARD THE SAYING "the damage is in the accusation," you'll know what this section is about. When the Sarbanes-Oxley Act was passed in 2002, companies found themselves scrambling to publish corporate ethics statements and codes of conduct to make it safe for employees to disclose financial improprieties—anonymously if necessary—that could damage a company or materially affect its published financial reports. That code of ethics, however, extended well beyond the immediate area of financial impropriety and incorporated other areas of "ethical business practices," including an organization's equal employment policies and guarantees of a workplace free from harassment and retaliation.

Corporate ethics statements made it safe to disclose all sorts of workplace improprieties—financial, systems related, or human—that threatened the safety or well-being of the workplace. And since employees had the discretion to escalate matters anonymously, a Pandora's box was opened that allowed workers to share concerns, and sometimes rumors and character attacks, with impunity. Likewise, because of the whistleblower protections

INDIVIDUAL CRISES . 65 .

contained in the act and in many companies' written policies, workers figured out before too long that engaging in the prover- bial *preemptive strike*—"I'll complain about my boss's *conduct* before she has a chance to complain about my job *performance*"— became a new tightrope act for operational leaders and human resource managers to cross as workers protected themselves with an "invisible cloak" of retaliation protection should the company later come back and attempt to dismiss, lay off, or otherwise disci- pline them after filing a complaint.

This idea of companies accepting anonymous complaints has a healthy side to it, of course. Employees who fear retaliation can still escalate matters of concern to senior management, often doing so using a nontraceable cell phone number. Yet all good things can be abused once people figure out how to game the sys- tem. In this case, how does a responsible employer handle it when it suspects that the nameless voice behind an anonymous com- plaint may actually be engaging in character assassination against a targeted supervisor? And how do you protect yourself if you find yourself on the "sharp end of the investigation spear" with numer- ous, unsubstantiated claims being levied against you?

This isn't easy for your company: finding that delicate balance between the individual privacy rights of complainants and what could appear to be mean-spirited slander toward the alleged wrongdoer (often the supervisor) places every department head and human resources manager in an ethical quandary, besides placing the company in a compromising legal position. Attacking workplace problems like this directly and appropriately poses exceptional challenges to even the strongest companies and indi- vidual leaders alike, so an approach that combines legal guidance and common sense will work best.

And it won't be easy for you either. Anonymous attacks could hit very close to home and feel exceptionally personal. For instance, an allegation that someone is embezzling company funds or falsify- ing time cards is fairly straightforward to investigate and verify. But what about an anonymous letter that alleges that supervisor X is sleeping with his subordinate? And what if that anonymous complaint appears in the ombudsman's mailbox at the same time that the supervisor's wife receives an anonymous text message alleging that her husband is sleeping with that same subordinate? That's when things can get ugly and personal, and the targeted supervisor will often feel he's being attacked at work at the same time that he's attempting desperately to repair his personal relationship with this wife on the home front. Now it's more important than ever to understand how to play your hand correctly and partner with the company investigators, typically human resources in conjunction with in-house or outside legal counsel.

Following are reasonable steps that you can follow to protect yourself and your organization if you feel you are being unfairly targeted by an anonymous complainant:

Rule 1: Keep your cool. Don't overreact to a situation like this. True, it may hurt deeply and leave you feeling profoundly disappointed in your team, but this isn't about your feelings; it's about your role as an objective leader within your organization and your willingness to partner with human resources and/or legal to protect the company (and yourself, of course).

Rule 2: Partner closely—and I mean closely—with human resources. Follow HR's lead every step of the way. HR may need to have you work remotely or not work at all one day so they can remove you from the premises to conduct an objective investigation (that is, so that you will not be able to influence it by your mere presence). If you're placed on "administrative, investigatory leave," go along with it willingly. Your job is to do whatever it takes to make the investigation easier on the HR team.

Rule 3: Do nothing to appear to conduct your own mini investigation into who on your team (or outside your team) may be raising these allegations. You are not to speak about this with anyone on your team or with any of your peers. Consider yourself "frozen" until the investigation is concluded: do your work and nothing more. If anyone brings up the topic, simply tell them that you're not at liberty to discuss it.

Rule 4:   Admit any wrongdoing that may have occurred when you speak with the HR fact finder. Be willing to share any specific circumstances where people may have taken what you said or did out of context. By admitting partial responsibility for a situation gone wrong, you'll actually come across as more objective and credible. Lying under these circumstances will likely result in immediate dismissal of employment.

Rule 5:   When it's your turn to be interviewed (and defend yourself), remember to encourage the HR fact finder to speak with everyone on your team, your peers, and anyone else who may know about the allegation or have witnessed any particular events in question. This is not the time to be shy or shield yourself from others—it's the time for you to involve others in getting to the truth and remaining as transparent as possible. Provide detailed responses as well as emails or other proof that demonstrates your innocence in the matter. Follow a rule of full cooperation and honesty. Nothing will build your credibility faster.

Finally, assuming that the investigation concludes with no wrongdoing found, encourage HR to hold a staff meeting with you, your immediate superior, and your team to share the results of the investigation. (No details—simply the overall findings and conclusion of the investigation.) This isn't intended to violate your privacy rights or air unfounded allegations against you publicly. It's to help the team heal. In many instances, this is far better than sweeping the whole matter under the rug and pretending that it never happened. Understand that this may be the hardest part of all because it requires your working with team members openly going forward, even if you feel vulnerable because someone did so much to damage your credibility and reputation and to possibly get you fired. You have to be the "bigger person" here. Once the team acknowledges that the investigation led to no findings, healing can begin.

A simple closure measure from HR might sound like this:

As I believe you're all aware, human resources has been conducting an investigation for the past two days regarding anonymous complaints that were made against John Doe in terms of his management, leadership, and communication style. We conducted a full investigation, and we looked into every allegation and spoke with every witness who may have had some knowledge of these claims as identified by the original anonymous complainant as well as those of you who were also identified as potential secondary witnesses.

The investigation revealed that while certain comments may have been taken out of context and ill motives may have been ascribed, there really was no finding of wrongdoing here. The witnesses identified by the original anonymous complainant did not corroborate the allegations. And as such, we've fulfilled our commitment as a responsible employer to conduct a thorough investigation in a timely manner and reach a reasonable conclusion.

But I'm not comfortable just closing out this investigation without addressing what really happened here. We don't know who filed the original allegation, and we have no need for that information at this point. But I want to remind you all that real damage can be done to someone's career and personal life when anonymous complaints are made behind the scenes with apparent impunity. I'm very disappointed in how this matter was escalated: the allegations appear to have been grossly exaggerated, the witnesses couldn't support the allegations, and this felt like a very personal attack against John.

John, I want to apologize to you on behalf of the team for what occurred here. I think you deserve to hear that publicly, and I remind everyone in this room to treat others as you would like to be treated yourself. If you have legitimate issues and concerns, feel free to raise them openly or file your complaints anonymously—but please remember that there are real people whose careers may be placed at risk, and I expect you all to act in a more responsible manner in the future. Remember as well that a knowingly false complaint is a violation of our company's code of conduct and could result in immediate termination. We clearly take these matters very seriously.

This investigation is officially closed. This meeting was an attempt to heal the wound that's dividing this team right now. I have higher expectations of you as a team than you've displayed in this situation, and I hope you all take the time to consider how this might have felt to John and other members of the team.

With this public apology to the wronged supervisor in place and an opportunity to reset group expectations, you'll stand the greatest chance of healing the wound while enforcing your company's escalation policy and whistleblower protections. Addressing the matter openly and honestly will provide a healing touch that will go a long way in preventing future whimsical attacks from behind an anonymous curtain while allowing your team to rebuild fractured relationships and reinstitute a sense of healthy camaraderie.

12

BEING SET UP FOR A CLAIM
OF "PRETALIATION"

LET'S BEGIN THIS SECTION WITH A case study I share with my students at UCLA Extension when I teach in the HR certification program. I want you to be me at an earlier point in my career: director of human resources responsible for employee relations. Here's the scenario: I was sitting in my office on a Tuesday late afternoon when a vice president of legal affairs stopped by to speak with me. (We'll call him Raul.) He said that he happened to be on my part of the campus and thought he'd drop by to say hi and share a problem he was having with one of his direct reports, the recently hired director of legal affairs. (We'll call her Eden.) Raul began to tell me about problems with Eden's performance. She'd been with our organization for only two months and seemed to not be taking her responsibilities seriously. For example, she wasn't returning clients' calls in a timely manner; her contract work wasn't tight or well thought through, causing additional rewrites; she wasn't putting in the hours that were required of the role; and she wasn't able to answer clients' basic questions about contract status, necessitating that the clients raise their questions to Raul, the VP, who soon realized that Eden should be able to answer many of the questions being asked.

I asked Raul what he wanted to do at this point and how I could help, and he told me there wasn't anything to do just yet. He wanted to speak with his boss, the departmental senior vice president, to get her take on the matter. At that point, they would both come back to me with a recommended plan of action for the new hire, likely later that week. Raul gave me the heads-up, though, that it would likely result in some form of discipline—either a written warning or a formal extension of Eden's initial "probation" period. I thanked Raul for coming in and told him I'd make myself available whenever he and his boss were ready to address this. Easy enough.

Now, guess who came to visit me first thing the next morning? You guessed it: Eden, the director. But when she came in, she appeared downright angry. Her conversation sounded like this: "I have to make a formal complaint about my supervisor, Raul. I just can't take it anymore. He's very condescending toward me as a woman, he shows a bold male Latino 'bravado' or 'machismo' in everything he does and puts down my ideas. I feel like he treats me *less than*, and I see that he doesn't treat other males that way. Overall, I feel like I'm being discriminated against because of my gender, and I don't know if this new relationship is going to work out."

Okay, now here's the test question. Remember, you're me in this scenario, the HR director minding my own business in my office when I had my first visit with the VP on Tuesday afternoon and now the director on Wednesday morning: do I tell the director that her boss was in my office the night before complaining about her job performance, or do I not mention that at all? In other words, while she's complaining about his conduct, should I bring up that he's already put me on notice about her performance and is considering writing her up or extending her probation?

First, an acknowledgment: this is a particularly tough case study, and it's open to different interpretations. But it's real, so it's worth considering. And as you might expect, there's a good deal of disagreement among the students in class, either for or against disclosing the VP's visit the afternoon before. On the one hand, certain students argue that the VP's concerns about Eden's performance are relevant to the situation at hand. After all, this is about their mutual relationship, and his behavior toward her may show signs of frustration or stress because of her substandard job performance. On the other hand, certain students argue that one issue has nothing to do with the other. There shouldn't be any mitigating considerations for a supervisor's behavior, especially when discrimination or harassment may be in play. Therefore, the latter group of students argues that no mention of the VP's visit the night before should be included in your conversation with the director on Wednesday morning.

What say you? What would you have done if you were me, sitting in that meeting with the director that Wednesday morning and listening to her complaints about her boss's alleged conduct? (Please think about this before you read any further.)

Okay, the answer behind the curtain is: I disclosed that her boss met with me the night before to discuss his concerns about her job performance. I also shared that he was planning on speaking with the SVP/department head before the end of the week and getting back to me about either issuing a disciplinary notice to Eden or extending her initial probationary period (or both).

Why would I do that? I'm glad you asked, and this is the lesson and moral of the story. Workplace communication, generally speaking, is about transparency. Behavior and performance issues often overlap. In a spirit of full transparency and goodwill, I needed to let Eden know about my conversation with Raul the night before because it was simply the right thing to do. After all, her job may be on the line at this point. Further, her boss's boss is getting involved. Therefore, to sweep the matter under the rug and make no mention of it would be doing her a disservice in a way, as she wouldn't be fully informed about the totality of events at play in this situation.

But there's another critical reason to disclose the boss's concerns about her performance: *the record*. The record being created is a critical consideration in everything you do as a leader in corporate America. When in doubt, always consider what the record will look like if you act in one way versus another. Here were my thoughts at the time: If I share Raul's concerns about Eden's performance, then she'll have a fuller picture and understanding of what's going on and what may be affecting his communications with her. If she fully understands that he's already come to HR to express his concerns with her job performance, then she'll have a better understanding of the seriousness of the situation and be given a "fighting chance" to save her job (if she chooses to).

In comparison, if I mention nothing about Raul's visit the night before and simply listen to Eden's complaints about his conduct, then there's additional risk involved as far as the record is concerned. First, she won't know of his concerns, and she could later come back and accuse me of denying her a fair chance of salvaging her job by sharing what I knew at the time relative to her boss's impressions about her problematic performance. Even more significantly, she could reason that she (a) came to human resources to complain about her boss's conduct on Wednesday and then (b) got written up and had her initial probationary period extended on Friday. Do you see the potential damage to the record in this second consideration? She could easily reason that retaliation is at hand for her having filed a good-faith complaint about her supervisor. By disclosing the full picture, she at least realized that there were concerns about her performance that preceded her complaint to human resources, and that's a critical element and consideration should the case ever proceed to litigation.

Of course, I added to my conversation with Eden that I wanted to hear her side of the story in full, that I would take notes of everything she had to say, and that I'd ask her for witnesses who could corroborate her impressions of her boss's behavior so that I could conduct a formal investigation. But in my mind, she had to know about this visit the afternoon before so that she understood that any adverse action that might come her way from the VP and the SVP in her department was not in retaliation of her complaint to HR that morning. *That's* the importance of honesty and transparency when it comes to the record being created.

Here's where the VP was lucky: he just happened to stop by on Tuesday afternoon to share his concerns about Eden's performance with me. Had he not done so, the only information I would have had would have come from Eden on Wednesday morning when she filed a formal complaint against her supervisor. Think about it from my (the HR) perspective: if you, the operational leader, speak to me about a subordinate's substandard job performance, that sets me in motion in one particular direction (that is, I have to help support you with turning around an employee's performance). In comparison, if the employee speaks to me first and complains about your conduct, especially using terms like *discrimination*, *harassment*, or *retaliation*, then that sets me in motion in a totally different direction (that is, I have to investigate a complaint about a manager's alleged discriminatory conduct).

The lesson: *run*, don't walk, to HR when you have challenges with an employee's performance. Make HR your ally early on. As the middle person involved, I have no way of judging who may be telling the truth in a scenario like this. True, Eden's supervisor Raul may demonstrate inappropriate or dismissive behavior toward her because of her gender. Likewise true, however, is that employees are sophisticated consumers and often realize that if they can complain about a supervisor's *conduct* before that supervisor has a chance to complain about their *performance*, then their preemptive strike of what's known as *pretaliation* can help them protect their jobs. After all, they know that it's more difficult for a company to take adverse action (like termination) against a worker who recently complained about their boss's conduct using the "d" (discrimination) word.

Managers are best partnering with their bosses and with HR whenever their gut or intuition tells them that a performance issue may rise to the level of disciplinary action or termination. Do so as quickly as possible to avoid the potential of workers—suspecting that you may be preparing to discipline or terminate them about their performance—seizing an opportunity to steer the record in their favor. No, this doesn't happen all that often to individual managers, but you'd be surprised how many times human resources people experience it across the enterprise. The goal, therefore, it to get ahead of the issue and train managers to partner with HR transparently rather than hide any departmental concerns from HR. Leadership is a team sport. Your immediate superior and your HR representative are your first lines of defense should someone attempt to "pretaliate" by alleging inappropriate conduct on your part when you sense that a legitimate performance issue may be at hand.

13

DEALING EFFECTIVELY WITH
ATTITUDE PROBLEMS

ONE OF THE MOST COMMON CHALLENGES facing managers lies in dealing with employee attitude problems, typically evidenced when employees roll their eyes, sigh, or use antagonistic body language. Trying to stop such "silent" behavior is difficult because employees can so easily deny it. Frequently, managers tend to avoid confronting employees who "cop a 'tude" because the path of least resistance is avoidance and because the whole matter seems so slippery. After all, as a manager, you don't want to come across as touchy or overly sensitive. Still, feelings of resentment may linger, and pent-up emotions result in a public shouting match when some proverbial last straw is broken. By then the situation is out of control.

There are two key points to keep in mind when attempting to eradicate this all-too-common workplace problem. First, tell people in private how you *perceive* their actions and how they make you feel. Be specific and paint a picture with words so that they clearly understand the behaviors in question. Ask for her help in solving the perception problem that exists, and make a mutual commitment to hear that person's side of the story and better the situation.

Second, avoid the term *attitude* in your discussion and replace it with words like *behavior* and *conduct,* which are much more neutral and objective. The word *attitude* is subjective and inflammatory and typically escalates disagreement by fostering feelings of resentment and anger. More important, courts have interpreted *attitude problems* as being mere differences of opinion or personality conflicts. It is therefore critical that you avoid that specific term in any of your conversations or disciplinary documentation.

When attempting to fix a communication problem that exists with one of your staff members, approach the matter by painting a picture with words like this:

Lisa, I need your help. You know they say that perception is reality until proven otherwise. I often feel like you're either angry with me or angry with the rest of the team. I may be off in my assumption, but that's an honest assessment of the impression you sometimes give off. I don't know if anything's bothering you or if you feel that I can be more supportive of you in any way, but please let me know if that's the case.

Otherwise, though, please understand that you make me feel embarrassed in front of other members of the staff when you roll your eyes upward, sigh, and then say, "Okay, I'll get it done!" with a harrumph. Your body language is also confrontational when you cock your head back and place your hands on your hips. I'm not sure if you're aware you're doing any of these things or if you do them purposely to place others on the offensive, but either way, it makes it difficult at times to partner with you. And everyone on the team is responsible for creating a friendly and inclusive workplace, you and me included.

Do you feel it's inappropriate for me to ask you to complete your work on time? Should I even have to follow up with you regarding project completion deadlines, or should it be your responsibility to keep me abreast of the status of your projects? Even more significantly, *how would you feel* if you were the supervisor and one of your staff members responded that way to you in front of others?

Likewise, *how would it make you feel if* I responded to your questions with that tone in my voice or that body language? Wouldn't you feel that I was disrespectful or condescending toward you, especially if I did it in front of the rest of the team?

Is it reasonable that I ask for a commitment from you to avoid any perception of condescension in your responses or tone of voice, "being bothered" to do something, or responding aggressively to others' questions? Even more important, will you make a commitment to me now that you'll assume partial responsibility for this perception problem that exists so that we'll never have to discuss it again?

Notice the highlights in the paragraph above: "You make me feel . . ." and "How would you feel if . . ." are common phrases that invoke feelings of introspection in others and help them assume partial responsibility for things gone wrong. Feelings aren't right or wrong—they just are. When combining such phrases with an opening statement like "There's a difference in perception here," employees are usually more willing to hear your side of the story objectively. After all, there are two sides to every story, and employees typically won't deny that they're partially responsible for the problem if it's presented in the right way. What they often want, however, is to be heard and to gain your attention as their manager. Therefore, seize this opportunity to fix the problem verbally by declaring a truce and listening with an objective ear. End your conversation by requesting a commitment that you'll never have to address the matter again.

What's critical is that you don't allow this type of conduct to continue after your initial conversation takes place. This is not the type of conversation that needs to happen more than once. Don't expect less from your employees than you expect from yourself. If the matter continues to escalate, your response should be in writing in the form of a progressive disciplinary warning. Because it's conduct related, you have the discretion to skip the first step in your company's progressive discipline program (the documented verbal warning) and escalate directly to a written (second-level) warning. Why? First, because you have more discretion to escalate disciplinary matters when inappropriate workplace conduct is at hand. Second, because you've already had a detailed conversation about this, which can count as your initial verbal warning. Just be sure to document the date and time of the original conversation in the written warning to make the clearest record possible.

14

PERFORMANCE APPRAISAL BOMBSHELLS
Delivering Bad News for the First Time During the Annual Performance Review

THIS MAY NOT SOUND LIKE A TRUE "crisis" at first, but once you realize the gravity of the situation, a healthy sense of fear, disappointment, and yes—even guilt—will likely set in. Let's assume you have a problematic employee who's been with the company for ages, demonstrates a bit of an entitlement and fierce resistance to change, and has built an invisible wall to fend off peers and associates. Next, you realize you've been guilty of sweeping things under the rug and leaving unaddressed those matters that should have been handled three or four iterations of managers ago. Finally, your immediate boss or human resources informs you that the organization is now taking a much more serious approach to annual performance reviews and expects you to document that the individual should fail this year's review for ongoing performance and conduct problems. Oh, and let's assume that you know they're right but were hoping to pretty much issue the same (passing) review as last year and be done with it. Okay, now you can panic!

Why? Because many organizations are taking serious looks at their performance management programs to spike employee performance, team productivity, and bottom-line results. As such, they're asking for real, accurate, and real-time feedback in the annual performance review, even if you haven't been addressing performance or conduct challenges adequately throughout the year. The bottom line: you know that your employee will feel blindsided by this and ask why you didn't mention these problems when they occurred and simply waited to document them in the annual review, and worst of all will ask whether you're trying to build a paper trail that leads to termination (which may be accurate).

Even without such a sudden change of corporate heart as to what the performance review exercise is supposed to accomplish, you may simply feel that you cannot issue a passing score in good conscience when the individual fails on so many different levels— quality, quantity, customer care, and internal communications and behavior. How do you "fail someone" when you rightfully haven't addressed the issues throughout the performance period? You know by heart that people should never be surprised on their annual performance reviews, but you also suspect that many employees' scores are regularly inflated at your organization and at other organizations where you've worked in the past. When it's time for the rubber to meet the proverbial road at performance review time and you have to issue poor scores due to problematic performance or conduct that was not discussed at the time they occurred, you'll likely have to assume responsibility for your failure to communicate properly in real time but issue the "bombshell" annual performance appraisal nevertheless. No, this won't be easy, but there are ways to do this that make the process more tolerable and reasonable.

First, understand that you're not alone. By far one of the biggest mistakes that managers make lies in inflating grades on annual performance reviews. The path of least resistance is avoidance, and in order to minimize confrontation, many managers give *meets expectations* scores to underachievers or workers with poor behavioral records. This same documentation, however, can come back to haunt you should the organization later look to terminate. Why? Because with no records of progressive disciplinary documentation and only "acceptable" performance reviews, it would be difficult to terminate the individual for cause or suddenly invoke a layoff or position elimination to remove the individual from your organization. (Remember, layoffs typically require "peer group analysis" to determine who the least qualified individual is to assume the remaining job duties in a particular job classification. If the employee in question has significant tenure and no disciplinary history, you'll likely be required to choose someone else in that job classification to lay off—not the individual you were hoping to remove from your team.)

Therefore, as a general rule, if you suspect that you may have to terminate someone in the upcoming year, you should ensure the performance review accurately depicts why the employee's performance and/or conduct *does not meet expectations*. An objective performance review with concrete examples of an employee's shortcomings is a critical tool that supervisors can leverage to correct an employee's performance or conduct. And, if the performance or conduct does not improve, the performance review, combined with other progressive disciplinary measures, lays the groundwork for a defensible business decision to terminate the individual for cause or lay him off during a corporate downsizing. *That's* how important annual performance reviews are in terms of defending a company's actions relative to terminations and layoffs.

When you suspect that you'll need to introduce new negative information on an employee's annual review, call in human resources as quickly as possible. If your company doesn't have an HR department, check with your immediate supervisor, and enlist your legal team's help. Many HR departments will have the resources to help you construct a well-written review that introduces these new elements. In certain cases, HR may recommend including progressive disciplinary language in the annual review, turning the review into a documented warning. HR can help you document a performance improvement plan, the company's expectations, and consequence language that makes clear that immediate and sustained improvement is required and may result in termination if not attained. In certain cases, HR will also be able to coach the employee or offer outside training resources that help your company demonstrate its willingness to rehabilitate flagging performers. All in, however, you'll want a strong partnership with HR or legal to gain approval of your draft before it's shared with the employee.

With the approved documentation in hand, your next step will be to meet with the employee and explain the communication gap—in other words, why there is substantial documentation demonstrating that the individual has not met minimal performance expectations when you haven't discussed problems together at the time they occurred. When that's the case, be sure and assume responsibility for not having shared this negative feedback at the time it occurred. Here's what it might sound like when you explain that at the beginning of the sit-down meeting:

Roger, I recognize that we haven't formally discussed your getting along well with others over the past year, but I felt it appropriate to bring this issue to your attention during the annual performance review because it's so serious and such a critical aspect of your overall contribution to the department. In fact, it could have a significant effect on your longer-term career potential if it's left unaddressed. Likewise, I've turned a blind eye to a number of performance issues that have occurred throughout the review period in the form of missed calculations, errors, and necessary rework because you appear to have rushed through a number of assignments at different times. I know that you're aware that I feel like I have a continuous need to double-check most of your work, and the quantity and quality of errors remains of significant concern. We've discussed your not thinking things through on occasion or making the same error on monthly reports, and I'll need to document this in this year's review.

I'll start with an apology: I realize that I should have shared more of this with you at the time these incidents occurred, but I was guilty of avoiding the confrontation and hoping the problem would simply fix itself. I realize now that wasn't fair to you. That being said, we can't avoid the issue any longer. This performance review window is the ideal time to discuss my concerns because it's intended to provide feedback, reset expectations, and guide your career development going forward. Just so you're aware, I've discussed this with Sara, my boss and our department head, as she's expressed concerns about your performance and conduct as well. That being said, you're more than free to discuss this with her and escalate the matter to human resources once we're done here.

Further, I believe you're suffering from a perception-management problem: regardless of your intentions, people tend to avoid you. You come across as being angry or upset much of the time, confrontational, and at times, overly challenging. And people—me included—tend to cut a wide swath around you and do the work themselves rather than come to you for help. That's damaging the overall sense of morale and camaraderie in our department, Roger, and you're responsible for creating a friendly and inclusive work environment, just like everyone else. Your behavior is negating your overall performance contributions, as evidenced by the flare-ups that occur between you and your peers from time to time as well as some of the customer challenges you've experienced that I've had to step in to mediate.

I'll make a commitment to you now to bring these matters to your attention immediately whenever I notice them in the future, but my main message to you during this performance review is that you're not currently meeting company expectations overall because of these significant challenges. Again, I apologize for not addressing some of these situations on the spot at the time they occurred or expressing how much they concerned me, and I'll commit to you that I'll bring this to your attention whenever I see an issue from now on. But it's significant enough to formally document now and to reset expectations going forward. Let's look at how I documented this on the review itself and the examples, development plan, and future goals that I've outlined . . .

Resetting expectations going forward will likely not be so easy and face stiff resistance. The individual will likely disagree with your assessment and look to escalate the matter to the department head and/or to human resources, claiming it is unfair because you failed to discuss many of the documented issues at the time they occurred. That may be true, but you also have the right as the manager to "start somewhere." It won't be pretty doing it this way because you never want people feeling blindsided, but resetting your own commitment to share concerns at the time they occur will surely help.

Detail your expectations in the appraisal very clearly. List in very clear terms how you expect this individual to communicate with team members and customers, create a friendly and inclusive work environment, and resolve conflict in a constructive manner. Emphasize the positive benefits that will result from such a turn-around, including stronger teamwork, having one another's backs, and lightening up the overall mood in the office. But don't shy away from your responsibility: admit your shortcomings in not sharing your concerns earlier, but hold the individual accountable to a higher performance standard going forward and starting now. Expect some lingering resentment, but know that it will heal in time if you keep your end of the bargain in communicating future challenges as they occur.

15

HANDLING EMPLOYEES
WHO QUIT . . . THEN
CHANGE THEIR MINDS

EMPLOYEES GIVE NOTICE ALL THE TIME, RIGHT? There's not much to it: they walk in, hand over a letter of resignation, and offer two weeks of continued service out of courtesy and tradition so that you have some lead time to find a replacement. Granted, usually there's little more to do than say thanks for the person's service and prepare your strategy for backfilling the position and distributing the individual's work to the remaining team members until a replacement can be identified. But what if an employee who has had ongoing conduct problems quits but refuses to provide a final termination date? What if the person offers verbal notice but has done this before, and now you're afraid there will be a change of mind again within the two-week notice period? Would you rather the employee leave immediately rather than in two weeks? As you can see, the exit process can get a bit hairy depending on the circumstances. Let's address these not-so-uncommon scenarios.

First, if someone refuses to commit to a final separation date, that's not okay. They can't just walk in and tell you they're leaving without telling you when. Likewise, someone may walk into your office and tender notice ninety days from now (which just happens to coincide with their wedding date). Are you obligated to keep them?

Once an employee places you on notice of intending to leave the organization, you have a legitimate business need to question the exit plan and confirm timelines. After all, you're not obligated to employ an unexceptional worker who's buying time by remaining employed while waiting to get married, finish a bachelor's degree or fulfill any other personal obligation. Call the individual into your office and say that setting a specific date will help you plan for a successful transition. Pull out the calendar and determine together an appropriate end date that suits your needs. As for the individual who graciously offers ninety days' notice, simply say thanks for the generous offer of three months, but say that you plan on following the company's policy and past practice of accepting two weeks' notice. The person will be free to leave at that time and will be compensated for any work through that end date.

If you're in a situation where you'd rather send the employee home on the day of notice rather than in two weeks, you have every right to do so. This happens often with salespeople, especially when they're going to a competitor. Under those circumstances, however, it might make most sense for you to pay out the two-week notice period. Consider it a cheap insurance policy, because if you, rather than the employee, determine the date that the worker is to leave your company, you may have inadvertently transformed the *resignation* into a *discharge*, and the individual may be entitled to unemployment insurance benefits. Further, sending resigning employees home the same day without paying them through their two-week notice period could be viewed as a *wrongful termination* if your employee handbook states that you expect all terminating employees to provide your company with two weeks' notice. In such cases, the extra two weeks of pay function as insurance to ward off any potential wrongful-termination claims.

On the other hand, if an employee refuses to resign in writing and you suspect the person may have a change of heart or is otherwise appearing to be playing games, you have every right to confirm the verbal resignation in writing. A simple email or note might read something like this:

> Connor, I have accepted your verbal resignation today, January 30, and that means February 15 will be your last day with our company. You will be relieved of your duties on that day, and I will appreciate your cooperation over the next two weeks in reassigning your current workload and helping with the job posting. Thank you for your contribution to our company over the past two years, and I wish you well as you move forward and excel in your career.

Your written confirmation will serve as a proxy for his, and it will make it more difficult for Connor to change his mind one week later and attempt to keep his job.

What about the employee who gives notice and then changes her mind? Does she have a right to insist that you retain her before her two-week notice period runs out? It depends. You have the right, as an employer, to rely on the individual's resignation in good faith and end her employment on the agreed upon date. But how you *act in reliance* on the notice becomes a key issue in the eyes of the law. Specifically, if you haven't truly acted in reliance upon her resignation by posting her job, reassigning her work duties, and interviewing candidates, for example, then the employee may very well be free to rescind her resignation during the notice period.

The lesson? When a problematic and underperforming employee tenders notice, fill the position as quickly as possible, or at least demonstrate that you acted in good faith in reliance on that resignation notice by posting the job, redistributing the work, and beginning interviews. You'll have a much greater chance of warding off a wrongful-termination claim if you can show that you acted on the notice rather than simply accepting the resignation letter and filing it away. And who knows—you may be able to hire or promote someone into the soon-to-be-vacant role within that two-week notice period. At that point, all doors close to the individual who suddenly decides to rescind the resignation notice, no ifs, ands, or buts.

Next, let's expand upon our crises topics by considering departmental or team challenges that may likely come your way as you progress through your management career.

PART TWO

DEPARTMENTAL/ TEAM CRISES

16

TEAM-INTERVIEWING YOUR PROSPECTIVE BOSS
No Pressure!

WHEN YOUR DEPARTMENT HEAD LEAVES the organization and a search for a new director or vice president is launched, it's not uncommon for the team members to meet with the finalist candidates to assess their backgrounds and add their voice about who would be the best fit. Typically, the final decision will be reserved for executive management, but hearing from the department members is definitely a factor in the final consideration. It's generally considered healthy and transparent to have team members interview finalist candidates for their input. The opposite would be to have senior management conduct interviews, make the final selection, and introduce the new department head to your team on that individual's first day of employment. If your organization invites you and your team to interview finalists in advance and weigh in on their ultimate suitability, take advantage of the opportunity and appreciate the inclusive nature of this interviewing approach. After all, it's the ultimate show of respect for your input and recommendations.

When asked to participate in either a group or individual meeting with someone who's under consideration for the role of your next boss, how you approach the interview could make a lasting first impression on the candidate and provide your senior leadership team with insight into your people-discernment abilities. How can you delicately and respectfully glean important information about the individual's leadership, communication, and team-building styles? How do you go about asking questions that will help you come to an informed decision about what working with this individual is like in order to prepare your recommendation to your organization's senior leadership team?

OPENING QUESTION SALVOS

True, interviewing your prospective boss might feel awkward at first. Much will depend, of course, on whether you're meeting with the potential boss one-on-one or in a group. If you're meeting with the individual one-on-one, be sure to have your questions lined up clearly so that a natural rhythm and flow occurs throughout the dialogue. If you're meeting as a group, be sure to coordinate who will ask which questions or will cover particular types of questions (for example, career history, team communication style, approach to the first ninety days, and the like). Opening questions can be softer and open ended to get to know the individual more personally. They can then be followed by more specific "drill down" questions that can be prepared in advance. Following are some group openers that may make candidates feel at home but also let them know you've prepared adequately for this meeting and have a well-thought-out strategy for selecting candidates:

1. Charlotte, I know it's a bit awkward for us to interview our future boss, but I appreciate that our organization encourages us to do so as a team. Is this something you've done at organizations where you've worked in the past, and have you sat in our shoes in a similar situation? If so, how did you approach it?

2. If you don't mind our asking, how did you find out about this opportunity, and what initially attracted you to our company?

3. Most of us have been here for at least five years, so we sometimes lose sight of what's going on in the outside world. Can you share with us what criteria you're using in selecting your next position, company, or even industry relative to what you're seeing out there in the job market these days?

GETTING TO THE HEART OF THE MATTER

Once the polite openers and inviting introductions have launched a respectful conversation, it is time to get to the heart of the matter: the individual's philosophy of leadership and prior experience leading teams in similar situations. The following questions attempt to dive a bit deeper into the individual's philosophy about leadership, communication, and team building as well as prior experience and expectations:

4. We prepared for this interview as a group in advance of today's meeting and determined that what keeps us happy and sticking around is our strong sense of independence and autonomy. Have you worked with groups that have longer tenure and a fairly deep level of expertise in their field, and if so, how would you manage that type of team?

5. In terms of your communication style, do you tend to hold weekly staff meetings, quarterly one-on-ones, and the like, or do you tend not to schedule your meetings in such a structured way?

6. What's your philosophy on performance reviews? Do you love them or hate them, or are you somewhere in

between? How would you advise us to make the most out of professional and career-development opportunities while working for you?

7. Do you prefer for your team to set goals and, if so, do you measure and evaluate them monthly, quarterly, or annually? Likewise, how do you measure and track success?

8. What would you add or subtract to your current team (or a prior team) to strengthen performance or productivity?

9. What's your general approach to addressing problematic performance issues? What can we expect in terms of your style when dealing with interpersonal conflict, and what's your philosophy surrounding "mistakes"?

10. Would you consider yourself more of a laissez-faire leader, or do you prefer providing ongoing structure, feedback, and direction? How hands on is your leadership style?

11. How would you prefer that we keep you in the loop and feed information to you? Do you like informal visits in your office or being copied on emails, or would you be interested in joining us in our client meetings?

CLOSING THE INTERVIEW

Finally, close out the interview by inviting the individual to ask you open-ended questions about your individual or team dynamic, overall performance level, or the culture of the division or department you're working in. It's important that this is a two-way street and transparent discussion for both sides equally. As such, your closing question might sound like this:

Charlotte, we've asked you a number of questions to get a feel for your leadership, communication, and team-building style. What can we answer for you in terms of our culture, our way of doing things, how we get along with one another, and the like?

Interviewing your future boss may feel like an awkward request on senior management's part, but you should appreciate when your company encourages it—the request is based on trust and respect for the work you do. The candidate gets to know the team, the team members have some say over who ultimately gets selected for the role, and senior management benefits from the team's insight. It's a triple win based on trust, respect, and transparency.

17

INHERITING A NEW TEAM
A Blessing and a Curse

INHERITING AN EMPLOYEE FROM another department or even from another organization can create special challenges, depending on the reason for the transfer. Whether it's due to a merger or acquisition or a simple departmental reorganization to improve efficiencies, managers sometimes face the prospect of inheriting a group of direct reports overnight. The matter can become particularly thorny if you're inheriting a "bumped" employee from another unit because of union contract demands. First, you may be integrating more than one person into your team all at once. Second, you may be inheriting an individual or a group that may be used to a totally different style of managing.

You will have to answer several delicate questions and keep a few critical rules in mind: Did the prior management team make promises of raises or promotions? Are you bound by those commitments, and if not, how do you reset expectations? How do you appraise these inherited individuals when it's performance-appraisal time and you've only been supervising them for a few months? And, what about inheriting an employee who is known to be a troublemaker or who comes over to your group on final written warning status? Finally, what about the resentment that will surely exist if someone from your team had to be laid off because the union contract demanded that employees who were laid off elsewhere were permitted to "bump" lesser-tenured people out of their positions in other departments? As you might guess, the circumstances may vary widely and can lead to an awful lot of tension and resentment.

The upside is that having a larger staff could provide extra "hands on deck" to keep the work flowing more smoothly in your area. Of course, the bigger your staff, the greater your résumé value tends to be. And don't forget the career development advantages of showing how you've led teams through dynamic change in a postmerger or integration environment. Even being able to tell the tale of how you calmed people's nerves when a beloved coworker was laid off because someone with greater seniority in the organization (whose position was eliminated) bumped your team member out of the organization? (Union contracts typically allow workers with greater seniority to "bump" out individuals in the same classification elsewhere within the organization. In other words, the elimination of a health unit secretary may have occurred in your hospital's radiation oncology unit, but the person whose position was eliminated can then bump someone in, say, the bone marrow transplant unit in the same classification but with lesser tenure.)

INTEGRATING NEWCOMERS

When you first learn that a new team or individual is being reassigned to your unit, don't panic—just do your homework. You may not be given the choice to say no, so think strategically about the move's benefits and plan proactively for its challenges. Likewise, be sure to partner with your boss, your department head, and human resources to ensure that you have all the facts necessary about the individual or group of employees involved.

This type of merging of people from different areas is typically referred to as *cultural integration* because it's all about protecting and preserving the culture that you've created with your original group while welcoming the positive aspects of the new group's style. Cultural integration starts by doing your due diligence up front and gathering the necessary data to determine the group's level of productivity and its style of working. Reviewing résumés, performance reviews, and disciplinary records is a logical place to start, as is speaking with current (and soon-to-be-former) supervisors. In fact, performance appraisals are the sweet spot of the pre-integration process since they, more than anything else, can provide clear documentation about an individual's performance, career progression potential, and areas for development. If performance appraisal is done correctly in the organization, those appraisals become an invaluable tool in picking up where the former management team left off.

CHECKING INTERNAL REFERENCES

When you interview the prior supervisor(s), ask questions that focus on the individual's or team's overall strengths, achievements, cohesiveness, and areas for professional development and performance improvement. Keeping in mind that personalities play a part in team cohesiveness and some of this judgment may be subjective, you might find it useful to include questions such as:

If you had to rehire any one of these individuals, who would be the first person you would call and why?

Who shows the most potential from a succession-planning standpoint in terms of career progression?

Who tends to be the "highest need" or "highest maintenance" person in the group?

Are there any individuals whom you'd advise me to be careful with or pay special attention to?

Are there any special circumstances with any of these individuals that I should be aware of, especially in terms of their expectations moving into our department?

Note that if the individual was bumped into your department under the union contract provisions, it might be wise to ask if the person expressed any remorse for having to lay someone else off with lesser seniority or considered accepting a layoff package rather than forcing someone else to be laid off elsewhere in the organization. This, of course, is not a critical factor, but it might be helpful to know if this individual has a high level of self-awareness or a healthy sense of selflessness.

CONSTRUCTIVE APPROACHES TO PERFORMANCE APPRAISALS

What happens if the transition to your new team occurs just before the annual performance appraisal is due? Performance appraisals are always challenging, but they become doubly difficult if you haven't had enough time to really evaluate the individual's performance. You may not be given the option of passing on this exercise by simply marking "too new to rate" on the appraisal template, so feel free to speak with prior supervisors within your company and find out how they would have rated the individual. In fact, it's not at all uncommon to split a review between two supervisors who happened to oversee an individual's work throughout the same appraisal period.

For example, if you will have supervised a group of newly inherited employees for two months of a twelve-month evaluation period, invite the prior supervisor to conduct the appraisal with you. Simply add narrative notes under both your names outlining your respective roles and time frames and explain to the individual that the numerical score that you came up with reflects both supervisors' opinions. Of course, that's all well and good unless the individual feels that the prior supervisor unfairly disliked him or her. If the individual expresses that concern, explain that this shared review process is common within your company and that all individuals in the group are being handled the same way. Of course, you'll be open to reinventing your relationship with this individual over time and will keep an open mind in the upcoming year.

THE CHALLENGES OF DIFFERING MANAGEMENT STYLES

Assuming you've done your homework in conducting pretransfer interviews with prior supervisors and in reviewing résumés and performance appraisals, then the creative but most challenging part begins. How do you integrate different work styles? For example, if your group enjoys open communication, an environment where their suggestions and recommendations are heard, and an overall culture of empowerment and shared decision-making, how do you adopt a group that is used to "doing what it's told"?

If you're used to eliciting feedback and suggestions from your team and enjoy a healthy sense of camaraderie, how do you integrate workers who lack trust in management and place doubt in even your most benevolent intentions? Fear not. There's light at the end of this tunnel too. You can't expect everyone to take to your management style right away. First of all, everyone will be worried about their jobs, and people will be walking on eggshells waiting to see what you're like and how the rest of the team interacts with them. Just remember that it may have taken a long while to get them to the point where they are now—it may take almost as long to get them to a new way of thinking.

Your surest bet will be to set your expectations to clearly err on the side of overcommunicating and sharing your values up front. What are your key expectations for everyone on the existing team? What are your five or ten most important *rules of the road* for your existing team that you want these new staffers to be aware of and abide by? What are your "hot buttons" and how can new transferees avoid "stepping on landmines" within the group? Share this type of information generously so that people know where they stand and what to expect. New relationships like this often require more support, structure, direction, and feedback. Once things are clearly coming together and you're comfortable with your newly merged team's interaction and productivity, then you can step back and take a more laissez-faire, hands-off approach to managing them.

INHERITING EMPLOYEES WITH
DISCIPLINARY CHALLENGES

"My boss promised me a 10 percent merit raise next year. Is that still on?" "I've been told I'll be promoted on my anniversary, which happens to be next month. What would you like my new title to be?" "Yes, it's true that I'm on final written warning for what my boss called substandard job performance, but she just didn't like me." These individual challenges could often take up more of your time and cause you more angst than the whole cultural-integration process of merging your new and old teams.

When one employee is a squeaky wheel, dedicate your time to hearing the case and tending to the individual's needs, but promise nothing until you've had a chance to research the situation thoroughly and through as many sources as possible. What prior management promised in terms of promotions and large salary increases may in fact hold true if it's documented and if your human resource and finance departments have given final approval. As such, putting such changes through will not affect your budget because the variance will have been approved as part of the team integration.

More often than not, though, you will find that such claims are based on assumptions on the employee's part, so be sure to temper ambitions while you look into the matter further. Unfortunately, you may have the unpleasant chore of communicating to your new employee that former management, HR, and finance do not agree that this was a "done deal," so the huge merit increase and/or promotion won't be happening as the employee expects. In cases like this, let the individual know exactly whom you spoke with, what they said, and why there may have been confusion. Confirm that all parties agree with the decision, and invite the employee to speak directly with those individuals himself. Just remember that you weren't part of that decision; you're simply communicating what was communicated to you, and you'll be open to evaluating the situation with a fresh set of eyes going forward.

Sometimes, though, it will be more than hurt feelings or disappointment that you will be inheriting. Candidates who transfer to your group on final written warning for substandard job performance, attendance, or inappropriate workplace conduct may cause specific challenges. When that's the case, make copies of the written and final written warnings, share them with the employee up front in a private meeting, and talk about them openly. In most cases, it's best to get things like that out in the open and to discuss them rationally, adult to adult.

There are typically two sides to every story, and the validity of the documents isn't in question: as far as you're concerned, they're valid because they are in the employee's file with the employee's signature (and possibly rebuttal). What you want to look for now is how the individual responds to those warnings: if the person is very defensive and quick to blame others, you may have someone who suffers from "victim syndrome" and who fails to take responsibility for their own actions. In comparison, if the person readily admits mistakes, assumes responsibility for them, and is committed to avoiding those mistakes in the future, you're halfway there. That's because people who readily admit that they were the cause of a perception problem—even if they don't agree with the facts— demonstrate a high level of business maturity and self-awareness and are much more prone to seeing the bigger picture and not repeating past mistakes.

These scenarios that are sometimes forced upon you can be challenging, especially if you like your current team and don't want the added responsibility of integrating others into the close-knit environment you've worked so hard to cultivate. But don't underestimate the value of this opportunity. You will rarely be given such a chance to shine as a leader; your résumé will have a nice new juicy bullet point to discuss for years to come, and you may just find that today's most sought after attribute—the ability to lead others through transition and demonstrate key leadership skills in a changing business environment—is a hidden strength you can apply in any workplace.

18

MEDIATING EMPLOYEE DISPUTES
When Employees Refuse to Acknowledge One Another and "Just Want to Do Their Job and Be Left Alone"

IT'S SAID THAT THERE ARE two kinds of employees who quit: those who quit and leave and those who quit and stay. It's also said that the difference between an active job seeker and a passive job seeker is one bad day in the office. In light of the remote work trends that took root after the COVID pandemic of the early 2020s, so much changed so quickly, and managers were forced to adapt to a whole new work world. So where does that leave you—the line manager with very little time to achieve higher output and quality ratings with fewer resources—in terms of managing and leading your group forward? After all, you may get along great with your subordinates. Sometimes, though, they just can't seem to get along with one another. Broken trust among staff members, like old wounds, can run deep. Mastering the skill of reinventing relationships with trust and empathy that can work wonders on your teams (and on your leadership abilities) over time.

Every line manager in corporate America has felt frustrated over employee tensions and unresolved conflict that negatively affect the work environment. And with the critical need to retain top performers, managers have to find ways to get their people "plugged in" again or else face premature turnover. The reality, though, is that your staff members will almost always take the path of least resistance with one another—avoidance—rather than address problem issues head-on. You, as manager, have to then intervene in a mediating role to ensure that a lack of communication doesn't lead to performance problems, poor cross-team communication, or turnover.

MEDIATE AND INTERVENE WISELY

Pretending that a problem doesn't exist or allowing staff members to work out problems on their own may be a safe strategy when a new interpersonal conflict first arises; however, once that initial frustration has festered over time in the workplace, it becomes time to step in. The key question is, how do you balance individual privacy with workplace needs and avoid appearing to play favorites? After all, you see them avoiding one another. It's obvious that they look down at their shoes when they pass each other in the hallway rather than saying good morning. In short, you can sometimes cut the tension with a knife when two people aren't getting along, and don't think for a minute that the rest of the team doesn't sense it either. Two warring parties can easily throw the balance of the entire team off and perpetuate drama and angst for everyone.

Remember that your job is *not* to motivate your staff. Motivation is internal and is therefore the responsibility of each individual employee (yourself included). On the other hand, as a manager, you're charged with the responsibility of creating a work environment in which people can motivate themselves. That kind of work environment exists when people feel like they make a difference— the so-called psychic income that keeps people loyally employed when companies down the street appear to be paying higher wages for the same work. They feel like you, as their manager, have their back and can do their best work every day with peace of mind. And while they may get that great feeling from you, it may get trounced by that uncomfortable feeling they get from their coworker day in and day out.

When two of your staff members are "at war," meet with each individually. Privately find out Oliver's side of the story before meeting individually with Emma. In your meeting with Oliver, ask him why Emma may be feeling the way she does. Ask Oliver what he'd like to see happen ideally in terms of his relationship with Emma, and then ask him what he'd be willing to change about his own behavior to elicit a different response from Emma in the future. Afterward hold the same meeting with Emma in terms of her relationship with Oliver.

Let both know that you want to meet with them together in your office to open the lines of communication. First, however, they need to know that you're listening to them individually in an attempt to understand their perspective, so they feel heard and understood. (They also therefore feel like you're on their side, which you are.) Second, they need to know that you will share their feedback with the other person in advance of the group meeting so that both sides can think about the other person's side of the story. Nothing helps more than getting each to walk a mile in the other's moccasins, so to speak, because this raises awareness and empathy on both sides before the group meeting. Once they've heard the other person's side of the story, they can see matters more clearly and make themselves part of the solution.

Simply open the meeting with Oliver this way:

Oliver, in this one-on-one meeting, I want to listen carefully to everything you have to say. I'm going to take notes, I may ask some clarifying questions, but my goal is to understand your perspective regarding the ongoing tensions with Emma. Here's the key, though: everything you tell me in this meeting is what I'll share with

Emma when I meet with her later this afternoon. This way, she'll understand the *what* of what's going on, and we can come together as a group in the morning and solve the *how*. In other words, we need to get everything out in the open in a spirit of full transparency so that we can fix this once and for all.

The same goes for Emma: I'll meet with, listen carefully, and take notes of what she has to say and what her perception of the matter is. But she'll also be told that I'll be meeting with you right after that meeting to explain to you her side of the story and how she sees things. Once you're both fully informed of the other person's side of the story, we can come together tomorrow morning to discuss how we're going to fix things moving forward. Does that sound like a fair, reasonable, and transparent approach? [*Yes.*]

When you meet with Emma, explain the situation the exact same way so both sides understand how you're handling this and what's expected of them.

When you open the meeting with your two subordinates the following morning, share the rules of the meeting:

First, I wanted you both to hear the other person's perspective to raise your awareness of how he or she may be feeling. Getting to walk in others' shoes is healthy in situations like this because it raises your self-awareness and helps you see the problem more objectively. After all, we're adults and we can fix this. I also wanted you both to sleep on this for a night so we could have a fresh look, now having a much better sense of the other person's side of the story.

Next, as far as this group meeting, you shouldn't hold anything back. This is your chance to get it all out in the open, and if you withhold anything, then you'll have missed a golden opportunity to share your side of the story. This is a once-in-a-career opportunity for you both to fix this: you're not going to get another chance to readdress these issues after today, and it's on both of you to make this work. After our meeting today, I'm rewelcoming you both to the company as if it were your first day of employment. I'm also holding you both equally accountable for reinventing your working relationship from that point forward, both for your own sake as well as the team's.

Finally, everything you share has to be said with the other person's best interests in mind and in a spirit of constructive feedback. There is no attacking and no need for defending anyone's actions; we're simply coming together as adults to fix a problem that's been holding us back as a team. This is really more a sensitivity session where you both get to walk a mile in the other's shoes and hear firsthand how the other is feeling. At that point, however, I'm going to ask you for a commitment to ensure that you'll assume good intentions going forward and, more important, that we won't have to have another meeting like this. I'm afraid that if that becomes the case, it will likely be in the form of disciplinary action, which we want to avoid at all costs, agreed? [*Yes.*]

Setting up a meeting with those ground rules automatically deescalates feelings of angst or tension in the participants. It also gives you the chance to take a gentle approach to interpersonal issues that, like scars, sometimes run long and deep.

GET THEM TALKING TO EACH OTHER—NOT TO YOU

During the group meeting, you'll notice typically that each employee will first address his or her concerns directly to you— the mediator. It will be as if the other person weren't even there in the room. Third person "he-she" discussions need to be changed into first-person "I-you" dialogue. To accomplish this shift, simply stop the conversation as soon as one of the participants begins speaking about the other in the third person. Ask the individual to speak directly to the other person as if *you* weren't there. That may appear a little challenging for the participants at first, especially if emotions are running high, but direct communication works best. After all, you're helping them fix *their* problem.

In addition, you should encourage your two staff members to use the phrases "this is how I feel" and "can you understand why I would feel that way?" Feelings aren't right or wrong—they just are. Since perception is reality until proven otherwise, it's each individual's responsibility to sensitize the other regarding the existence of the perceptions that have developed over time.

More important, remember that guilt works better than anger in the workplace. Anger is external—"it's the other person's fault; I'm the victim here" goes the typical train of thought. When someone is in anger mode, there is no assumption of responsibility—simply blame. Self-justification is easy when anger is at hand, and communication shuts down because the individual is acting "on principle."

Guilt, on the other hand, is internal. This isn't the old-fashioned "guilt" that's intended to make people feel bad about themselves; it's more about awareness. Guilt is a "moral emotion" that helps people look inward and assume partial responsibility for an imperfect situation. That element of accountability is the seed of goodwill that helps heal old wounds. For example, if Oliver feels bad about his relationship with Emma, shares with her why he feels the way he does, and admits that it takes two to tango and that he's part of the problem, then Emma will likely respond in kind to the olive branch that Oliver is offering (and vice versa).

END THE MEETING WITH NEW EXPECTATIONS AND A CHANCE TO HEAL

Once you've "pierced the heart" of the combatants, the battle is won. You'll know you're there when they're talking to each other, agreeing that they've got a problem on their hands, and demonstrating a willingness to fix it. These kinds of management interventions aren't normally investigations of fact-finding. Instead, they're sensitivity training sessions where goodwill and openness naturally heal the wounds associated with ego and "principle."

Conclude the meeting this way:

Emma and Oliver, you've both heard the other side of the story now. I'm not asking you to hold hands and sing "kumbaya" together, and I don't expect you to go bowling together after work tonight. But I do expect you to openly communicate so that the work in our department isn't negatively affected. I'm likewise holding you both accountable for making it more comfortable for your teammates to be in the same room with you. The comments from others about "cutting the atmosphere with a knife" when you're together or the "walking on eggshells" feeling people get when you're together in a group meeting needs to end immediately. Is that a fair ask on my part? [Yes.]

The final questions I have to ask each of you are, now that you've heard the other person's perceptions of what's going on, what are you willing to change in terms of your own behavior that will elicit a different response in the other person in the future? My other question is, how should I, as your manager, react if this situation were to rear its ugly head again?

And voilà—you'll have given each employee his or her "day in court," so to speak, where each vents and shares perceptions of the problem. You'll end the meeting on a constructive note where both agree to change their behavior. And you'll also create a "healthy sense of paranoia" where both realize that if the problem surfaces again, there will be a more formal management response—most likely in the form of progressive discipline. Congratulations, you've treated your warring parties as adults and held them accountable for fixing the PR or perception problem on their hands.

Remember that a key rule of workplace due process is that an employee should always be given a chance to respond to a charge—a charge levied by a supervisor or a peer. When tensions build up among employees, isolation results. Isolation, in turn, leads to a "checkout" mentality with which employees report to work every day believing that they simply have to "put their time in." "No one knows or cares what I do around here—my opinion doesn't matter" is an all-too-common complaint. In such cases, premature turnover, excessive absenteeism, workers' comp stress claims, and even lawsuits related to hostile work environment claims may result.

The solution? Allow adults to hash out their differences in a controlled, safe environment. No matter how much you care, you can't manage *their* differences. Only they can do that. Still, you can provide a mechanism for solving employee disputes that brings out the best in people. Establishing a culture of openness means confronting "people problems" in an environment that maintains the individual's dignity. It enhances your position as a leader and establishes your reputation as a fair arbiter of disagreements—truly a management trait that's hard to find at other companies where the "grass may be greener." There's no better formula for employee retention than treating people with respect, dignity, and a caring ear.

19

TURNING AROUND A
DYSFUNCTIONAL TEAM
(a.k.a. Mastering Toxic Team Turnarounds)

NEWLY CREATED DEPARTMENTS AND/OR newly minted managers often find themselves in dire straits after assuming the helm of a new group because of interpersonal conflict, misaligned talent, or organizational structures that lack efficiency and fail to mesh with their customers' needs. When such a situation rises to the level of an urgent distress call, it becomes time to take a candid look at either reinventing the structure of the group or replacing certain key individuals within it.

As a new manager or department head possibly faced with a department that's about to implode, you'll want to conduct a departmental structural and workflow analysis with your boss and key direct reports to determine areas of overlap and areas where additional resources might be needed. That's often the best time to launch both a series of training workshops on leadership and communication in conjunction with formal weekly meetings to ensure that all voices are heard in an effort to make "fixing the crisis" a shared goal. In addition, in a fairly short amount of time, and with the right help and guidance, you'll be well on your way to determining whether you've got the right players in place to move your newly created department forward to meet the immediate challenges ahead. Likewise, you'll discover who's holding the team back and undermining the team's efforts to perform at a higher level.

PHASE 1:
THE STRUCTURAL AUDIT

A simple organizational analysis is typically the best place to start when faced with the urgent need for immediate turnaround. Your immediate supervisor and HR team are critical allies at a time like this. Drawing from their experience and guidance is the first benefit; keeping them in the loop in a spirit of full transparency is the second (and most crucial). Training improves individual performance, typically by building a particular individual's skill set, whereas organizational design looks at the structural system in place to determine whether the organization has proper alignment and efficiency. You can do both exercises simultaneously. Critical team problems can often have more to do with systems than individuals. But you have to be prepared to assess and address both: structure plus individual conduct. In short, if the system and structure of your workflow paradigm are off, you could have Einstein in your department and not see success.

When conducting a candid review of your department's current structure, keep it simple: map out, on butcher block paper if that's all that's available, your entire workflow process, from inception through end result. Map out all contiguous areas where your employees touch the process and add value. Your rudimentary organizational analysis should indicate fairly quickly where people and processes overlap, conflict, or need more resources.

Next, weave in the roles of ancillary support departments (for example, finance, information technology, and customer service), external vendors, and ultimately customers and key stakeholders.

Finally, overlay areas where conflict and staff complaints seem to converge so that you could physically see the areas of tension. (Mark those with an asterisk.)

The next day, roll out your workflow draft to the rest of your staff—those actually in the trenches—and ask them to comment on your senior team's initial insights. Drill deeper until the majority agree on the pressure points squeezing off productivity and ask for suggestions on how to reinvent the workflow to ensure smoother operations. Finally, ask for internal leaders to volunteer· to assume responsibility for fixing the smallest and most manageable parts of the dysfunction in the system. Such "stretch assignments" should be able to be accomplished within a relatively short period of time and will provide for concrete, positive outcomes that all could see. You can then prepare to assess the team's findings regarding misalignment, over- or understaffing, and problematic touch points with your immediate supervisor and/or with human resources.

PHASE 2:
SIMULTANEOUS LEADERSHIP AND COMMUNICATION TRAINING

Next, propose to hold a series of three or four short, ninety-minute lunch-and-learns to discuss leadership, communication, and team building. Your company's learning and development department may have "canned" training workshops on hand, or you may want to invite in an external training organization to establish your new expectations in terms of individual and team performance and conduct. Be sure to leave plenty of time to discuss the topics raised in the workshop in an attempt to relate the rules and lessons to your group and customize the materials to your needs. This becomes your platform for high levels of group interaction and peer reinforcement.

Depending on your structure, you can begin with management training and then progress to staff training. Simple management workshops may include topics such as "High Performance Management Practices at XYZ Corporation," "Legal Aspects of Supervision and Management in [state]," "Power Recruiting and High-Impact Interviewing Strategies," "Mastering Progressive Discipline and Structuring Terminations," and "Managers as Mediators—Conflict Resolution in the Workplace." Staff workshops might include topics such as "Leadership 101—Communication, Team Building, and Leadership," "Our Code of Conduct and Expectations Regarding Employee Behavior in the Workplace," "Conflict Management Essentials," "Active Listening Even When It's Difficult to Listen," "Navigating Change Effectively," and others.

The list goes on, of course, but one training workshop per week over a four-week period should get your team off to a solid start in terms of outlining your expectations and providing all your group leaders with the basic tools necessary to excel in their roles.

A natural by-product that you could expect from these types of training interventions will be requests for more formal feedback and communication. Once the request comes your way, grant it: there's no better way to get people out of their foxholes to safely volunteer their opinions or to stop their griping about others' shortcomings than by encouraging them to share their opinions and hear others' suggestions. Training builds energy and momentum and poses the challenge of how to apply the newly learned content to the workplace. That tends to be fun and exciting for staff members and gets their creative juices flowing. Sure, there will be roadblocks along the way, but areas of critical shortcomings will likely be exposed before too long, providing you with additional information on where to focus your leadership efforts.

Remember that only very mature teams who have worked together side by side and who trust one another will benefit from a laissez-faire management style, and those are almost always the exception. Most departments require more formal feedback, structure, and direction to excel on an ongoing basis. And if people come together only when there's a problem, then conflict becomes associated with all meetings. But if people come together in a regularly structured setting, then conflict need not enter into the equation. And even when it does, there will be more trust and goodwill because both sides get to express their opinions and assume ownership for the solution.

What if you hear resistance to this suggestion from certain members of the team? "We don't have time for meetings—if we did, then none of these problems would have arisen in the first place" goes the common objection. Explain away employees' fears by simply stating that you're keeping these meetings going only through this "crisis" stage. Once you see that regular and open communication is ongoing, then you could "kick off the training wheels" of weekly training meetings and allow employees to revert to a more laissez-faire style of communication and leadership (that is, without formal structure and direction).

PHASE 3:
THE PEOPLE "FIT FACTOR" REVIEW

Whether you're a new manager to the group or you've worked with these team members for years, watching employees behave in this new environment with heightened expectations may go a long way in helping you determine who's a fit and who may be out of place.

Some people naturally resist change and self-select out of the change process. Others "get it" and rise to the occasion, demonstrating discretionary energy and effort to accomplish the predetermined goals. Extreme times call for extreme measures, and only under those circumstances do you often get the chance to see the real person behind the facade. The leaders will find ways to motivate themselves in light of the group's changing needs, while

others will simply opt out or demonstrate an entitlement mentality, revealing their ultimate lack of fit in the renewed and reinvig-
orated work environment.

Once again, there's a very simple litmus test to apply to determine who gets to stay and who might be better off leaving the
company, called the "Fall of the Planet Test." Here's how it works:
categorize all the players on your team by answering the
following:

If [NAME] fell off the planet tomorrow, I would . . .

1.   absolutely panic because I don't know how all the work
     would get done and how I'd be successful. After all, I rely
     on her so much both as a leader and individual contribu-
     tor that I couldn't face losing her.
2.   eventually notice that she was gone, but probably not
     until a week or so down the road (or longer).
3.   jump for joy, because I'd finally be able to get control of
     the group back and not have to hear his constant whin-
     ing or worry about his gossiping and driving a wedge
     between the other staff members.

Clearly, the third option represents your initial area of focus
with your HR team to either initiate a conversation with the individual to consider exploring opportunities outside the company or
to begin the progressive discipline process and issue written warnings and substandard annual performance reviews, as necessary.

With those key problematic individuals on the way toward termination or resignation (shy of an immediate and sustained turnaround), you can then focus your attention on the rest of the team.
People will know that you mean business when they see you
addressing the problematic performers who have been permitted
to weigh the team down for so long. And they'll often raise their
level of self-expectations to meet your expectations once they
know you're fully in the game. The rising tide lifts all boats once

the most problematic performers are either removed or turn around their inappropriate workplace conduct or substandard job performance. You can then make it safe for people to do their best work every day with peace of mind, knowing that you hold everyone equally to the highest expectations.

This cycle allows you to grow and build on your team's strengths and then recruit new players who demonstrate increased pride in their work, engagement, and overall job satisfaction. And voilà— the performance cycle, which often goes on for months or years without much notice, gets refreshed and reviewed anew, all because of the *urgency* that faced you suddenly. Or maybe we should call it the *opportunity* that forced you to look openly at your practices, structure, and tolerance for mediocre performance or inappropriate workplace conduct.

Dire straits may cause more drama and adrenaline rush than you care for at any given time, but let cooler heads prevail: sometimes the need for immediate turnaround of people, systems, and structures provides you with the greatest ability and maximum discretion to reinvent and reevaluate who you are as a leader and communicator. And that's where business is at its height: by creating challenges that help you become everything you were meant to be and by redefining yourself in light of your company's greatest challenges. Rising to the occasion may be the greatest way to move from the brink of failure to the edge of ultimate success.

20

DEALING WITH BURNOUT
Reenergizing Individual High Performers
Who May Be Losing Their Mojo

TOP PERFORMERS WILL ALWAYS BE résumé builders, looking to fuel their need for achievement at every turn. And while no job is great enough for the human spirit, certain conditions help top performers thrive, while others can squelch their creativity and productivity. COVID pandemics and large-scale economic recessions aside, when people's ambitions get placed on hold while they tread water in their careers, how do you identify those who may be quiet quitting or vulnerable to becoming "recruiter's bait"? More important, what can you do now to reinvigorate and reinvent their loyalty to your organization, so they don't leave when temptation calls? And how do you turn around teams that may be suffering from the same fate—lost interest and simply "going through the motions"? We'll cover the individual top performer first in this section, and then we'll move to the team approach in the next section.

First, remember that it's not so much employee *satisfaction* that's at issue as much as employee *engagement*. Keeping subordinates engaged in their work, helping them feel like they make a true difference, and indirectly helping them build their résumés and skill sets is the fodder of great leaders. In fact, the glue that binds someone to any company at any given time is, first, the relationship with their immediate manager and, second, the learning curve. Help overachievers to better themselves while benefiting your organization, and they'll be both satisfied and engaged. No amount of money will be able to entice them away.

IDENTIFYING COMMON SIGNS OF DISENGAGEMENT

Signs of moderate employee dissatisfaction abound at any given time. In fact, some labor pundits believe that people are most responsive to learning when they are moderately dissatisfied. That seems to be the push necessary to force people to step up to the next level in their careers. But too much dissatisfaction can be paralyzing. Once an "us-versus-them" entitlement mentality takes hold in your employee's mindset, it's difficult going back. The grass tends to become a lot greener anywhere other than at your company. That disengagement may tend to show itself in subtle as well as concrete ways.

What can a high disengagement level look like? It's different for different individuals and very personalized, which is why it's important that you get to know and spend one-on-one time with your direct reports. People remain engaged when they receive recognition and appreciation for a job well done. They're satisfied when they experience open communication and trust with their immediate managers, and they excel when they believe that they've got longer-term opportunities available to them beyond their current role in the organization. In short, there is a "psychic income" from work that makes people feel socially accepted and respected. Meeting the needs of this psychic income may indeed be more effective when it comes to retention than meeting the monetary income needs of most individuals because happy employees won't necessarily walk away from a good thing for a 15–20 percent raise elsewhere, which might bring with it a new manager who breathes fire and throws chairs.

Disengagement may show itself in a number of common ways, including a sudden nine-to-five mentality, an unwillingness to participate in social events outside of the office, or a tendency to "fox hole" oneself apart from one's peers. It becomes most noticeable when someone who's normally outgoing and enthusiastic seems to fall by the wayside and has nothing positive to contribute. Sometimes it shows itself quietly with raised eyeballs and sighs of apathy, and other times it results in open challenges to authority or shouting matches with peers. You'll not always know concretely if someone isn't happy, but your gut may tell you that something's changed. Whether the change is obvious or intuitive, assume that you're going to lose your superstar once opportunity comes knocking because work at your office or on your shop floor just isn't fun, rewarding, or exciting for that individual anymore.

APPROACHING YOUR TARGET AUDIENCE WISELY

Reengaging the superstar isn't all that hard to do if you, the manager, want to turn the individual around. The team can then be turned around one person at a time in addition to as a group. But always start with your star performers. Further, ask them for their ideas and their support in turning the rest of the group around. There are a myriad of books available on tips for motivating those around and beneath you, but the most effective strategies focus on the particular individual's needs. The key issue to ask yourself is, "Is there *trust* in the relationship?" If the answer is yes, then assume you could fix just about anything. If the answer is no, then you may have to postpone this activity for the time being until a greater sense of trust and respect can be initiated, both individually with key players and as a team overall.

Assuming that trust is indeed present in your relationship with your top performer, then the first move will be yours as the manager to raise a potentially uncomfortable subject this way:

Samantha, I've read all the stats that say that 50-plus percent of all US workers would change jobs if they could. I know you've been in your current role for four years now, and we haven't had much to offer you beyond our standard annual 3 percent merit increase, but you know how much I value your work and our friendship. Let me ask you this: on a scale of 1 to 10, 10 being you'd jump ship tomorrow if you had the chance, where would you rank yourself?

Expect some type of mitigated response from your employee as most people don't want to tell their bosses outright that they're a 10 on that scale and looking to make a change as soon as something crosses their horizon. But if trust exists in the relationship, many a loyal subordinate may say that if an opportunity to assume broader responsibilities, a higher title, and/or more money surfaces and they're tapped on the shoulder to pursue it, they should for the sake of their careers and families. (Assume that will make them an 8 on the scale.)

REENGAGEMENT 101

Bingo—your fact-finding mission is paying off! Now is the time to spring into action and implement a reengagement plan to greatly increase your chances of retaining this individual despite external job offers. Where do you start? That's simple: with your heart. State:

Samantha, I'll make no bones about it—I want to keep you. I see you as an integral part of the future of this company and our department. I realize we may not have any promotional opportunities for you right now, and I can't tell you where our year-end merit budgets will be allocated, but I can tell you that I want to help prepare you for greater responsibilities within the firm, and I'd like to speak with you now about how to do that.

With such a solid verbal commitment (and hopefully an equally solid performance review and development plan on file), it's time to get creative. This creativity will be a function of your industry, geography, and company history as well as your subordinate's personal interests, but let's take a look at an example from the discipline of human resources management.

Your director of staffing is doing a stellar job identifying talent and closing offers with difficult-to-find job candidates, but you suspect that she may be recruited by competitors who know of her reputation. Besides, you suspect that she may feel that her position is becoming less challenging and more of a "maintenance mode" type of job. Maybe this individual wants to eventually run her own HR department, or maybe she prefers to remain in the subdiscipline of recruitment over the long term. Following are creative alternatives that should motivate her to stay with your company for her own good despite an onslaught of job offers that may come her way:

Scenario 1: Samantha, I realize that your next move in career progression will be to move beyond recruitment into more of an HR generalist role so that you could ultimately head your own department. Let me tell you where I need your help as I pursue new initiatives within our group. First, it's time for us to take another baseline look at our entire department—from compensation and benefits to training, employee relations, and HR systems. I'd like you to spearhead that fact-finding initiative, work closely with all the group heads to benchmark their current practices, and then develop a market comparison so that we know where we stand relative to our peers and competitors. By the end of this six-month project, you'll be as savvy about the overall HR operation as I am, and at that point I could show you line-by-line how that audit will provide us with tremendous opportunities for operational improvements and increased efficiencies. I'll also ask you to present your findings to our senior management team. It'll be a very time-intensive task, and it will no doubt take you away from your immediate recruitment responsibilities fairly often, but I guess my question to you is, are you up for the task and willing to join me in this new initiative?

Scenario 2: Samantha, I realize that you enjoy recruitment and you're certainly stellar at it, but I'd like to see you move in some new directions that will really complement your overall approach to staffing and selection and give you a much broader appreciation of your specialty. First of all, one of the biggest trends in HR's future lies in international expansion. Although our firm doesn't have overseas operations, I'm going to recommend that you enroll in an international HR course at the local college so that you can gain an appreciation of recruitment practices in Europe, Asia, and Latin America. Once you see how staffing as well as other HR generalist functions are performed abroad, you'll gain some greater insights into the work you do here for us domestically.

Second, in addition to that international HR course, I'd like to spend some time with you reviewing our organization's financials and human capital metrics. One of the things I've benefited most from in my career was my understanding of enterprise valuations, income statements, and balance sheets, because once you understand what to look for in those kinds of financial statements, you become much more astute at forecasting workforce planning needs. Combined with an HR scorecard to see how we're increasing the efficiency and effectiveness of our organization's human capital, you'll be all charged up and ready to go as far as driving your career to new levels of achievement. Are you game?

By making individual commitments like these to your key "keepers," you'll be helping them gain skills, knowledge, and competencies that they didn't formally possess. You'll also identify skill gaps and developmental opportunities to motivate them and enhance your own reputation as a true leader and career coach. It's a win-win for all because your proactive outreach will have kept a top performer from leaving. In addition, you will have saved the company the time and expense of having to recruit and train a replacement, and you will have reengaged someone who, consciously or not, may have simply been cruising along unaware of their own career desires and needs. In essence, you'll have initiated a "counteroffer negotiation" before it was ever needed and in a much friendlier light. Challenging your employees to reengage in the workplace will no doubt make your own career a lot more rewarding and fun. You may just find that creating new career opportunities for those you care most about in the workplace will create ripple effects throughout your team and allow you to build stronger one-on-one relationships with the rest of the crew.

21

CONQUERING "QUIET QUITTING"
Energizing a Team That's Slipping in Performance and Productivity

QUIET QUITTING DESCRIBES THE psychological withdrawal of an employee from their organization, resulting from not being engaged at work or having a poor work-life balance. The employee does not actually leave the organization, but they're no longer giving their best efforts. And what starts at the individual level can quickly spread to the entire team. The principles involved in working with individuals apply to teams as well. Of course, teams can be harder to "fix" because of their size and the disparate needs of its members. If your goal is to start with the highest performer first, then it makes sense to move next to one-on-one discussions with your second- and third-highest performers, for example. Encourage those top members of your team to partner with and support you in turning around the broader team as a whole. Further, once you've reached those top members of your team, you can hold a group meeting that invites everyone to schedule time to meet with you individually, based on the expectations you set. Here's what your team meeting opener might sound like:

Everyone, I called this meeting to discuss something that I'm feeling and sensing: we might be feeling less than energized or otherwise losing our sense of excitement about what we're doing here every day for this organization. I may be off in my assumption, but truth be told, I'm feeling it a bit too. We work too hard to feel like we're losing our mojo or simply going through the motions, and I want us to move in a new and more creative direction, at least for a short period of time, to spike interest and engagement levels. Here's what I'm thinking:

First, I'm handing out a one-sheet that I want you to think about. I'll walk you through it, but overall, I want you to schedule a one-on-one meeting with me to discuss what's most important to you from this sheet. If you have a quick look at it, you'll see there are six categories of motivators I've outlined:

1. Career progression and opportunities for promotion and advancement
2. Work-life balance/control/flexibility, especially between your job and family life
3. Lateral opportunities for broadened responsibilities and skill building, including exposure to other areas of our department or company
4. Acquisition of new technical skills and exposure to new systems, including new certifications or licenses
5. Development of stronger leadership, management, and administrative skills (like moving from being a teacher to a principal or a stockbroker to a branch manager)
6. Money and other forms of compensation

Of course, there can be other categories I haven't thought of, so feel free to add anything I may have missed. Likewise, I can't guarantee anything, but I can make a commitment to each of you individually to help you pursue your career goals and professional interests further. So please add this to your to-do list and schedule a thirty-minute meeting with me over the next two weeks to review and share your findings. I'd like to complete all one-on-one meetings by [DATE], so please be sure and book time on my calendar as your schedule allows.

But wait, there's more! Besides discussing your career focus, I want to do a greater deep dive into the company. It's time that we put on our research hats and create a competition—final prize to be decided—about our organization and who can bring new news to the table that's most interesting. Here's how it works:

My goal is to turn you all into corporate futurists. (Yes, that's a real job, and it's typically held by economists at large banks, investment firms, and think tanks.)

Scour the internet for current trends and patterns in our industry, especially those that can impact our career trajectory in [DISCIPLINE/DEPARTMENT] for better or worse. Conduct multiple searches on Google, Glassdoor, and YouTube to learn more about our organization and our competitors. What are people saying about us? How do our Glassdoor ratings from prior employees and anonymous coworkers reflect the reality you see around here every day? And what, if anything, can we do to improve what's being said about us? Likewise, who are our closest competitors, both slightly larger and slightly smaller than us? What niche do they focus on that's different from ours? With a greater understanding of our niche and reputation as a company, we can develop new and creative ideas about how our department contributes to our organization's bottom line and—who knows—come up with new ideas for reinventing what we're doing.

Next, I want you all to research the Bureau of Labor Statistics' *Occupational Outlook Handbook* at www.bls.gov/ooh. Tell me about jobs in our area of specialty versus the overall growth of jobs in America over the next ten years. Which industries will have the greatest demand for our roles, and where will the growth be for people who do what we do? Does it make sense to make tweaks or pivots in your specialty area that will result in greater job opportunities in the future? No more bump-on-a-log career management:

we really have to research where the opportunities will be coming from by industry over the next decade.

Finally, I want suggestions from you in terms of what we could be doing differently to spice things up around here, at least for the next three months. It's time to reengage and gain greater awareness of what we're doing and why we're doing it. A little due diligence into our industry, company, and reputation can go a long way in spurring new ideas and helping us reinvent ourselves. But most important to me is the six-point checklist that I've asked you to consider regarding your own career goals and motivations. Let's work together to build something that means something to you at this point in your career—again, with no promises but certainly good intentions. And let's gain a thirty-thousand-foot view of our industry and company to understand how to perform better "in the day-to-day weeds," so to speak. Hint: the first-place prize for whoever comes up with the best research or ideas for increasing our ability to make things better will make you very happy. That's all I'm saying for now and more on that soon. I'll look forward to your calendar invitations over the next two weeks as well as research findings and suggestions!

If your company is publicly traded, instruct your team to research what's being said about your stock on Yahoo! Finance and other prominent sites. If you're a nonprofit, ask them to research GuideStar and Charity Navigator to see how your organization is performing relative to its peers. A simple Google search can reveal tremendous amounts of information, and a curious and informed team can often find new ways of reengaging in their work and proffering new solutions to real-world challenges that they may not have known about otherwise. The power to motivate your team simply lies in placing opportunities before them to learn and grow. Making them responsible for the due diligence and digging creates an environment where workers can motivate themselves. Your job is simply to point them in the right direction and then gently step out of the way. (PS: Try to make the prize something that adds value to their careers: maybe a day at an off-site leadership training workshop or opportunity to visit the corporate headquarters.)

QUIET FIRING—A COROLLARY TO QUIET QUITTING WITH SEVERELY DAMAGING POTENTIAL

Quiet firing describes how managers fail to adequately provide coaching, support, and career development to an employee, which results in pushing the employee out of an organization. In a worst-case scenario, quiet firing happens when managers create the circumstances where employees have truly toxic or miserable experiences at work as a way to squeeze them out. Needless to say, such practices aren't ethical or productive and can lead to legal claims of "constructive discharge," meaning the employee quits but that any reasonable person would have quit under the same or similar circumstances (creating liability for the organization similar to "wrongful discharge"). At the very least, it tarnishes your and your company's reputation as a good place to work and poisons team trust. At worst, it can upend an otherwise successful manager's career by leading to disciplinary action, up to and including dismissal of employment.

22

BUDGET LIMITS AND NO
ROOM TO GROW YOUR PEOPLE
Motivating Without Money and Keeping Top
Performers Engaged When There's No Way Up

THE TITLE OF THIS SECTION IS pretty self-explanatory and potentially scary. Talk about a crisis! The reality for so many managers in corporate America is that they'll lose their best and brightest talent once employees feel that they're capped out or otherwise not making enough progression in their careers to justify remaining with the organization. And that's fair: workers, especially top performers, will naturally want more over time, which typically includes titles and compensation. At some point, your organization will likely be capped out in terms of what you can offer. How do companies keep great workers when budget and promotional limits stifle vertical growth?

First, let's be clear about two things:

- People join companies but leave managers.
- The relationship to the boss and the learning curve are the two most critical aspects of employee retention.

Therefore, unlimited growth potential isn't required in most situations when it comes to retaining top performers who are otherwise feeling connected to their work and fully engaged. In other words, they experience self-fulfillment in their contribution levels, their relationship with their boss, and the positive difference they believe they make every day. Compensation usually comes in around fourth when exiting employees are polled about why they're opting to leave their company. Lack of appreciation, recognition, and communication usually come in somewhere between first and second place.

Next, Marcus Buckingham's and Curt Coffman's bestselling book, *First Break All the Rules: What the World's Greatest Managers Do Differently* (Pocket Books, 2005), proved over years of research and countless interviews with managers and staffers alike that people don't quit their companies, they quit their bosses. Think about it: job applicants join companies, wanting to become part of their growth and success, to associate the name-brand recognition of that organization with their bio, résumé, and LinkedIn profile, only to flee one or two years later from a "crazy boss." People have gone on to say that they hate an entire Fortune 500 company because they were so angry at the boss they had at the time. Bottom line: compensation and vertical promotions may be a motivator in certain cases, but you have to see past that initial excuse to examine whether the real, underlying reason for an employee's departure has to do with the relationship with the boss. Likewise, workers may feel like they're treading water in their career, doing the same work they've been doing for years with little opportunity for growth, challenge, or professional development, which also leads to regrettable turnover.

Let's start with one basic assumption: your job as a manager is *not* to motivate your staff. Motivation is internal; people are responsible for motivating themselves. Instead, you're responsible for creating an environment in which people can motivate themselves. It's an important concept to understand because the weight of the world isn't on your shoulders to keep people happy. Few companies have unlimited opportunities to promote people internally, yet they benefit from a long-tenured staff. Many have withheld equity adjustments and even annual merit pool increases because the bottom line has been squeezed so tightly. More important, there exists an underlying tension that corporate America is about to burst—whether that stems from the stock market falling, trade tariffs being instituted, or prices shooting through the roof.

Therefore, now is the time to look at the latter half of the "recruitment and *retention*" equation. The time to begin recognizing, appreciating, and motivating your staff is now. That doesn't mean you have to bring your corporate pom-poms to work and play cheerleader. There are, however, several relatively simple ways that could help you create an environment in which people can motivate, reinvigorate, and reinvent themselves.

INCREASE OPPORTUNITIES
FOR DELEGATION

I know what you're thinking—they have too much work already! But when done right, delegation provides on-the-job training that can challenge and motivate people exponentially—as long as what they're working on ties into their longer-term career goals. This isn't about delegating minor tasks: it's about putting people in position to gain hands-on experience doing what they're most interested in. "Delegation," in this case, refers to stretch assignments in which employees can "get their hands dirty" learning about and gaining exposure to other parts of or functions within the organization that they find exciting from a career-development standpoint. Far better than any "book learning" or canned workshop, hands-on exposure rotates people into positions of pure learning and growth that's meaningful to them personally.

Does your recruiter want to learn more about human resources in general? Assign that individual the task of conducting a departmental baseline audit to capture the broader picture of the department's effectiveness. Would it make sense for the individual to spend a half day every week over the next quarter shadowing her peers in other areas of HR to learn firsthand what they deal with and how they handle challenges that come their way? Is your recruiter a high-potential performer who wants to visit the corporate headquarters and get to know her international recruitment peers overseas? You won't know until you ask, but delegating or exposing the individual to other areas of the organization can go a long way (with low expense) to reengage and retain talent.

START A BOOK OF THE QUARTER CLUB

You've heard of the Book of the Month Club. Well, that schedule may be a little too aggressive for your team, but if you're looking to stimulate your staff and challenge them to look outside the box, then this "best practice" may win some big fans for you. Simply decide on one book that you'd all like to complete within, say, sixty or ninety days. Assign each member of your staff a chapter, and have that individual discuss the merits of the chapter in your weekly staff meeting. The real challenge will lie in getting your employees to apply the theoretical knowledge from the book to the day-to-day workplace. The company should pay for the books, but $100 will never be as well spent or have such a potential return on investment. Note: some authors will even join you to host a meet-the-author meeting, so don't be afraid to reach out on LinkedIn and introduce the idea.

INTRODUCE ROTATIONAL STAFF
MEETING LEADERSHIP

One thing that staffers often look for in an ideal employer is leadership development opportunities. Place employees into rotational leadership roles that help them grow and develop professionally. Specifically, allow each of your employees to run a weekly staff meeting—its structure, delineation of responsibilities to others, and follow-up. Placing future leaders into management development roles is probably the most important benefit that you have to offer your people. Besides, it's much easier to complain than it is to fix the problem. People responsible for attempting to fix problems are less likely to blindly blame others because they're more sensitive to the challenges involved in rendering a solution.

EXPLORE EXTERNAL TRAINING WORKSHOPS,
CERTIFICATIONS, AND LICENSES

Assume that many of your best employees will be résumé builders: They'll stay long enough to prove their worth so long as they're on the fast track. Once they feel blocked from upward mobility, new learning, or greater responsibilities, however, they may look elsewhere rather than forgo their personal agendas. The key is to allow all your employees a chance to make a difference and do their very best work every day. People are much more inclined to feel like they're making a positive contribution to your organization if they're in a learning curve. So even if you can't promote them because of budget or head-count restrictions, you can still challenge them to challenge themselves.

Training organizations offer hundreds of situation-specific seminars via Web-based e-learning self-study courses like finance for non–financial managers, foreign language acquisition, and software certification. Two or three seminars per employee per year may add very little to your overhead budget and allow employees a one- or two-day "sabbatical" to reflect on their careers as well as to reinvent themselves in light of your organization's changing needs. And remember that LinkedIn Learning certificates of completion map over to people's LinkedIn profiles with the click of a button, demonstrating their breadth of technical experience and desire to learn more.

HOLD ONE-ON-ONE QUARTERLY PROGRESS MEETINGS

Scheduling a thirty-minute meeting with each of your direct reports will help you, as a leader, build stronger relationships and learn what each individual values. Better yet—have your employees schedule time on your calendar, prepare the agenda, and lead the conversation. You can review progress toward established goals, discuss where goals may need to be tweaked, ask about professional development opportunities, and find out how you can provide greater organizational exposure or build stronger technical skills. Most important, take the time and make the space to listen. What you talk about on the shop floor or in the office corridor is *not* what this is about: this is personal. This is about them: their self-assessment of their work, their identifying where they need greater support, structure, and direction; their progress toward goals, and their identifying where they need help. Placing yourself into the role of mentor and coach this way says a lot about how much you care.

General motivation techniques like these are great, but you won't know what makes an individual tick until you spend one-on-one time listening. Effective leadership is based on personal relationships, and you won't really know how your individual staff members are unless you ask and make it safe for them to provide a sincere answer. People are, after all, motivated by very different things, and true motivation and bonding happens at a personal as well as at the team level. If you could build a program at no cost or at a very low cost to turn your people back on, then you'll likely avoid a crisis of excessive turnover and strengthen your reputation as an outstanding leader. In today's business environment of scarce resources, payroll increases, or promotional opportunities, you'll have provided your staff with the two key elements of any retention program: a personal commitment and relationship as well as a learning curve and constantly evolving and challenging work environment.

SPECIAL NOTE: SALARY PLANS

Despite tight budgets and limited compensation opportunities, there will certainly be times when an "equity adjustment" is appropriate. Equity adjustments are increases in employees' base salary and/or total compensation (that is, including bonus targets) that reflect the general marketplace. When you find that a particular employee has "fallen behind the market" in compensation but don't have the budget currently to award an increase, consider placing the individual on a "salary plan," which typically creates opportunities to "bring the employee to market" over six-, twelve-, and eighteen-month periods. You can share your intentions with an employee without making promises. Be sure to get explicit approval—typically in email format—from your supervisor, department head, and human resources before sharing any of this with a member of your staff. Assuming all the advance approvals are in place, however, you can simply inform the individual as follows:

> While we can't do anything right now to increase your salary, I've gotten approval to work with our compensation team on reviewing your compensation three times over the next eighteen months. I can't promise that there will be increases at those junctures and can't commit to how much they'll be, but we appreciate and value

you and want to make sure you're being compensated competitively. You've got my commitment—as well as our department head's and the human resources department's commitment—to review your salary again in those shorter intervals. We call it a "salary plan," and it's intended to increase employees' total compensation over a fairly short period of time. I'm sorry we can't do anything right now, but please accept this goodwill gesture that reflects our good faith intentions of partnering with you on something that we know is important to you but is likewise really important to us.

23

OVERCOMING CUSTOMER SERVICE CRISES
A Case for Values-Based Leadership

NOT ALL TEAM AND DEPARTMENTAL crises are internal. Some, in fact, may be external, particularly with consumers, customers, or clients. How do you know when this crisis needs to be addressed? Simple: falling sales, rising customer complaints, a spike in product returns, and other telltale signs of an unsuccessful customer experience can show themselves quickly or gradually over time. When faced with this sort of critical challenge, organizations typically rely on customer service training as a remedy. "Back to basics" training is certainly a good idea, but it may not pierce the hearts of the team members who may be harboring feelings of resentment, frustration, and anger based on the way they perceive customers as treating them. This is an ideal opportunity for values-based leadership: an opportunity for you to share and document your core values and what you expect from everyone on the team and also hold yourself accountable to. When people gain a greater understanding of your core beliefs relative to how to deal with one another or how to interact with customers, they tend to assume responsibility for fixing the problem, if for no other reason than you've made it *personal* to them. That's something that no amount of formal training can achieve on its own.

Achieving service excellence is very challenging when dealing with angry customers. Late deliveries, product defects, and billing errors may not be your customer service team's fault, and frustration from dealing with angry clients can boil over into anger if not addressed quickly and proactively. Yet customer service is a partnership. It's actually an opportunity to bond the customer with your company by demonstrating excellence in care that accompanies the product—no matter who may be at fault. Heading off customer service challenges typically works best when you go back to basics: share your beliefs—in writing—with the team and discuss your philosophy, your values, and what's made you successful over the years.

Acknowledge the challenges that may be at hand in particularly thorny circumstances, but discuss the significance of *turnaround relationships* in your employees' careers—their ability to make "true believers" out of initially hostile and unreasonable customers. These are the tales we'll tell decades later when thinking about that particular organization or job. Everyone prides themselves on how they were able to *slay a dragon* in particularly thorny situations, and now is the time to stand out and step up and become a *client whisperer*. Here's what your presentation and documented values one-sheet might look and sound like.

Everyone, I sense that the level of frustration is high right now. There's no judgment here—only observation. I can hear it on the phone calls and can feel it even in our own interactions with one another. I know that customer care is something you got into because you enjoy solving problems and building relationships, but when the numbers of problems get too out of hand, when the tone of the complaints we receive reaches a certain pitch, it's time to get back to basics. I haven't shared this sheet I'm about to pass out with you up to now. It reflects my goals, career aspirations as a leader and customer care specialist, and my values.

I put this down in writing to help us all gain a healthier perspective on who we are and what we're doing. More important, I find that a values one-sheet like this is more important than anything you'll receive in training or in an employee handbook because it's more sincere, personal, and focused than anything you'll read in a training manual. I also think it will give us a broader perspective and serve as a tool to help us focus our energies and efforts going forward.

I'll pass it out now and would like to review it with you all line by line. I'd also like to hear your thoughts and suggestions as we make our way through the document. We can amend it going forward and make it our own mantra toward service excellence. Let's take this one line at a time and work our way through it together.

PAUL'S RULES AND VALUES ON OUTSTANDING CUSTOMER CARE	
RULE	**INTERPRETATION**
Rule 1: Always have one another's backs. We're one team and one company, and we support one another in all circumstances.	We don't assign blame to other parts of the organization or criticize other departments. We don't shift blame or infer that the customer made a mistake or failed to interpret the instructions correctly. We're simply here to solve a mutual problem and help remind customers why they chose our company and our product in the first place.
Rule 2: Stay positive and proactive and take ownership of the problem.	We don't make statements to customers like "Calm down," which is patronizing, or deflect responsibility. Instead, remain positive and take full ownership of the problem. Focus on solutions rather than who or what caused the problem.
Rule 3: Communicate with empathy.	Listen with your eyes and heart in addition to your ears to defuse frustration. Ensure customers feel heard and permit them to vent initially. Remember that the customer isn't upset with you, only with the situation. Don't overpromise fee reimbursements, same-day deliveries, or expedited shipments. Make your word your bond.

PAUL'S RULES AND VALUES ON OUTSTANDING CUSTOMER CARE	
RULE (CONT.)	**INTERPRETATION (CONT.)**
Rule 4: Investigate problems thoroughly and explore alternative solutions.	Ease the tension and partner together to find an appropriate solution. Ask specific who-what-where-when-why questions to clarify the challenge. Repeat and clarify the problem once you have a fuller understanding. Help the customer while involving them in the solution.
Rule 5: Escalate appropriately.	Underpromise and overdeliver. Apologize for their having to experience this. Make yourself the point person for follow-up. But know when to escalate the matter to a higher tier for swifter or more efficient resolution. Stop bullying behavior on the customer's part if their conduct is unprofessional or inappropriate. Welcome partnership with a supervisor or alternative tier to resolve roadblocks, and always have each other's backs.

You can then close out your meeting after answering questions like this:

Folks, these challenges can be difficult at times, and I want you to know that I have your back. My goal is to help you do your very best work every day with peace of mind. The customer isn't always right, especially when their behavior is inappropriate or disrespectful. But it's time we all up our game and increase our level of customer care and performance and productivity. I'm resetting my expectations so you can reset yours. Pretty much any challenge I've faced throughout my career can be captured in this one-sheet and the guidance it provides.

I'm here whenever you run into challenges that you feel you cannot handle on your own, but I expect you to explore every alternative available before escalating things to me while doing so with the utmost respect and empathy. Please keep this one-sheet front and center on your desk going forward. We'll use it to diagnose any situations gone wrong and to leverage our customer care levels going forward. Otherwise, I'm glad I had the opportunity to share my career and personal values with you on this, and I'm happy to answer any questions that you can think of once you sleep on this.

Resetting expectations by sharing your values is often the most impactful way of reinvigorating your team to reach higher levels of performance. Values make expectations personal, and it's much harder for staff members to violate their boss's personal values than it is a company policy or procedure. Open communication, defusing customer complaints, making the customers part of the solution by offering them alternatives, and making yourself the point person to resolve any issues going forward is the gold standard of customer care. Spike your team's enthusiasm for resolving problems and remind them of their commitment to customer service to help them reinvent themselves in light of your heightened expectations.

24

MULTIPLE GENERATIONS AT WORK
Bringing Peace to Five Generations of Traditionalists, Boomers, Xs, Ys, and Zs

FOR THE FIRST TIME IN US HISTORY, five generations coexist in the workplace:

- The Traditionalist/Silent/Veterans Generation: Born 1928– 1945 (fifty-five million)
- The Baby Boom Generation: Born 1946–1964 (seventy-five million)
- The Baby Bust Generation (Gen X): Born 1965–1980 (forty-four million)
- Millennials (Gen Y): Born 1981–1996 (eighty million)
- Zoomers (Gen Z): Born 1996–2012 (sixty-eight million)

Note that, as of this writing, millennials and Zoomers make up approximately 38 percent of the US workforce, and that percentage is increasing quickly as the baby boomers move toward full retirement in 2029.

In fairness, the workplace has never been a single-generation monopoly. Junior workers have always come in to gain experience and work toward advancement. Senior workers have always served as supervisors and mentors. And there's always been some tension between the two. And that's to be expected. But workplaces generally employed Americans from two or (at maximum) three generations, not five. As one might expect, this phenomenon affects the workforce in both subtle and overt ways, especially when compounded by rapid changes in technology and communication tools.

Depending on the line of work you are in as well as your industry, finding employees working well into their seventies is relatively common. Looking at the massive Gen Y alone (eighty million), you can see why college competition is higher than it's ever been and why new entrants into the workforce abound. Could there be a potential clash of generations if not managed correctly? Yes. But can you make this a critical personal value that you share with your team if faced with this situation? Of course! Let's discuss what this might look like in your office or on your shop floor.

GENERATIONAL SNAPSHOTS

First, some stark differences: the Silent Generation, born during the Great Depression and World War II years, believes in doing what you're told and respects a command-and-control structure that values top-down leadership. This generation views conformity as a virtue and values self-sacrifice and communal responsibility. They experienced the post–World War II financial boom that led to higher education and a golden age of prosperity.

Boomers likewise believed in the American dream, but many remain at work since pensions all but vanished during their lifetimes. As a cohort, they are known to relish authority and seek out power.

Gen X, born during the Vietnam era and into the late '70s, faced multiple recessions and layoffs and experienced challenges obtaining and holding on to meaningful employment and career paths for themselves.

Gen Y millennials, also known as the "Net Generation," are associated with a sense of empowerment (sometimes interpreted as entitlement) that spurs them to see experiences that transcend the ideals of a traditional career path. This generation has become more peaceful about letting go of jobs and perceives lack of job security as normal. They believe that businesses should focus on corporate social responsibility and environmentalism, not just on profit.

Gen Z has forced companies to rethink flexibility, open space office configurations, and remote working relationships—the first truly global generation, adapting to fake news, mass shootings, and destabilized politics. This generational cohort has no knowledge of the world as it existed before smartphones. Looking across these vastly different timelines, workplace experiences, and generational values, as well as significant differences in technical capabilities, you can see the vast divides that separate us. Unless we ensure that they don't.

SOLUTIONS TO MULTIGENERATIONAL WORKFORCE CHALLENGES

With such an eclectic mix of generations, worldviews, and experiences, how can any manager hope to create harmony and alignment in the workplace? Success in this realm, as in so many others, stems from open and honest communication, respect, and commitment. While differences will clearly exist in terms of views on authority, leadership and communication styles, and feelings about work-life balance, the following factors may foster a positive atmosphere in your workplace:

- *Cross-generational mentoring and coaching:* This helps acclimate older workers to new experiences and helps younger workers gain wisdom as they benefit from older workers' experiences. (Watch the movie *The Intern* with

Robert DeNiro and Anne Hathaway working together as a team: you'll love the message and see how both generations helped one another not only survive but thrive.)

- *Collaborative and rotational work assignments and projects:* These bring people together quite naturally and align them in a common cause. Remain cognizant of building teams with this type of diversity in mind. Diverse ideas and opinions tend to strengthen a team's final recommendations because of the inclusive nature of so many disparate points of view.

- *Flexible work schedules:* These offer new alternatives to getting work done thanks to technology. The COVID-19 pandemic in the early 2020s made remote work a staple of business life worldwide. Encourage flexible teams and multiple outlets for communication and remote team building to capitalize on this post-pandemic trend, which appears to create greater performance and productivity than traditional nine-to-five work settings.

- *Opportunities to cross-train on the latest technologies:* In-house technical training is helpful to any team, but it's an excellent stretch assignment for high-potential employees who enjoy teaching and public speaking. Don't be surprised to see members of elder generations picking up and mastering the newest and greatest technology, especially if the teacher can make it fun!

- *Training workshops on leadership and communication:* Any of the content from this book or any in the *Paul Falcone Workplace Leadership Series* can be used to develop ideas and discussion points regarding leadership and communication. Get people talking about communication in terms of what works best and what can be changed or tweaked. Encourage open discussions about how to ratchet communication up a notch in your shop. Create the space to sit around the proverbial campfire where elders can pass wisdom down to the younger generations. Encourage team

members to let one another know how they prefer to
communicate. By sharing how—and how often—they plan
to be in touch with one another, teams can anticipate and
avoid communication gaps before they occur.

- *A social atmosphere of community at work, including
  environmental awareness and social causes that make the
  world a better place*: Millennials and Gen Z make up
  38 percent of the workforce as of this writing. In the next
  decade, that figure will shoot up to 58 percent. It's in every
  organization's best interest to get to know this powerful
  combination and what its top priorities are: diversity and
  inclusion, good corporate citizenship, the environment,
  career and professional development, and diversity of
  thoughts, ideas, and voices. Make these staples of your
  organizational voice and pronounce them loudly during the
  recruitment process.

- *Team-building events that heighten awareness of others'
  backgrounds*: There are myriad books written on
  team-building exercises, and many can be found online.
  Bond your teams by addressing differences and developing
  areas of agreement and commonality. Add a "What Can We
  Learn from One Another?" exercise to keep the door open
  to new possibilities for increased interaction and learning.

- *Networks of cross-functional councils and boards that serve as
  a primary source of leadership and decision-making*:
  Committee work naturally brings people together from
  across organizations. It represents an excellent opportunity
  for high-profile exposure as well as an opportunity to truly
  make a difference in your organization's future.
  Committees also give senior leaders an opportunity to pass
  along wisdom to younger generations, ensuring a healthy
  transition of power in succession planning.

- *Social networking tools that build relationships, increase
  collaboration, and enhance employee engagement*: New tools
  are rampant in the workplace—communication tools,

performance feedback apps, employee recognition software, and even robotics and smart apps that mimic human behavior and project future outcomes. Get on board by sharing, teaching, and having fun with new tools and apps, but remember that nothing replaces good old-fashioned human communication and connection.

Despite our vast differences, it's important to remember that generations can work together effectively. Each brings a unique viewpoint and skill set to the table. And if they can be persuaded to communicate openly with one another and respect their differences, there is no workplace challenge that a diverse but united team can't master. Our diversity of thoughts, ideas, and voices is our strength, especially if departmental and team managers can leverage and harness our differences to produce team harmony and more thought-out and steeled recommendations.

To foster a more collaborative environment, embrace employees' differences, not from a sense of toleration but as a source of strength. Leverage the energy and creative enthusiasm that the newest generations bring to the workplace. Support today's leaders by helping them understand and appreciate the many generations within their workforces, and prepare tomorrow's leaders to build stronger muscle around inclusion and respect. Think carefully about succession planning, and coach up-and-coming "high-potential" employees, or "Hi-Pos," to work effectively with all the generations they interact with and lead. And know that many of the ideas outlined previously work just as well in a remote environment as they do in person. Thanks to technology, the ability to communicate and bond from a distance has never been stronger.

25

DEALING EFFECTIVELY
WITH DIFFICULT BEHAVIOR
FROM DIVERSE TEAMS

MANAGING A MULTIGENERATIONAL TEAM is not uncommon but carries with it certain risks that you need to be aware of and prepared for. You need to understand the diversity of your employees and apply various strategies to avoid conflict between them. If you tap into the potential of this diversity, you'll create a more productive, collaborative, and innovative work environment. Your key to success lies in managing your team in a way that ensures that they feel included, respected, and supported—both individually and as a team. Generational differences affect everything from work ethic to communication style to learning methods and collaboration preferences. Let's look at these differences briefly.

Generational differences in work ethic speak to the functions of authority, structure, feedback, sacrifice, flexibility, and openness to change. There are even remarkable differences in assumptions and expectations when it comes to the role of the individual versus the team. Likewise, communication channels range from in-person to remote to electronic (texting, instant messaging, email, and social media). Further, the generations may have different learning preferences—formal in-person training versus online, step-by-step linear learning versus the tech savvy, on-demand video approach—and have different levels of comfort with asynchronous learning and distance-led or self-paced training. Finally, approaches and assumptions toward multitasking and collaboration can be very different among baby boomers, millennials, and zoomers, depending on each team member's comfort with interactive tools and natural learning styles. In short, this can get complicated, so it's important that you identify the structure of your team by generation and look to take the best from everyone to strengthen the overall team dynamic and culture.

According to the ACORN principles, companies that successfully nurture cross-generational workplaces exhibit five common approaches to making their environments generationally comfortable and focused on high levels of performance and productivity. These five approaches successfully accommodate differences, exhibit flexibility, emphasize respectful relations, and focus on retaining talented and gifted employees. The acronym ACORN stands for:

- Accommodating employee differences
- Creating workplace choices
- Operating from a flexible management style
- Respecting employees
- Nourishing Retention (via, among other things, mentoring and training)

Generationally friendly companies allow the workplace to shape itself around the work they do, the customers they serve, and the people they employ. Dress policies tend to be casual, bureaucracy is decreased, and the atmosphere is relaxed and informal. Their approach to diversity and inclusion considers a number of different elements that incorporate these ACORN tenets.

First, they decide how to select participants for various intermittent leadership roles based on their willingness to commit time. For example, natural-born teachers from all generational cohorts may be selected to train, tell stories, and elicit the best that their generation has to offer in a spirit of fun, goodwill, and heightened awareness. For a great example of what this might look like, watch the movie *The Intern* with Robert DeNiro and Anne Hathaway. Even seventy-year-old interns in a dot-com start-up may have lots to offer younger coworkers in terms of the best that their generation has to offer.

Second, generationally friendly organizations ensure that communication allows for give and take. If they're clear on the why behind what needs to be done, they can comfortably delegate the where, when, and how.

Third, they are clear about all goals up front, which is a critical component of their corporate culture (starting in new-hire orientation).

Fourth, they follow up at intervals and offer to help. No one is just "thrown out there" to figure things out on their own, sink-or-swim style. Instead, these organizations pride themselves on their healthy culture and sense of camaraderie, bolstered by their focus on teamwork.

Finally, they constantly monitor and evaluate progress to ensure no one gets lost in the shuffle.

Do such organizations truly exist that incorporate these various values, beliefs, and cultures? Of course. Look first to Ben & Jerry's (the Vermont-based ice cream manufacturer). Whether its employees are dressing up for Elvis Day or Corporate America Day, its Joy Gang remains focused on making work fun, scheduling cross-generational appreciation activities, and ensuring relaxed participation and creativity. Apple, Amazon, and Costco, to name a few, are "generational enterprises" that exhibit high levels of maturity and emotional intelligence. On a practical basis, that means they value and further the ability of employees to recognize their emotions and those of others, discern between different feelings and identify them appropriately, use emotional information to guide thinking and behavior, and manage and adjust emotions to adapt to environments or achieve people's goals.

And this isn't just a nice-to-have. To point 5 previously mentioned in the ACORN principles, it's all about retention. Americans are working longer, which is critical to staffing success in light of (a) the baby boomers' ongoing retirement (through 2029), (b) the dearth of available talent from Gen X (the baby bust generation, which was roughly half the size of the baby boom), (c) the Great Resignation and the Gray Resignation, which followed the COVID pandemic and hastened retirements and career-path changes like never before, and (d) the quiet quitting concept where many workers placed boundaries on how much they would be willing to sacrifice for their companies at the expense of their physical and mental health. Demographics is destiny, and the approach of making companies stronger through their employees' differences can be a brilliant strategy to ensure longevity, retention, and a healthy culture simultaneously.

In short, wise organizations looking to leverage generational differences and create a more inclusive work environment focus on:

- creating opportunities for bridges and connections between the various generation groups of employees based on their commonalities, communication preferences, and distinct advantages
- focusing on organizational attitudes for work styles, financial and nonfinancial rewards and recognition, and motivators that match generational expectations and lifestyles
- leveraging the best that each generation has to offer to support workplace initiatives and corporate goals by promoting, highlighting, and celebrating the values of each generational group

This isn't utopia; it's simply a smart business strategy. Evaluate your organization's balance of generational presence and determine how to create the optimal circumstances and opportunities to bring out the best in everyone in a true spirit of inclusion and belonging. You'll simultaneously address the long-term labor shortage challenges that face us and take advantage of the rising age of retirement.

"For older workers, their younger colleagues offer an opportunity to pass on their skills and knowledge (79%) and for the creativity they bring to the work environment (73%). For younger workers, older colleagues are valued for their skill as teachers (77%), for providing an opportunity to consider a different perspective (76%), and for making the workplace more productive (69%)." —**AARP** (See https://knowledgecompass.com/the-generational-enterprise-challenges-and-values/.)

26

YOUR ROLE AND LIMITS DURING WORKPLACE INVESTIGATIONS
Be Careful Not to Cause Another Crisis!

DEPARTMENTS COME UNDER INVESTIGATION from time to time. An anonymous complaint, hotline tip, allegation against a coworker or manager, and the like are not all that uncommon. How you handle the matter as a manager is critical to an investigation's success. Even more important, misbehavior or inappropriate conduct during a formal workplace investigation tends to result in serious consequences for anyone who runs afoul of the guidelines and expectations that corporate HR or legal departments have in place for how internal investigations are to be handled. The challenge? HR and legal departments typically provide scant instruction for managers and expect them to "know this stuff" intuitively, even if they've never been trained on it before. Hence, the value of this portion of the book because there's actually a lot to know.

WORKPLACE INVESTIGATION DOS AND DON'TS

The first rule is the most critical: thou shalt not conduct thine own investigation. In other words, particularly if the allegations are against you personally, do not—and I repeat, *do not*—attempt to find out who's saying what to the investigators. Conducting mini investigations is a serious code of conduct (ethical) offense that could result in your own immediate dismissal. Investigators, by definition, must be neutral finders of fact and must be guided by an attorney to keep the investigation privileged. Any appearance of a manager unduly influencing the results of an investigation or discussing confidential matters with other employees without authorization to do so will subject the manager to disciplinary action and even termination for violating the company's investigation policy, processes, and directives, and for jeopardizing the credibility of the entire investigation. Ouch! This is not a place for errors or assumptions. If investigators do not share this with you at the time you are briefed at the onset of the investigation, please ask about it to ensure they know that you are aware of this critical fact.

Second, take good notes of everything the investigators tell you at the onset of the investigation. You must understand their instructions literally and word for word. Follow their instructions to a tee, even if they ask you to remain away from work for the day while they conduct their interviews. This is not uncommon if the allegation is against you as the manager: removing the manager from the workplace while they conduct their interviews ensures greater transparency and honesty in witnesses' responses because you are not there to unduly influence the tone and tenor of those responses. Being asked to remain home the day of the team interviews does not mean you are guilty: it's a simple method for conducting interviews that ensures greater process integrity and objectivity.

EMPLOYING THE ATTORNEY-CLIENT PRIVILEGE CORRECTLY

Third, when asked to respond to questions in writing as part of an investigation conducted by your company's internal or external counsel, use "Privileged and Confidential—Attorney-Client Privileged Communication" in your email subject line. Here's how it works: Attorney-client privilege is a method of keeping an investigation confidential and privileged. If the investigation is not privileged, then the investigation and all of the communication created in the course of the investigation are "discoverable," meaning that a plaintiff's attorney looking to sue your organization can access the information and disclose it in a court of law. Instead, you want to prevent that from happening, whenever possible, by keeping the communication privileged between the company and the company's attorney. Marking the communication "Attorney-Client Privileged" is one way to help preserve it.

Likewise, limit the communication to your attorney and those individuals your attorney authorizes you to talk to. If you include a dozen people in the email correspondence, for example, a plaintiff's attorney could argue that it wasn't ever intended to be "privileged" since you copied multiple people who were not under the umbrella of the attorney-client privilege.

Write "Privileged and Confidential—Attorney-Client Privileged Communication" at the top of your email in bold print, address it only to your in-house legal counsel or defense attorney (and anyone else your attorney instructs you to copy), and ask your defense attorney/recipient for legal advice and recommendations in the body of your communication (such as, "Please let me know what you'd recommend after analyzing and evaluating this new information").

Note that the privilege only works if an attorney is included and is providing legal advice in the communication; in other words, you cannot invoke the attorney-client privilege by simply writing to your boss (who isn't an attorney) and marking the communication "Attorney-Client Privileged." Further, understand that judges may allow or deny requests to keep documents privileged, and the company may, at some later point, agree to waive the attorney-client privilege. Therefore, always assume that what you write could be discoverable by a plaintiff's attorney and shared with a jury at some point during the litigation process. When in doubt, pick up the phone and call the attorney first (the recipient of your email) with questions before clicking the send button.

27

F-BOMBS AND PROFANE LANGUAGE
Putting a Quick End to Bad Habits

AS THE SAYING GOES, it's sometimes not *what* you say but *how* you say it (and whom you say it to). For example, if an employee stubs his finger in the drawer and shouts, "Oh, f---!" that could be a disciplinary offense that results in a written warning, but it's very unlikely to be cause for termination.

On the other hand, if your subordinate looks at you, his manager, and shouts, "F--- you!" then it's pretty safe to assume you have a summary dismissal on your hands. Egregious and insubordinate conduct aimed at the supervisor personally allows you little room as an employer to reason, "Well, I'll just give him a warning this time so that he doesn't do that again." If a company were to waive terminating an individual under such circumstances, it could be remiss in its responsibilities for two reasons: First, it would appear irresponsible to allow such inappropriate conduct to potentially continue and it would create a record of its failure to act. Second, it could create a problematic precedent for future occurrences of gross insubordination and potentially harassing behavior. After all, if the company didn't terminate under those circumstances, what would justify a termination for someone else in the future?

When an individual takes pride in using language that's more colorful than you'd like, and especially if a member of your team puts you on notice that he's not comfortable hearing that type of language in the workplace any longer, respond to the offending employee this way:

Jim, I called this meeting with you in private in my office because we've got a situation that's come up that I'll need your help in resolving. Up to now, you've been pretty loose with your language, and I know you tend to use colorful words to make others laugh, including the proverbial F-bomb. And while we all appreciate your sense of humor, we've been put on notice that some folks on the team feel like it's getting out of hand. Whenever we're put on notice as a company that language or behavior potentially offends anyone, we've got to notch things back a bit so that everyone feels comfortable again. I'll need your help in fixing this perception problem that exists, and I'd like your commitment now that we won't be hearing any further expletives or inappropriate sayings from this point forward. Will you support me in that?

That's a very reasonable opener and one that most people will be able to accommodate.

THE "EVERYONE'S BEING OVERLY SENSITIVE" SELF-DEFENSE

What happens, however, if Jim tells you that he really can't help himself? In fact, he's not even aware of when he's using foul language because it's such an integral part of who he is. His family used that language from the time he was born, his friends used that kind of language when he was growing up, and well, there's really not too much he can do about it. Besides, we're all friends in the group, aren't we? Can't we all agree to just keep things the same? What's all the fuss about anyway? Why are people suddenly being so oversensitive? When the justifications and rationalizations come into play, it's time to lay down the law a bit more sternly:

> Jim, you're not hearing me. This isn't about you any longer—it's about your coworkers and our company. When someone puts us on notice that they're not comfortable with the curses and loose banter and offensive jokes that have arguably become pervasive in the workplace, there's a whole new paradigm in play. At this point, we no longer have the discretion to laugh it off and ignore it. If we do, we can have a hostile work environment claim levied at us, and as you know, hostile work environment claims are a subset of sexual harassment, which falls under our company's antidiscrimination policy.
>
> In short, we're putting you on notice that the language and behavior have to stop immediately. If you really feel you can't accommodate our request, then you may have to make an employment decision. If you honestly can't or won't stop at this point, you'll either have to resign or be terminated for cause should this occur again.
>
> I don't like having this conversation with you because you're an excellent worker and one of our most popular employees, but you've got to understand this and get it right: as much as we enjoy working with you, we can't allow you to expose our organization to a hostile work environment claim.
>
> In that case, here's what the record would look like: Employees inform company that they're no longer comfortable with foul language and inappropriate jokes made by Jim Smith. Company does nothing to amend Jim Smith's behavior and allows the foul language to continue. Employees who lodged the original complaint sue the company for failing to take reasonable action to fix the problem. Do you see the challenge we're facing and why I need your help now?

Once you couch the legal concerns in such a straightforward manner, even the most steadfast offenders will likely take this more seriously.

THE APPEAL TO PERSONAL LIABILITY

If you need any additional fodder to convince Jim of the urgent need to change his behavior, you can include the following:

Oh, and Jim, there's one more thing: I'm not saying this to frighten you, but I want you to be fully educated on the matter. If the company were to be sued, you would also likely be named as an individual defendant in the lawsuit. In fact, in cases where the company warns the employee and the employee refuses to change his ways, he may be considered to be "acting outside the course and scope of his employment." And under those circumstances, the company's legal team wouldn't necessarily protect you. You'd have to find your own defense attorney and pay the damages that arise from the claim.

There are actually two separate legal issues here, Jim: First, there's the concept of personal liability. Second, there's the "out of scope" concept, which speaks to whether the organization will indemnify an employee if that individual is held personally liable. In most states, you could be sued for up to $50,000 of your own money for what they call *managerial bad acts* or *outside the course and scope of your employment*. In some states like California, there's no monetary limit. You don't want to go anywhere near either of these two legal scenarios. We don't pay you enough money to risk your home and your bank account for work-related lawsuits, so any time you find yourself slipping back into your old ways, be sure and stop by my office so that I can remind you about the risks you're assuming when it comes to foul language in the workplace.

DOCUMENTATION OPTIONS WHEN YOUR MESSAGE JUST ISN'T SINKING IN

If he doesn't take you seriously after that discussion and persists in his argument that this is all silly, put your concerns and expectations in written form, either as a formal written warning or letter of clarification (which doesn't contain any consequence language stating that "failure to demonstrate immediate and sustained improvement may result in further action, up to and including dismissal"). Seeing things in writing often escalates the sense of urgency. It might likewise make sense to address the team openly about this (without referencing Jim's role). Your communication might sound like this:

> Everyone, I called this meeting because I want to put into place a practice that's become a bit too casual or nonchalant in our daily communications with one another. I've heard F-bombs and other expletives shared openly, often with the intention of getting a laugh. I'm no longer comfortable with it. While at first, I thought it was funny, it feels like it's gotten out of hand. I don't want people thinking less of us as a department because we have "potty mouths" or otherwise demonstrate disrespectful behavior toward one another and toward the organization as a whole. In short, I want the foul language to end, starting now. And I'd like your commitment right here and now that you'll adopt this new approach willingly as a team and that we'll never have to have a conversation like this again. Do I have your commitment? [*Yes.*] Thank you. Does anyone have any questions? [*No.*]

Boom—situation resolved. In real life, it really is that easy. After all, if you heard your boss have that discussion with your team, would you be inclined to adhere to her instructions or would you flout them, daring others to hold you accountable? You can typically tell by the tone in someone's voice and by the solemnity of the message's content when a hard line is drawn in the sand. Few will risk challenging a directive like this, especially when employees know better. Foul language is tolerated until it is no longer tolerated. It's your job as a first-time manager to avoid this crisis by addressing the matter clearly and setting expectations wisely. Under most circumstances, this will be a "one-and-done" conversation with immediate results. If that's not the case, then formal disciplinary action will likely become your next logical tool for handling the matter responsibly.

28

WELCOMING BACK PROBLEMATIC WORKERS FROM LONGER-TERM LEAVES OF ABSENCE

WANT TO KNOW ABOUT A crisis you couldn't see coming? Try returning a problematic worker to the team after that person was on a long-term leave of absence. When problematic employees go out on leave, normalcy can return. People communicate more openly, laughter is heard, that tense feeling of walking on eggshells evaporates when that particular employee isn't present. Things can finally return to normal, and the team gets used to the new normal fairly quickly. Six months later, an announcement is made that the problematic employee has been cleared to return to work. Panic sets in: Are we going to go back to that feeling of walking on eggshells? Will that individual start pitting people against one another like he used to do in the past? Is the drama about to return with a vengeance? Soon, you start hearing banter like, "If he returns, I'm going to start looking for a new job." Even you're nervous about how things are going to change (for the worse) with this individual returning to the workplace. What's a first-time manager to do to avert a crisis that could upend your entire team's balance and peace of mind?

First, understand that the problem employee who's been out on an extended leave of absence has likely felt isolated, rejected, and otherwise scorned by the group over time. After all, the best defense is a good offense, so if the isolated worker can figure out how to attack his opponents or enemies proactively, they will be too occupied with defending themselves to stage an attack of their own. This "strategic offensive principle" is more common in the workplace than we like to imagine. The question is, once you recognize it, how do you go about trying to fix it?

Second, realize that it takes two to tango. Even if you weren't the supervisor when this individual was having ongoing challenges with the other team members in the unit, you need to assume partial responsibility for the situation in order to heal it. (In this case, you're assuming responsibility as the company for anything that might have gone wrong, whether you were present or not.) Once you're in that mindset, you can consider how to extend the olive branch and bring that worker back into the fold. In short, the person's return to work can be a brand-new beginning for everyone. But everyone has to make themselves part of the solution for the healing to begin. No easy task, but that's why you purchased this book! Let's go through this by the numbers . . .

STEP 1:
SCHEDULE A MEETING WITH YOUR TEAM TO ANNOUNCE THE INDIVIDUAL'S RETURN AND TO SET EXPECTATIONS PROPERLY

In calling the meeting, determine who should be present. Naturally, the team of coworkers should be present to hear the same message from you. Next, you might want to include your boss and your HR representative as well so that there's total alignment of message. In fact, it would be a great idea to share your intended approach with your boss and with HR so that you have full buy-in before you step into the room. Note that your supervisor may pass on the opportunity, as may HR. That's okay but running your ideas past them and inviting them is a wise move on your part because it shows full transparency and excellent partnership on your part.

STEP 2:
CONDUCT THE TEAM PREP MEETING
WITH TRANSPARENCY AND EMPATHY

All, I'm calling this meeting to get us all on the same page about something I'm going to need your help with, partnership, and full cooperation. Anthony Ellis is scheduled to return to work next Monday, and I want to make sure we're fully aware of his return and in alignment in terms of how we're going to approach this.

First, I'm aware that there were issues with Anthony's relationships with many of you in addition to what many of you considered inappropriate conduct on his behalf at the time he left. And I'm not going to ask you to do anything that I'm not likewise going to ask of him when he returns. But this is a new opportunity to reinvent and strengthen our team, and I'm choosing not to sweep this under the rug and simply permit him to return to work without saying anything to anyone. Instead, we need to make sure we all have clear expectations of how to handle matters going forward, and I want you to hear from me that I'm dedicated to returning Anthony to our unit with a full sense of goodwill and openness.

Second, at the time he left, there was a healthy amount of drama going on, as I recall, and you may recall. What I can't allow to happen is that we all snap back into defense mode, allow frustration from old memories to have free rein, and hope for the best but expect the worst. I just don't operate that way, and I don't expect any of you want to go back to that either.

Here are my thoughts: I'm not asking you to forget everything that happened. And I realize you'll likely feel cautious and defensive around Anthony, especially when you first see him. But I'm going to ask you all to let the past go for all intents and purposes. There's no need to rehash any of the drama that we were experiencing when Anthony was with us last. I'm likewise going to ask him not to pick up where he left off and simply attribute what happened to a disagreement in thoughts and approaches to a problem. But raising those old issues will help no one, so I'm holding everyone accountable for dropping those issues that were in play at the time he left. Am I crystal clear on that? [Yes.]

Third, I want you to know what I plan on sharing with Anthony when we meet one-on-one in my office on Monday morning. I'm planning on telling him that we're specifically not picking up where we left off. Whatever was a concern at the time he left is now forgotten and is not to be addressed going forward. Once I have his confirmation that he agrees with that, I'm going to tell him that I'm committed to welcoming him back to the team as a fully contributing member. I'll confirm for him that I'll have his back and support him in any way I can. I'll let him know that I met with you all to announce his return, so everyone is aware of his return, and I set expectations for the rest of the team to avoid picking up where we left off as well.

Finally, I'm going to ask him how we can heal. I'll tell him I want him to feel included and accepted in the group, that I'm committed to his successful return, and that I'm here to ensure everyone's success. And over time, I hope that everyone will become more comfortable with one another in light of the situation that involved us all six months ago at the time he went out on leave. Overall, I'm leading with my heart and assuming good intentions, and I want everyone to follow my lead.

That being said, if there are any conflicts that pop up, I want to be involved immediately. I don't expect everyone to forgive and forget as if nothing happened, but I expect everyone to assume good intentions and err on the side of compassion. As much as I tend to address any open items rather than dismiss them, in this case, I see no benefit to pick up where we left off—nothing good can come of that approach, if no other reason, it's old and there's no benefit to conjuring up old resentments. I expect a clean start for our department as if it's everyone's first day and I'm welcoming you all to the company. I likewise expect everyone to treat and be treated with respect and dignity. Do I have your group commitment to moving forward in this way?

The answer from the team will likely be yes, but you can expect some resistance. "We hear you, Paul, but Anthony caused a lot of ill will. I won't rehash the problematic behaviors that caused our department to practically implode at the time, and we can assume good intentions, as you're instructing us. But it's got to go both ways—he has to be held accountable to these very same standards or else this isn't going to work." To that point, you can assure the team that everyone will be held equally accountable. Likewise, since you are mandating that any issues that surface be brought to your immediate attention, you are making yourself primarily responsible for the solution. That's a healthy role for you to take in a problematic situation like this where sides were so clearly drawn in the past.

Hold your one-on-one meeting with Anthony when he returns outlining these same expectations previously mentioned. Once you're done, you might call a brief staff meeting—preferably with donuts or scones or other treats—to welcome Anthony back to the team. In that meeting, you can update Anthony on the status of some of the larger projects that the team is working on along with any other significant changes over the past six months. End by confirming what Anthony will be working on, when the next staff meeting is scheduled, and what you plan on talking about then. This way, there's little need to exchange niceties, and you can keep it all business. That's probably the wisest approach to a potentially stressful meeting where you're reintroducing a team member who left last under extreme conditions and where currents of resentment may still fester under the surface. Stay with your weekly staff meeting schedule but check in regularly with staff to ensure no drama is creeping in or otherwise showing itself. Letting some time pass—under a heavy amount of structure, direction, and feedback from you—will hopefully normalize feelings and allow the healing to begin.

29

STOPPING BULLYING AND HARASSMENT ON YOUR TEAM ONCE AND FOR ALL

BULLYING AND HARASSMENT REPRESENT real legal risks to your organization. Sure, you probably have policies that define harassment and discrimination, and it's not uncommon for employers to mandate this type of training, both for management teams and line staff. Training—often via video—certainly teaches what the types of harassing behaviors are and includes definitions and more. But this cognitive approach to turning around situations only goes so far. To truly fix this problem once and for all, you need to make it emotional by piercing people's hearts and resetting expectations and consequences. Insecure adults may taunt and tease others in an exercise of power through humiliation, and it's not a far stretch of the imagination to see how this could lead to a hostile work environment claim. Any incident in which a worker is abused, threatened, intimidated, teased, or ridiculed could be considered intrusive and harassing behavior, and such emotional and psychological violence should be taken very seriously. The aggression may be verbal, physical (as in blocking someone's way), or visual (as in leering or staring someone down). The challenge with bullying, however, is that because it can be subtle and easily denied, it can be difficult to prove, especially when peers cover for one another or witnesses refuse to get involved.

When a staff member complains to you, the manager, about feeling stripped of his or her dignity or otherwise publicly humiliated by a peer, you may very well have a bullying situation on your hands. Bullying in the workplace destroys morale for those who witness it and may expose your company to significant financial damages. Employees will often fear going directly to their supervisor or HR to complain about a peer for fear of retaliation. Even if no formal complaints are made by the staff member who was subjected to the harmful behavior, proactively addressing any incidents as soon as they surface is important:

> Liam, I called this meeting with you this afternoon because I'm concerned about your conduct during this morning's staff meeting. I saw you engage in something I would call a "public humiliation session" with Eddie, and from what I could see, your attacks were intended to strip him of his dignity in front of the rest of the group. Can you picture the meeting and specifically what I'm talking about?

At this point, Liam may launch into an all-out defense to justify his actions: "Eddie did one of the stupidest things I've ever seen. He called a client on the phone and said—" Your best response is to stop him right there:

> Liam, this isn't about the merits of your argument, and I certainly don't need a justification of any sort for your behavior. Whatever Eddie did or didn't do is not why we're here. We're here about you and the perception you created in my eyes and in others' eyes that your behavior was menacing, mean-spirited, and personal.
>
> Let me be clear: Treating your peers with disdain or contempt for any reason and under any circumstances violates company policy. More significantly, it makes me lose faith in your ability to

contribute to this organization positively and in your ultimate suitability for the position you're in.

Here's how I see it and how I feel you should see it from now on: stripping people of their dignity or humiliating them publicly is no longer an option for you. Simply take that tool out of your toolbox and throw it away. It's not useful here or at any other organization where you work for the rest of your career.

Further, you're responsible for your own perception management. Perception is reality until proven otherwise, and you're responsible for creating a friendly and welcoming environment, just like I am, and every other member of this company is. Your role is not to judge others, make them feel like less of a person, or humiliate them or publicly humiliate them. In fact, that's the opposite of what your role is, which potentially makes you a net negative and a liability to the organization.

If I had to describe your behavior today, I would say that you humiliated, overruled, ignored, and isolated a team member in front of his peers. That's bad for morale, needless to say, and creates a culture based on fear. As a company, we pay for that over time in terms of lost efficiency, turnover, absenteeism, and unnecessary separation packages and lawsuits. In short, this morning you created a tremendous liability for our company, both in terms of stress-related health and safety exposure, as well as in the potential for a hostile work environment claim, which violates our organization's antidiscrimination and antiharassment policies. I'm here to make sure that something like that never happens again. Am I clear? [*Yes.*]

I'm choosing not to put this in a written warning form at this point, Liam. I want you to consider this a coaching and mentoring moment to help raise your awareness, because something like this, if left unaddressed, could hold you back for the rest of your career. You've got too much potential to let this tragic flaw get in your way, and I hope you'll always think back on this meeting and appreciate the time we're sharing right now to help you readjust your approach to building strong teams, selfless leadership, and having others' backs. Just know that if I ever again have to address this with you, it will be in the form of formal progressive discipline. Do I have your commitment that we'll never have to have a discussion like this again? [Yes.] Excellent. Thank you very much.

This was a fairly direct and confrontational response on your part. But remember that you need both a carrot and a stick to be an effective leader. When you sense that someone purposely acts in a mean-spirited way, no number of carrots will turn around an errant performer. Once that individual hears how seriously you're taking this, what your expectations are, and what the consequences will be should this occur again, you'll likely end this type of humiliating behavior once and for all. In fact, adding comments like "There's no place for this type of behavior in my shop" or "What you did really offended me and other members of the team" will cement the seriousness of Liam's lack of judgment and discretion in his handling of this.

People talk. Liam will likely share some elements of your discussion with his peers, no doubt harrumphing and complaining about it. Still, word will get out about the clarity of your message and expectations. More important, people will see Liam's changed behavior as proof of your intervention. In the end, permitting one member of your team to bully another will kill camaraderie and teamwork faster than just about anything. Addressing the matter immediately and turning it around, in comparison, will demonstrate your willingness to address problems head-on. Constructive confrontation plays an important role in your management career and is an important tool to have at the ready in your leadership toolbox. When it comes to bullying, harassment, and other potentially discriminatory challenges, spare little in making your feelings—and the consequences of future infractions—known.

30

MAKING IT SAFE FOR EMPLOYEES TO VENT ABOUT NON-JOB-RELATED CONCERNS

WORKERS ARE TIRED. Some are generally scared, worried about pandemics, geopolitics and global aggressions, climate crisis, the meteoric changes in technology that impact everything from how they buy groceries to how they order fast food, and their ability to find meaningful work to feed their families. Not to mention the politics coming out of Washington, DC, which are leaving many Americans feeling frustrated and angry. Worst of all, workers can't seem to leave this at the door when they arrive in the office or on the shop floor every morning. US workers are frazzled, frustrated, and angst ridden, and it's showing itself more and more in the workplace in terms of microaggressions, objectionable behavior, and even outright confrontation.

Whether in the boardroom, the breakroom, or at the kitchen table, workers remain challenged to drown out the noise that keeps shouting at them from social media, cable news, the internet, and so many other sources. Companies have to approach these challenges in an emotionally intelligent way, weighing the pros and cons of making formal announcements as opposed to stepping back from the fray and sweeping these social issues under the rug. Yet many of today's most profound and compelling issues are exacerbated in the workplace because of a lack of bona fide communication. There can be real benefits associated with a safe forum for employees to express their thoughts and feelings— provided that there are ground rules that include treating one another with respect, trust, and fairness, and abiding by the guidance provided by the individual who is leading the session.

Religion and politics discussions historically do not belong in the workplace. Period. Companies rarely make formal statements surrounding such topics for practical reasons of not alienating potential consumers, customers, clients, or other stakeholders. But fundamental principles and core values are being challenged and upended at a record pace, and whether you believe such changes are positive or negative, the pace and substance of change is forcing CEOs and corporations to rethink their traditional private postures. Workers, especially Gen Yers and Gen Zers, want their employers to take a social stand, bringing to the forefront "personal" matters that affect their demeanor in the workplace, including abortion rights and reproductive health, gay and transgender rights, and gun control, among others. In short, these are fundamental identity challenges to assumptions and core values that many believed were guaranteed, at least in terms of their lifetime experiences. Aggressive responses are becoming more commonplace and carrying over into the workplace, and the traditional rules of etiquette and professionalism are suffering as a result.

PRACTICAL SOLUTIONS TO LETTING OFF STEAM

Is it healthy to invite employees to attend a "safe zone" meeting where they can express their frustration and vent their feelings about human rights, international relations, or politics? It depends. One thing's for sure: you'd better tread carefully, because once you open this Pandora's box, there's no going back. Watching large corporations take a stand on issues such as gender identity or gay marriage speaks volumes about their values and beliefs in terms of corporate social responsibility. But at what cost? How many potential consumers, customers, or clients will feel alienated or consider taking their business elsewhere? Extreme times call for extreme measures, but you can expect corporate responses to run the gamut—from bold embracement of social beliefs now under threat to total avoidance of anything that doesn't have to do specifically with business. On a more micro level, it becomes critical that you give thought to how you wish to handle this for your team or department.

Creating the space for employees to vent their frustrations in a safe setting can open the lines of communication for employees at all levels to share their thoughts about a wide range of issues, concerns, and disappointments whether emanating from society at large or from their jobs. In terms of structure, it's typically better to have a smaller group, since this provides increased opportunities for individual communication while reducing the likelihood of disruptive behaviors that can develop in a larger group, especially when dealing with sensitive topics. Be sure and speak with your boss and/or human resources before you move down this path, but if you're going to make it safe for employees to vent, add definitive rules and guardrails like this:

> Everyone, I invited you to this meeting on a voluntary basis to discuss—in a very professional and respectful manner—how you're feeling. So much is changing before our very eyes . . . truths, laws, and rules we've held as givens our entire lives. I sense an underlying tone of anger and aggression, not just in our department or company but in society as a whole. I want to make it safe for you to express your concerns, but we have to do so carefully. As such, before we begin talking about how you're feeling and what you're experiencing, I'll ask you to follow some simple rules:

First, there can be no attacking and there's no need for defending. We're here to support one another and make sure we can lower the level of tension that sometimes arises within our team.

Second, this can't be about personal opinions: only about how we're feeling about the pace of change and how it affects us. In other words, if you're shocked by politics, angry at our nation's financial situation, exhausted from pandemics, or simply frustrated about the amount of work or stress you're experiencing, I'd welcome your sharing it here in a safe setting. But this isn't a forum for debating your personal opinions. I have to make sure we're all clear and in agreement on that.

Third, I get to blow the whistle and act as referee if anything gets too hot or contentious. In such cases, my pressing the relief valve has to be respected by everyone in the room. Is that fair? [*Yes.*]

The more advance buy-in you have from the team before the meeting begins, the greater the chances that hot feelings won't escalate into conflict, which is exactly what you're trying to avoid. But your staff members will likely appreciate that you recognize the frustration they're feeling—the eight-hundred-pound gorilla in the room—and you're willing to take some risk and make it safe for them to express themselves. You can then close the meeting as follows:

Folks, I hear you. And I think we've done a good job hearing one another just now. I'm sorry for what we're all going through. And I'm realistic enough to realize that one sit-down meeting as a team isn't going to resolve these ongoing issues and the frustrations that we're all experiencing, no matter what side of the divide we fall on. But it does give us a chance to reset expectations regarding civil and professional behavior toward one another, and to understand that there's a lot more that we have in common than sets us apart.

I actually have a homework assignment for you to consider, I'm not going to check back with you on this, but it's likely the case that none of us has ever experienced this level of profound change to our core beliefs and values. Make your voices heard: Reach out to the president at WhiteHouse.gov, reach out to your senator and congressional representative on their websites to express your concerns. One voice can't change the world, but large numbers of unified voices may certainly affect decisions and voting records.

Finally, let's all agree to take it down a notch when dealing with one another. As the saying goes, each to their own without judgment. What you want for yourself give to another. And when in doubt, err on the side of compassion. There's an awful lot of confusion out there, and this is unfortunately something our nation and our world have to go through right now. But we're in control of minimizing its effects on our coworkers, and a little bit of goodwill can go a long way nowadays. With that, I'll end the meeting and remind you all that you're safe and respected here and that you're equally responsible for making everyone else feel safe and respected as well.

Making it safe for employees to talk about their frustrations with non–work-related matters may have seemed unnecessary or even downright foolish in the past as a management practice or initiative. But ignoring the matter and failing to address the belligerent behaviors that have become way too common in many workplaces may be missing the moment in terms of what's needed in today's world. Gain advance approval of your intended staff meeting, set your ground rules clearly, and reset expectations. Your employees will likely appreciate the gesture and appreciate your bold leadership. And you may very well avoid a crisis of simmering conflict and confrontation that's just waiting to explode onto the scene.

PART THREE

COMPANY
CRISES

31

TALENT SCARCITY
Creative Alternatives When Job
Applicants Are Nowhere to Be Found

THE COVID-19 PANDEMIC OPENED OUR EYES as employers to what true labor scarcity looked and felt like. Most executives would describe it as scary: organizations kept their doors open in early 2020 through the disabling period of the pandemic, only to find no human beings to do the work once the public returned to the scene to begin purchasing. A new phrase was coined—the *sansdemic*—meaning "without people"—that kept companies on the brink of closure while determining who would do the work to increase revenue after several years of income scarcity. COVID taught many of us that life wasn't a game, that this isn't a dress rehearsal, and that, after watching over a million Americans lose their lives to the disease, life is too short to waste any precious time in jobs or careers that lacked a greater purpose or otherwise worked us to death.

People opted to leave their current positions and not look back. The reasoning went something like this: "I don't know what I'm going to do, but I can guarantee you that it won't be [BLANK]." You can fill in that blank with whatever job the person held previous to the pandemic: nursing assistant, waiter, corporate executive, or the like. The disconnect came with the fact that companies typically look to hire people with previous experience. Once you realize that candidates with previous experience are no longer looking to work in that field and there's no qualified talent available to apply for your job openings, then the crisis reaction kicks into effect. You can't manufacture widgets, deliver food to tables, or accept new hospital patients if your core employees are gone and there's no one to replace them.

The Great Resignation was the term used to describe this massive cultural transformation and disruption. For workers in their fifties who were nearing retirement but opted to leave and start their own business or retire early, the term Gray Resignation was coined. And for workers fortunate enough to work through the pandemic but who were exhausted because of massive overtime, double shifts, seven-day workweeks, and a lack of appreciation for going above and beyond, "quiet quitting" came into play, meaning workers had reached their "mental max" and drew firm mental lines in the sand about what they would or would not do going forward. "I'm not going to kill myself on this job anymore. Life is too short, and I've got to worry about me, my family, and my health. I'm not going to work all this overtime, no matter how much pressure my company puts on me or how few people are available to backfill any of our open jobs" went the reasoning.

The COVID-caused job scarcity, however, simply cracked open the door and shone a sliver of light on what was to come. Demographers, social scientists, and labor economists (a.k.a. "corporate futurists") will tell you that the "population explosion" we've become accustomed to—read that as unlimited human capital talent—is coming to a swift end. Think about it: from the time of Christ until the eighteenth century, the world population fluctuated between two hundred and seven hundred million people. By the early 1800s, the planet hit one billion people. Then the Industrial Revolution came onto the scene in the eighteenth century and hit its full stride in America in the 1870s and continued through World War II. At that time, there were less than three billion humans on the planet. By the 1970s, there were four billion, the 1980s reached five billion, and the late 1990s witnessed six billion. By 2011, there were seven billion, and on November 15, 2022, the global population reached eight billion. That means that in the 1970s, there were roughly half as many human beings on the planet as there are today. Now *that's* a population explosion and a dynamic labor pool!

Corporate futurists will tell you today, however, that because of declining global birth rates, it will now take over two hundred years for the human population to double again. They will likewise tell you that labor scarcity will be the single most defining element of the twenty-first century. Per George Friedman in his bestselling book *The Next 100 Years: A Forecast for the 21st Century,* "By 2050, advanced industrial countries will be losing population at a dramatic rate. . . . In the first half of the century, the population bust will create a major labor shortage in advanced industrial countries. Today, developed countries see the problem as keeping immigrants out. Later in the first half of the twenty-first century, the problem will be persuading them to come." Demographics is destiny, and despite shorter windows of high unemployment that will surely come our way due to local economic disruptions from time to time, the overwhelming trend toward labor scarcity makes employee engagement and retention more critical than ever.

TALENT SCARCITY DRIVES THE DEI&B MOVEMENT (AMONG OTHER NEEDS)

Talent scarcity is a key driver behind the DEI&B (diversity, equity, inclusion, and belonging) movement: DEI&B is smart business not only because it's the right thing to do and because it's a core value of millennials and Gen Z—after all, all voices deserve to be heard and granted a seat at the table—but diversity outreach is at the core of identifying talent moving forward. The labor force participation rate in the United States reached its height around 2000 at about 67 percent but has—with slight exception—declined ever since, thanks mostly to the 2007–2009 Great Recession and the onslaught of the COVID-19 pandemic in 2020. As of

2020, the labor force participation rate fell to around 60 percent and, according to the Bureau of Labor Statistics, will remain at around 60 percent through 2050.

Further, the reasons to develop a diverse talent pool go well beyond equal employment opportunity governmental obligations, which require that minority representation within the organization approximates their proportionate numbers in the comparable labor market. Today, underrepresented ethnic groups account for 30 percent of the total US population. By 2060, they are expected to reach 60 percent of the population. These groups have historically been overlooked but have a growing amount of buying power. As such, a diverse talent pool increases the range of human capital available to the organization while also better reflecting the buying habits of a more diverse consumer base.

To accommodate these shifts in demographic trends, companies will need to recruit and train a more diverse workforce. And with a more diverse workforce comes more diverse expectations on the part of workers that their employers should strive to meet. In short, building strategies of inclusion and belonging around a demographically diverse workforce is smart business in order to simply stay alive in light of the coming talent dearth. It stands to reason that creating professional networks, providing leadership training and mentoring, and accommodating families have been found to be effective ways to facilitate career development, avoid career plateaus, and reduce barriers to advancement.

But before we discuss engagement and retention, we have to acquire the talent despite today's shortages, which is where we can pick up our story from a practical standpoint.

DEMOGRAPHICS IS DESTINY

Baby Boomers were born between 1946 (the year after World War II ended) and 1964, when the birth control pill was introduced. Over those eighteen years, seventy-seven million babies were born, that is, ten thousand newborns per day. In 2011, however, something very critical happened that got barely any press: that first cohort of babies born in 1946 began to retire. Our reality now is that ten thousand citizens per day are retiring, many of whom are exiting the workforce between 2011 and 2029. In other words, we're only a little over halfway through this massive demographic shift and workplace exit as of this writing.

When the birth control pill was introduced in 1964, the Baby Boom Generation was replaced by the Baby Bust Generation (Generation X). Gen X only had forty-four million babies, relative to the baby boom's seventy-five million babies. Starting in the later 2020s, we're going to feel the massive loss of talent that will plague us for years to come. The one positive offset to this massive loss in talent? Gen Y (a.k.a. Millennials). Gen Y (born 1981–1996) boasts eighty million humans, and in 2020, millennials overtook Boomers as America's largest generation. Hence, it behooves employers to listen to the needs of this younger generation (along with the Zoomers), which represent the vein of new talent that will populate our companies.

WHAT THIS MEANS FOR YOU

First, big job boards like Indeed, CareerBuilder, ZipRecruiter, SimplyHired, Monster, and Dice (for technical computer talent), among others, will likely have challenges identifying the volume of talent needed for today's many employment openings. While job boards will likely remain "first stops" for companies with job postings, employers are turning to new boutique websites for their recruitment outreach efforts, which likewise serve their diversity and inclusion needs. Boutique job boards like VeteranJobs .net, HireOurHeroes.org, RecruitMilitary.com, DiversityJobs.com, DiversityEmployers.com, LatinoJobs.org, OverFiftyJobs.com, Black Careers.org, AsianHires.com, NativeJobs.org, LGBTjobsite.com, and WeHireWomen.com will likely expand your reach to tap qualified diverse talent. The Department of Labor's Job Accommodation Network (http://www.dol.gov/agencies/odep /resources/jan) is an excellent source for identifying job candidates with disabilities.

Likewise, social media sites like LinkedIn and Facebook will continue to expand their outreach for professional-level candidates. Both also offer functions that allow employers and recruiters to create targeted advertising campaigns designed to reach underrepresented groups. And customized mobile apps and web platforms will permit turnkey employment solutions for smaller companies, including payroll, benefits, workers' compensation, and overall "employment without boundaries." In other words, workers belonging to the vendor's payroll can work at multiple employers while the vendor remains the constant employer of record. Technology will continue to provide solutions to labor shortage problems, just as the nature of gig talent and portable benefits take root in the United States and elsewhere to source talent.

Your job? Research local resources, such as nursing, hospitality, or tech trade schools and professional development programs, including local training organizations like Workshops for Warriors. Community action agencies, civil rights organizations, and church groups within communities can help employers reach inner-city residents. Further, determine which job boards, social media sites, and web platforms may work best for your organization relative to your geographic location and the types of hires you make. Set your recruitment budget for the next quarter or year by exploring new sources of potential talent providers and funnels. Some will work better than others, but you won't know until you try out different options. Note that a recruitment advertising agency may also make total sense to help you with your strategic ad placement.

Finally, build a buddy onboarding program to ensure a sheltered transition for new hires to make it through their first three or six months (where so much turnover typically happens). Talent acquisition and retention remains a living, breathing part of your organizational culture. It also spells your long-term success, as talent remains companies' primary profit lever in the tight labor markets that are sure to follow. Maximize the chances for success on the front end of the employment relationship, and with that secured, move to your retention strategic planning. Keep in mind that talent acquisition is not a temporary crisis: it will undergird your organization's trajectory for years to come, and you—the first-time manager—will shepherd your company's most cherished resource—its people.

SPECIAL NOTE: ACCOMMODATING FAMILIES

If your organization offers any particular family-friendly benefits, advertise them broadly in your recruitment advertising campaigns and internal employee referral programs, especially programs that are designed to be mutually advantageous to career-oriented working mothers and their employers. This may include alternative career paths, extended leave, flextime, job sharing, relaxed dress codes, summer hours, and telecommuting. Some organizations provide take-home meals for those working overtime, subsidize babysitting, or offer job-finding assistance for spouses of employees who are relocated. Requiring workers to shut off their mobile devices after hours is another perk that organizations are increasingly giving to their employees. All help recipients balance career and family. And all square with Gen Y and Gen Z's desires for greater work-life-family balance and harmony.

32

DEALING WITH THE CHALLENGES
OF EXCESSIVE TURNOVER
Where Are They Going and
Why Are They Leaving Us?

A MAJOR CRISIS CAN COME out of the blue, especially when you find that you're losing some of your key players in a short period. The panic sounds something like this: "Paul, Sam, and Nina have all left in the past three months, and now Janet's just tendered two weeks' notice. What's going on? We can't afford to lose her, especially now that we've recently lost the other members of the team. What's going on? Stop whatever you're doing and find out why they're leaving us, where they're going, and what's driving them to look elsewhere in the first place!" And off you go . . . If you haven't conducted exit interviews or have exit data that points to these key individuals' primary and secondary reasons for leaving and feedback regarding the company, their supervisors, and their jobs, it can make it difficult to pull this data quickly. (Hint: It would be wise to create an online questionnaire for anyone who leaves the company voluntarily so that you can determine trends and patterns in employee turnover in addition to specific employees' reasons for leaving the organization.) Employee satisfaction surveys, which gauge how employees feel about the organization, their supervisor, their position, and other elements like benefits and training, and focus groups can go a long way in identifying pockets of problems throughout the organization before any real damage is done.

COMMON REASONS FOR LEAVING

The concept of employee retention has everything to do with the effort a company puts into keeping its employees. Employee turnover is what happens when employee-retention measures fail. Assuming you don't hold in-person exit interviews or have quantitative data to fall back on, it would make most sense to contact the employees who already left in addition to Nina (who's still employed with your organization, although in her notice period) to find out what drove or what's driving their desire to leave. There are predictable reasons why workers tend to leave companies:

- money and other forms of compensation
- lack of communication, recognition, or appreciation
- lack of training, learning opportunities, or career and professional development
- lack of upward mobility opportunities
- company culture, management, or working conditions
- overall lack of connection or engagement to the supervisor, company, or the position

Since the COVID pandemic in the early 2020s, a surprising number of workers left their organizations based on their employers' responses to the pandemic. Think about it: if employers refused to inform workers that someone was ill with COVID and simply swept it under the rug, jeopardizing workers' health and the well-being of their families, you could see why employees might have felt justified in walking away. Ditto for employers who suddenly stopped practical accommodations like remote work or hybrid work and prematurely snapped back into "Monday through

Friday 8 to 5" mode without exception, making them sound tone deaf to workers' needs. The Great Resignation was an attempt by employees to take back control of their work lives, to do more meaningful work, and to be part of a workplace that valued, respected, and trusted them. As of this writing, the hybrid model has taken hold and will likely remain in place for the foreseeable future.

Notice where "money and other forms of compensation" comes in on the list. Money has historically been the third or fourth reason or priority to justify someone's leaving an organization (after categories like lack of recognition or learning opportunities). The pandemic changed this as well. Workers not only mentally quit their current jobs in frustration over companies' handling of the COVID pandemic, they likewise demanded more money to justify the risk they believed they were taking in reporting to work every day. Combine this with the fact that workers' careers were basically on hold for those initial COVID years in terms of growing, learning, and developing new skills, and a massive scattergram of job changes took place in the United States and abroad, causing massive disruption all around. The solution? More competitive pay. And lots of it—from private sector employers, government legislation, and union demands. This diaspora of workers and the talent shortages that resulted after COVID are likely to continue throughout the decade. Companies will therefore be wise to track and pay attention to turnover and, in particular, reasons for leaving the organization, while looking to improve the employee experience overall (including competitive pay).

With individual information from Paul, Sam, Nina, and Janet, you'll be ready to report back to your boss with relevant and timely data as to their particular reasons for leaving the organization. Each case will likely be different. Look for trends and patterns in their responses to ensure that you're accounting for any common macro issues that may suddenly be driving talent out of the organization. Understand that personal concerns will likely come into play to some degree, including family challenges, spouse's employment, and outside interests. Finally, remember that the top contributors to a high employee-retention rate are a flexible work environment, adequate compensation, and recognition for achievements.

Such are the makings of strong and sincere relationships, proactive leadership, and team trust. In short, you won't know unless you ask. And you don't want to find this all out when Rose tenders her resignation. By understanding reasons for turnover and then proactively addressing employee engagement and job satisfaction with your staff members one-on-one, you'll have a far greater chance of stemming any unwanted or unforeseen turnover challenges that might otherwise come your way.

NOTE TO SELF . . .

Exceptional managers "grow talent" by making space for and listening to their employees' aspirations, acting as coaches and mentors, identifying and building on people's strengths, and providing continuous real-time feedback. Leading organizations focus on talent retention via soft skills training, mentoring, and accommodating families to facilitate more effective career development. For more insights on best practices in proactive leadership and talent development, reference the five short books in the *Paul Falcone Workplace Leadership Series*, which address effective hiring and onboarding, leadership offense and defense strategies, ethics and sustaining a moral workplace, and a special edition for new managers.

33

TURNING AROUND AN "AVOIDANCE CULTURE"
Accountability Is King but Only
If Managers Walk the Talk

CEOS AND BUSINESS OWNERS ARE OFTEN known for announcing proudly that they don't want "yes people" surrounding them and want people who will push back and tell them what they may not want to hear. And that's a great mantra to live by unless their statements are in reality hollow. In such cases, the "kill the messenger" syndrome grows and thrives so that no one wants to disagree with the CEO in practice. Likewise, CEOs and senior executives are often known for sweeping things under the rug and taking the path of least resistance—avoidance—rather than tackle problematic employee performance or conduct challenges head-on. When this becomes the pervasive and predictable senior leadership or business owner response, it often seeps into the culture, and avoidance becomes the norm. Finally, it's not uncommon to see both managers and staffers refuse to make decisions on anything. Their logic? "As long as I don't make any decisions, I can't make a mistake." That may be true, but depending on their position, such a philosophy can go a long way in damaging an organizational culture, sometimes beyond repair. After all, if no one takes responsibility and everyone passes the buck, the organization as a whole suffers from lack of accountability.

Regardless of the experience you have with those above you, you get to create your own mini culture within your department. True, you can't necessarily change your organization's cultural ecosystem, your CEO's approach to avoidance, or the general sense that you'll be the only manager in the organization that holds your employees to higher standards of accountability. But that's okay: do it anyway. Great leaders are great communicators, plain and simple. To justify not addressing problematic staff performance or behavior because you don't see your manager or peers doing so misses the whole point: this is your team, and you're responsible for its performance, productivity, and overall contributions to the organization.

Interestingly enough, cultures can change upward from the grass roots at times when individual managers reset the bar. Others recognize the problems associated with an avoidance culture as well but may not feel comfortable sticking their necks out, until they see one of their peers doing so in a healthy and constructive way. At that point, they may become "early adopters" in joining you in this much-needed culture shift, or they may wait for more momentum to kick in from others. Whatever the case, true leadership is selfless, caring, and focused on making your team members stronger players and contributors. You be the first domino. You set the tone for others—sometimes even for your boss and the owner of the company. It's a fair and transparent strategy that, when done right, will help you stand out as a rarity among your peers.

GUIDELINES FOR EFFECTIVE
COMMUNICATION WITH YOUR TEAM

I'm going to borrow phrases from my book *2600 Phrases for Setting Effective Performance Goals* to map out what this communication style might look like and how you can measure and shape what your organization is doing currently versus your own ideal of where you'd like your team or department to be:

1. Publicly recognize achievements and accomplishments often.
2. Celebrate success. Make your people's individual successes your team's success.
3. Deliver bad news in real time, constructively, and in a spirit of career and professional development to build your team's performance muscle.
4. Praise in public, censure in private.
5. Assume responsibility for problems when things go wrong, and provide immediate praise and recognition to others when things go right.
6. Create a work environment based on inclusiveness, welcoming others' suggestions and points of view—no matter what role they hold within the organization.
7. Listen actively with your eyes and heart in addition to your ears, ensuring that you truly hear what people are saying by leaning into a discussion to ensure that they feel heard.
8. Share information openly (to the extent possible) so that your team members understand the *why* behind your reasoning and can ask appropriate questions as they continue along in their own path of career development and learning.
9. Remember that thankfulness and appreciation are the most important values you can share with your team members and colleagues. Make gratitude the core foundation of your department's or team's culture.
10. Put others' needs ahead of your own and expect them to respond in kind (a.k.a. "selfless leadership," otherwise known as "servant leadership").
11. When dealing with others' shortcomings, always err on the side of compassion.

12.   Solicit ongoing feedback and suggestions from your team
       in terms of how you could do things differently as a leader,
       inspiring others to follow in your footsteps and making it
       safe to be "vulnerable" in a healthy sense.

There now, how did you do? More important, what can you
plan on changing? That's the key to everything in life, isn't it?
Assessing where you are currently and then resolving to make
things better for yourself and your team members. Finally, add the
word *accountability* to your leadership vocabulary. Far too many
managers and organizations as a whole tolerate selfish behaviors
on their employees' part. In fact, they accept behavior from team
members that they would never allow of themselves. Why?
Because the path of least resistance is avoidance. What's key is
how to couch your message so that employees understand that
you're doing this in their best interest. The next time you're in this
situation, try an approach as follows:

Michele, I need your help with something. Can I have your permission to share something with you that may not be aware of? [*Yes.*] I
feel at times that you're either mad at me or mad at the rest of the
team. And I can't tell when you're going to come across that way—it
seems to come out of the blue.

There's no blame or judgment here. I'm just sharing what I
observe from time to time, and in fairness, I'm not the only one.
Other members of the team have shared with me that they find it
difficult to work with you on occasion. The way they described it
was, "You're never going to know what mood Michele is in until you
can divine which way the wind is blowing. And it can change as
quickly as the wind as well."

I wanted to discuss this with you not as a punishment but a
means of career and professional development. They say that the
most important decisions about your career are made when you're
not in the room. That's as true for you as it is for me and for everyone else. I'm wondering how I can help you influence what's being

said about you in the room when you're not present. That might be a noble goal for you to consider in terms of your own career and professional development, and I'll be happy to support you with that so you can fix any perception problems here and now so that it never holds you back in your career.

We're all responsible for our own perception management, and that's why I'm thinking that you may not be aware of this or it's otherwise not on your radar screen. Prior managers may have not spoken to you about this, but in fairness, they likely weren't doing you or the rest of the team any favors. Your performance is strong, you know what you're doing, you make your area hum with productivity. But I have to share that others tend to avoid you—I do myself at times—because it can be easier to work around you rather than partner directly with you. And that's not fair to the rest of the team and will hold us all back.

I'd just ask that you give this some thought. I'd like to think that I could help you overcome this perception challenge that you're facing. I'd love to be that mentor and coach who helps you overcome something that you recognize in yourself that you may want to improve. And I'll make it safe for you to do so, right here and right now, so this never holds you back in your future. If your conduct and behavior can be raised to match the level of your individual performance, your career could skyrocket. I'd like to be that person for you, but only if you'll let me. Please consider this a first attempt at career coaching and professional development on my part. But I'll likewise need you to understand that I have to hold everyone on the team accountable for creating a friendly and inclusive work environment—that's only fair. Please give this some thought and follow up with me once you've had a chance to consider and sleep on it.

Well done. Quietly and respectfully said. Avoidance cultures are solved one person at a time. You offered yourself as a solution in the truest sense of selfless leadership. But you also let your employee know that the behavior would have to stop, one way or the other (that is, via joining you in a coaching relationship or fixing this perception problem on her own). Such are the makings of engaged first-time managers facing crises from within the team. That's the kind of critical leadership communication that sets up win-win situations for everyone, especially in this case for the rest of your team who will witness the changes in Michele's behavior thanks to your intervention.

34

GRADE INFLATION ON PERFORMANCE REVIEWS
A Land Mine Waiting to Explode

SPEAKING OF AVOIDANCE CULTURES, they show themselves best during annual performance review time. The path of least resistance is avoidance, and managers inflate grades to placate problematic workers, much to the managers' disadvantage later down the line. First, performance discussions should occur throughout the year in real time, whether providing recognition of a job well done or constructive feedback when things go south. Further, formal employee feedback sessions should occur quarterly. The pace of change is so swift these days that purely "annual" reviews don't come close to meeting employees' career and professional development needs. Third, managers don't understand how inflated grades are not only unfair to the employees themselves and indirectly to the rest of the team but how those exaggerations undermine the employee's record. The "record," in this case, can be used to justify a layoff or a termination for cause at some point in the future, but only if it's written accurately and truthfully (read that, without embellishment or exaggeration).

Here's how it works. When it comes to layoffs, employers must first demonstrate that there is a legitimate business need to eliminate a position (for example, due to budget restrictions or departmental restructuring). Second, they must then select "the least qualified individual to perform the remaining work after the layoff" from a peer group (assuming that there are multiple workers in that particular classification). How can you demonstrate who is the least qualified worker in that peer group to be selected for position elimination? By their performance record, including performance reviews and progressive discipline. Assuming there are no negative entries in the employee's record, then you may likely have to lay off your most recent hire in that selection pool. In other words, if documentation doesn't point to who is the least qualified individual based on performance, then the company will likely have to defer to seniority or tenure to select the individual to be laid off.

IMPORTANT NOTE WHEN IT COMES TO PERFORMANCE REVIEWS AND THEIR LINK TO LAYOFFS AND TERMINATIONS FOR CAUSE

Companies often make a common mistake based on a false assumption: they believe they can simply "lay off" anyone they want from a particular team or group, thereby making "layoffs" a more favorable alternative than terminations for cause (which require hard work on the manager's part in the form of mentoring, coaching, documenting progressive discipline, and issuing a failed annual review). Your employment defense attorney will likely recommend that you discipline and terminate a substandard job performer rather than attempt to lay off that person. Why? Because the person giving you all the problems will very likely not be the least-tenured member of the group.

And if no one within the group has been disciplined or issued a failed annual performance review—then tenure typically determines who you must "attach" to the eliminated position. When is this not the case? Either (a) when you are laying off someone in an individual contributor role with no peers (for example, a vice president of a department) or (b) when the person giving you all the problems happens to also be the least-tenured person in the department. But don't take this "path of least resistance" approach: instead, hold all your employees accountable via progressive disciplinary actions and professional development discussions. Attempting to "sweep them under the rug" by "packaging them out of the company" is expensive and carries with it other hidden risks that your defense attorney will likely make you aware of at the time of your request to "lay off" the individual.

Similarly, when it comes to terminations for cause, the record must justify the termination decision. That means there needs to be consistency between the annual performance reviews and progressive disciplinary actions to ensure that the worker was accorded "workplace due process" and treated fairly. For example, annual reviews are like battleships—they cover an entire year of performance. In comparison, progressive disciplinary actions are like PT boats—they zip through the individual's personnel record to demonstrate substandard job performance or inappropriate workplace conduct. As such, written warnings serve to *break the chain* of positive performance reviews and move the written record in a new direction. A written warning may represent only one bad day in the office, but if these occurrences become frequent and the employee progresses from verbal warning to written warning to final written warning, then once an incident violates the terms of the final written warning, termination is justified—despite years of acceptable performance reviews on record. Sounds simple enough, but here's where it tends to go wrong.

WHAT'S WRONG WITH THIS PICTURE?	
DATE	EMPLOYEE RECORD
August 20XX	Documented verbal warning (first written warning)
October 20XX	Written warning (second written warning)
December 20XX	Final written warning
February 20YY	Annual Performance Review: "Meets Expectations"

WHAT'S WRONG WITH THIS PICTURE?	
DATE (CONT.)	**EMPLOYEE RECORD (CONT.)**
March 20YY	Request to terminate

Unfortunately, by issuing a passing score during the annual review in February, it may negate the discipline that preceded it, making it difficult to terminate in March. After all, despite the verbal, written, and final written warnings that were issued, the annual review shows that the individual "met expectations" for the entire review year. In short, you'll have just placed a battleship in front of all those PT boats, confusing the record and potentially permitting a plaintiff attorney to argue that the individual did not understand that his job was in immediate jeopardy of being lost. As such, an argument will likely be made that you "denied the individual due process," which can then open the door to a wrongful termination claim.

Here's a general rule of thumb that you might want to consider following: if someone on your team logically shouldn't be around a year from now, then issuing a failed review score is important to do once the opportunity becomes available. From that failed annual performance review foundation, progressive discipline can then follow that points out future expectations and consequences that, if not met, will result in termination. Of course, issuing a failing score can be a challenge if the problematic performance or conduct hasn't really been addressed throughout the review year. In such cases, the review can be delayed for three months once you notify the individual verbally of the problems. Also, depending on the situation, it may be safe to proceed if you present things carefully and with a healthy dose of mea culpa ("my fault") for not sharing concerns earlier in the process. For sample language of what such a discussion could and should sound like, please reference my book *101 Tough Conversations to Have with Employees: A Manager's Guide to Performance, Conduct, and Discipline Challenges.*

The lesson? Sugarcoating performance reviews only perpetuates problems. Employees are permitted to get away with unacceptable performance or conduct yet are quietly denied career and professional development opportunities to demonstrate healthy turnaround. That's not fair to them. Meanwhile, teams are left lacking, wondering why management never addresses what is clearly an eight-hundred-pound gorilla in the room. And the organization is left defenseless because the worker was denied due process in the form of remedial corrective action, leading to potential claims of wrongful termination and discrimination. True, this may be the most challenging part of management. And it may not feel fair that you inherited or have to "clean up" a problem that's been allowed to persist for far too long. But it is both your responsibility and an opportunity to turn around an individual's poor performance, strengthen the team's common interests, and protect the organization from legal challenges down the road. Speak with your manager and HR business partner about your intentions with chronic underperformers, and know that you're doing the right thing for the right reason for all parties involved.

35

WAGE AND HOUR CRISES
Employee Classification, Overtime, and Rest and Meal Period Challenges

NO BOOK THAT PURPORTS TO COVER workplace crises would be complete without addressing the snare awaiting far too many employers out there: wage and hour challenges. Some crises blow up instantaneously, exploding onto the scene with immediacy and urgency that can take one's breath away. Wage and hour liability is different: it lurks below the surface, sometimes for years, before the problem is discovered and brought to management's attention. The problem, of course, is that once that crisis hits, companies have very little to defend themselves unless they've been managing timekeeping procedures exceptionally well for years. If not, the long arm of the law can stretch back up to four years (depending on the state) to scrutinize paper and electronic records looking for unpaid overtime, missing meal and rest period penalties, or other violations in wage and hour practices. Likewise, such investigations often result in class action wage and hour lawsuits, which can be extremely time consuming and expensive to defend with hefty damage settlement demands and attorneys' fees.

No doubt about it: in your shop, you want to keep wage and hour (timekeeping, overtime, employee classification, and rest and meal period adherence) clean and tidy. After all, managing overtime properly can be quite a daunting task for many managers who may not be aware of some of the intricacies and traps that await them within the wage and hour world. There are a number of quirky twists and turns in this particular area of employment law, and you can't be armed well enough in terms of protecting your organization from wage and hour liability.

DETERMINING EXEMPTION STATUS

Exemption status will always be your first hurdle. It's your company's responsibility to pay overtime to nonexempt workers for hours worked more than forty in a week (or in some states like California, more than eight in a day), and it all begins with classifying your employees properly. Federal and state laws provide a limited number of exempt categories, chief among them positions in executive, administrative, professional, computer professional, and certain sales roles. Most companies don't have any problems identifying their CEOs and vice presidents as "exempt" from the protections under the Fair Labor Standards Act (FLSA) of 1938, which established "overtime pay" as a penalty or tax during the Great Depression to employers for "stretching out" their existing clerical or manufacturing workforce and not adding new employees to the payroll. (Congress wanted companies to put workers back on the job at the time to climb out of the depression, but companies stubbornly resisted, forcing employees to work excessive overtime, double shifts, and sixth and seventh days.) Employers also pretty much get that clerks, receptionists, and laborers are indeed nonexempt. In other words, they're paid for their time (rather than for their work product or results), protected by the FLSA, and docked when they come in late but paid overtime for hours worked more than forty in a week.

But where this gets dicey is with "wobbler" job categories like coordinators, analysts, specialists, and administrators (and in some cases, assistant managers). Some companies classify these paraprofessional and junior management positions upward into the exempt category, while others place them downward into the nonexempt, overtime-eligible category. In some cases, the classification decision may withstand legal scrutiny, but just understand that if you're ever audited by the government or sued by a plaintiff attorney, a misclassification error may lead to an award of substantial wage liability, interest, penalties, and attorneys' fees.

The law presumes that an employee is nonexempt, and the burden will fall on your company to prove or otherwise demonstrate that the workers in question are indeed exempt from overtime pay. And if your company is deemed to be wrong in its classification decision, then the organization could end up with a massive back wages tab that governs the entire class of workers. The problem may be compounded by the lack of accurate time records showing how many hours the misclassified employees actually worked. Remember, all else being equal, the government liberally interprets the law to require companies to pay overtime so that workers aren't exploited or otherwise denied the additional overtime pay. Read that: when in doubt, classify workers as nonexempt and pay the overtime. It could save your organization massive back wages settlements. Better yet, update your job descriptions and have qualified legal counsel review them for proper exempt versus nonexempt classification. Attorneys can't protect your organization from a judge who disagrees with your classification status for these wobbler positions, but rest assured that your attorney will err on the side of caution and likely recommend that your organization designates any questionable classifications as nonexempt to avoid the liability of a class action lawsuit.

PAYING OVERTIME CORRECTLY

In terms of paying overtime correctly, it's important to understand that overtime premiums must be paid for all overtime worked, including unapproved overtime. In fact, you're allowed to discipline an employee for working unapproved overtime, but you're not allowed to withhold the overtime pay. That would be a classic wage and hour violation. Reciprocally, in most employment settings, you have the right to instruct employees to work overtime as the workload demands. That's a basic right of any supervisor, and employees who fail to make themselves available could likewise be held to be in violation of workplace conduct standards. Of course, before proceeding to disciplining someone formally for insubordination (that is, failure to follow a reasonable workplace directive), be sure to look at more practical issues like the reasonability of your request, the amount of notice you've given the employee, and how you would treat any and all similarly situated employees under the same circumstances. This will avoid perceptions of favoritism, bias, unfairness, and discrimination in the workplace.

You should also be aware that when calculating the overtime rate of pay, your company may also need to include consideration of variable pay, such as shift differentials, bonuses, commissions, or other incentive pay. In some cases, an employee who receives a bonus earns a higher overtime rate than one who does not.

The elephant in the room when it comes to wage and hour violations is that they lend themselves to class action lawsuits. In fact, plaintiff attorneys often question prospective nonexempt clients who come in looking for representation to pursue discrimination and wrongful termination claims to see whether they worked unpaid overtime hours or frequently skipped lunches and breaks without pay. If the answer is, "Yes, it was expected of us and happened all the time," you could very well see a class action wage and hour claim attached to your ex-employee's other legal charges. And costs add up quickly. Calculations typically go back several years, and it's not uncommon for damages resulting from unpaid overtime plus attorneys' fees to settle in the six- to seven-figure range, depending on the size of your company and the number of workers in the class.

The lesson here? Don't panic if one of your nonexempt employees misses a break or lunch period on occasion. But don't become known as a company in which skipped meals and breaks become the norm or where working unpaid overtime occurs on an "expected" basis. If you steer clear of developing that type of reputation by respecting the law and treating your nonexempt workers fairly, then occasional, nonsystemic lapses probably won't pose much of a serious legal risk.

AVOIDING "LUNCH AT THE DESK" SYNDROME

That being said, you should encourage your nonexempt team members to get away from the office (or at least their desk) during lunch and rest periods. If taking lunch at the desk becomes the norm or expectation, it will be assumed that your hourly staffers were expected to pick up the phone if it rang, keep an eye on email, or attend to other matters of business. And that, unfortunately, violates the definition of a true rest or meal period. If an employee performs any duty during an off-the-clock meal break, this may give rise to a claim for off-the-clock work. Moreover, in some cases, courts have held that meal breaks shortened too much by work should not have been off the clock at all; in other words, the entire meal period was invalidated.

Oh, and if you and your employees don't have a record of all the times they skipped their breaks and meal periods, then the courts or the Department of Labor will gladly share their calculation tools and tell you how much your company owes in back wages and attorneys' fees based on their estimates. Just remember that for nonexempt, hourly employees, breaks and lunches are for breaks and lunches—not for work. There's no need to surprise your organization with a class action wage and hour lawsuit because you failed to adhere to the law in this very fundamental respect.

Finally, ensure that you understand the basic rules and guidelines involved in regulating rest and meal periods. Some states, including California and a few other jurisdictions, have specific meal and rest break regulations. For example, in California, nonexempt employees must be provided one ten-minute duty-free paid rest period per four hours worked. If they involuntarily only take one or skip both, a rest period penalty may apply. (In California, for example, and depending on the wage order, a penalty equal to one hour of pay at the employee's regular rate of pay is added to the employee's pay for the day if the individual did not take two breaks because the individual was required to work through those rest periods.) Likewise, be sure you understand how meal periods work. (Again, in California, if the meal period [lunch] was missed or not taken by the end of the fifth hour or the meal period didn't last at least thirty minutes, a meal period penalty of one additional hour of pay at the employee's regular rate of pay would be due.) If you do the math, you'll see that sloppy rest and meal period administration can add up to two hours per day for California workers governed by particular wage orders. On an eight-hour day, those two additional hours of penalty pay can add 25 percent to the employer's payroll on a daily basis!

These rules are complex, no doubt. For example, generally speaking, if the employee missed taking a rest or meal period for personal reasons, the meal or rest penalty may not be owed. Proving that the missed break was for personal reasons may require additional documentation. Some organizations, in fact, include "attestation language" in their electronic timekeeping systems that asks employees to confirm that they took both rest periods and the full meal period when they clock out at the end of the shift. (This makes for an excellent record should the company be sued several years from now.) Attestation language likewise clarifies if missing a rest or meal period was the employee's choice or if it was required by management. In California, where the missed break was due to work requirements, the penalty is paid. Most employers will pay the worker unless there is evidence of a voluntary missed break. If such meal or rest break deviations keep happening, the employee may be disciplined, but the pay should never be withheld.

There are other rules, of course. How many rest and meal periods are required under ten- or twelve-hour shifts? Does an employee need to work a minimum number of hours before rest or meal periods come into play? What if you suspect that an employee is working off the clock in a remote work setting? Whatever the scenario, rest assured that plaintiff attorneys have seen them all and may be ready to pounce as soon as the opportunity presents itself. It's in your and your company's best interests to make sure that you are familiar with the rules and constantly on the lookout for exceptions. If you haven't been trained in this critical area, ask your employer to set up a wage and hour training workshop so that everyone on the management team is on the same page.

36

MANAGING BULLIES AND PASSIVE-AGGRESSIVE PERSONALITIES
Leadership Interventions to the Rescue

WHAT'S WORSE: passive-aggressive behavior or outright bullies and intimidators? Hint: it's a trick question because both are very harmful to employee trust and a healthy workplace culture. Interestingly enough, both challenges can be typically addressed and handled in a similar fashion.

Let's start with workplace bullies. Certain employees somehow feel they have the right to raise their voices, openly challenge their peers, and intimidate others. Worse, their peers never know what's going to set them off. They have to "divine" from the employees' actions whether the individual is in a good or bad mood that day, and anything can set them off at any time. Not quite fair to the rest of the team, is it?

Passive-aggressive types, in comparison, are lower key but have a way of demonstrating their anger or frustration in a much more controlled and nuanced way. While they appear quieter on the surface, their anger at coworkers can sometimes appear to seep out of their pores, and others are made to feel like they have to constantly walk on eggshells around such toxic personality types.

As a first-time manager, you have options, of course. First, you can allow the toxic behavior to continue without addressing it, hoping it will fix itself. Second, you can meet with and verbally place the employee on notice about being accountable for managing perceptions and for creating and sustaining a friendly and inclusive work environment. Then, if the employee fails to meet the expectations that you've outlined, you can move to documented disciplinary documentation, potentially laying the groundwork for an ultimate termination for cause. I don't know about you, but this second option is so much better than sweeping toxic behavior under the rug and hoping it simply goes away.

THE MOST COMMON BUT DAMAGING APPROACH TO HEALTHY EMPLOYEE RELATIONS

First, understand that the biggest challenge facing employers and well-intentioned managers lies in permitting the toxic behaviors to continue without addressing them. Unfortunately, problems typically continue, complaints arise, and staff members become frustrated with management's failure to address the problem, sometimes to the point where coworkers feel they have no choice but to leave the organization. But we're not done. Performance and productivity break down as well, as the team sets lines where it will interact with or avoid the bully or passive-aggressive coworker. Before you know it, communication starts to slip, and work begins to fall through the cracks. "If management isn't going to do anything about it, then I'm not going to worry about it," reason the bitter and frustrated team members.

There are a lot of problems with this fact pattern:

- It happens way too often. The manager doesn't do the job of addressing the toxic behavior and doesn't create a written record of the problem via progressive discipline. Hence, the manager doesn't initiate the record, and the coworkers are set to bear the brunt of the burden—in this case, by having to tolerate the employee's poor behavior.

- As pointed out earlier, the written record doesn't reflect the problematic behaviors at hand, and there's no written record that differentiates the bully or passive-aggressive worker from peers. As a result, even if a layoff were to occur, the bully would likely survive, and a more effective member of the team would need to be laid off (assuming the bully isn't the person with the least amount of tenure on the team).

- Employees complain to HR, frustrated that their manager has done little to nothing about the ongoing problem. HR can certainly try to help, but HR can't manage other departments' employees for them. If the complaints to HR then go unaddressed, team members are angry at both their manager and the company overall for failing to account for their basic needs.

This is where you come in. Don't sweep matters under the rug; don't look the other way. Don't practice "willful blindness" or "deliberate ignorance," where the monkey covers its eyes, ears, and mouth to avoid any involvement and simply knows nothing. Simply avoid the drama by addressing the problem. Handle matters like this head-on. Create the appropriate disciplinary record if you see inappropriate workplace conduct or substandard performance with any of your team members. Initiate the record and make HR your ally. With your manager and your HR representative on your side, you can proceed with confidence.

ACCOUNTABILITY FOR PERCEPTION MANAGEMENT

After looping in your supervisor and HR about your intended plan of action, meet with the employee and explain the "perception problem" that exists in terms of the disconnect with the person's conduct or performance and your expectations as manager. Explain that you've already spoken to your superior and to HR about this and they are aware of this meeting. Proceed as follows:

I'm holding you accountable for your own perception management. In other words, regardless of your intentions or how you believe you're coming across, complaints from your peers are taken seriously. Since there are specific trends and patterns in the feedback that I'm receiving about your conduct from the rest of the team, in conjunction with my own observation, I have to take this seriously.

[**Option A:** You've been described by others as a bully. I don't mean to hurt your feelings or disrespect you in any way by telling you this: it's what I've heard from peers of yours, and I've witnessed some of it myself. Words associated with your behavior include intimidating, confrontational, condescending, and mean. Basically, you've made others afraid of you, and that will never work to your advantage in the office or on the shop floor. I believe you're capable of exercising your leadership influence in a positive way. I believe you can take your natural abilities and build stronger teams, influence others to come to you for help when they're having difficulties with their work, and make others feel safe and secure in their working relationship with you. I'd like to be the manager who can help you accomplish that so you can get ahead in your career because of people, not despite them. But I have to hold you accountable for your own perception management, just like I do myself and everyone else. In short, you're responsible for your reputation and how others perceive your actions.]

[**Option B:** You're being described as someone who is passive-aggressive toward coworkers, meaning that you express your negative feelings about others indirectly rather than discussing your concerns openly. People have shared with me that you can be overly sarcastic, and you pretend to agree but then talk behind others' backs. I just saw you engage in what's known as "silent sabotage": you failed to follow through and then made excuses for why you didn't complete your work, despite agreeing to handle this portion of the project. It's all very unhealthy and not fair to your coworkers. And you're not even being fair to yourself because there appears to be some sort of self-sabotage going on here that you may not even be aware of. I have to hold you accountable for your own perception management, just like I do myself and everyone else. Simply stating that others are too sensitive or need to understand you better isn't the right mindset in situations like this.]

I'll be issuing a written warning for your ongoing conduct challenges. I wanted to meet with you first, however, to learn your side of the story and determine what, if any, mitigating circumstances there might be. Based on what you've told me, I don't see any exceptional circumstances, and I'll prepare the documentation and meet with you later this afternoon to review it. Still, I want you to learn from this; I want this to be a defining moment in your career that you can look back on one day and say, "Thank goodness my boss was there to point this out and set me straight on a new path." You can do this, and I'd like to be the mentor and coach to help you get there.

Allow space for feedback, listen to the individual's side of the story, and incorporate his responses into the written warning draft. For example, if he responds that his coworkers are being overly sensitive or disrespect him, include that in the documentation at well. By doing so, it demonstrates in documented format that you handled this like a responsible employer—you listened to the individual's side of the story and incorporated it into the document before issuing the warning. True, you may have some follow-up investigational work to do based on the individual's feedback, but HR or your boss can support you with that.

What's most important is that you'll have addressed the matter head-on. If there is no other lesson that you take away from this book, make this your key learning lesson. Constructive conversations and documented discipline are your leverage points when dealing with employees who demonstrate attitude problems, entitlement mentalities, or victim syndromes. Use your tools and resources wisely in cases like this. Holding others accountable does wonders for team morale, minimizes corporate liability, and helps your leadership reputation shine.

37

LESS-THAN-ETHICAL
CORPORATE BEHAVIOR
Navigating the Rapids of Shady
Decision-Making or Personalities

THIS TITLE PROBABLY CAUGHT YOUR ATTENTION. It's not uncommon for employees to sometimes experience less-than-ethical behavior on the organization's part. Coming to terms with those shortcomings could result in either looking the other way, quietly launching a job search, or blowing the whistle on the organization. No doubt about it: first-time managers may be faced with crises of all sorts when it comes to how the senior management team handles sensitive matters. What you might not have seen or witnessed as an individual contributor suddenly comes to the forefront when you become responsible for others.

The question becomes, how do you navigate these rapids when you're faced with circumstances that you believe are neither fair nor ethical (never mind unlawful)? Much has been written on topics like this in various books on ethics, including my book *Workplace Ethics: Mastering Ethical Leadership and Sustaining a Moral Workplace*. It's important that you're able to validate your feelings and find a disciplined way of evaluating "slippery slope" situations that may make or break your committed relationship to your company. Let's look at one such moral analysis construct together and see how it can help in trying times.

A SIMPLE TOOL FOR ETHICAL DECISION-MAKING

First, let's take some extremes off the table. Let's assume there is no theft, embezzlement, fraud, or forgery at hand. Likewise, we'll assume that the "dark triad" of personality traits from the world of psychology is not present in your CEO or boss: (a) narcissism (a pathological need for approval and self-aggrandizement); (b) Machiavellianism (a propensity for cold, calculating social manipulation); and (c) psychopathology (a predilection for ruthlessly exploiting others). We can likewise screen out bosses that are incapable of empathy, guilt, or shame or that otherwise destroy others' careers. Phew! With those egregious offenders out of the way for this exercise, we can look in a more nuanced way at lesser offenders who may nevertheless cross the line of your moral comfort zone.

Sexism, for example, is real and remains a pervasive, structural problem, especially in male-dominated fields. Psychologists have a concept called "pluralistic ignorance" that may describe a team's silence about out-of-control jokes and group behaviors. How about "lemmings" who refuse to rock the boat and do the right thing, either for fear of retribution or outright apathy? What about executive leadership teams with toxic cultures that "normalize" values that you would otherwise reject if you weren't on the payroll: At what point do you rationalize staying with the company? At what point do you decide to quit in order to advance your career? (Yes, quitting may advance your career—and your mental health—if you refuse to tolerate behaviors that are so utterly unhealthy that you choose to walk away from them rather than be subjected to them.) Make no doubt about it: ethical crises are real, and you will likely face many of them over the course of your career.

Personal reflection and career introspection are never needed more than when faced with such moral dilemmas. Your self-questioning under these circumstances might sound like this:

IDENTITY	Is this who I am or risk becoming? How does my decision square with my beliefs about compassion, respect, fairness, and truth? Who am I relative to this obstacle I'm facing and whom do I choose to be?
CONSCIENCE	Can I live with my conscience if I remain with this employer under these circumstances? What does my decision say about my character and self-respect and the trust that others place in me?
PRINCIPLE	Is there a core principle involved here that should never be compromised under any circumstances in order for me to remain true to myself? What if I compromise this principle: will I sacrifice any of my essential beliefs?
RATIONALIZATION	How do I justify this to myself? Do the rules not apply to me? Will anybody notice? Do I deserve better than this? Am I simply going along to get along? Are such rationalizations undermining my character?
COMMON SENSE	Is this consistent with how I want others to see me? Does any short-term gain justify the potential longer-term consequences? Is this consistent with the narrative I have of myself? Would someone refer to this situation if they had to provide a reference about my character?
CONSEQUENCES	What are the consequences involved if this is discovered? How can it damage my career? How can I explain this to a prospective employer if I stay or leave? Does this violate my basic sense of morality?

Reasoning about moral questions like this is profoundly complex. Yet using a consistent framework helps you feel more confident that you've thought through the various implications affecting your decision. The list above is only a suggestion: feel free to create your own. But you might want to type this out on your computer, write down your answers, and then sleep on them and have a fresh look in the morning. There are no absolute right or wrong

answers when considering such moral imperatives. Likewise, consult with your trusted partners, advisers, and mentors to gain
additional perspective on the matter, if possible.

When in doubt, however, there's a simple reliable solution that
will always serve you well and show you the way. Go with your
gut. Your conscience—that internal compass and guidance system that we were born with—will never let you down. You may
likewise refer to it as your spirit, your soul, or your "Spidey sense"
(popular among Spider-Man fans). Whatever you call it, trust it.
Analyze objectively first using a tool like the one previously mentioned: diagnostics are important. But when push comes to shove,
your answer will not come from your brain: it will come from your
heart. Emotion trumps cognition in matters relating to morals
and ethics. Your heart, more than anything, will help you address
and avert crises at work, at home, and anywhere in between. Your
heart will allow you to summon your character. In short, let your
soul call the shots when facing major life or career dilemmas.

For more information on workplace ethics and developing ethics
training programs as well as certifications, visit the Business Ethics
Resource Center (https://www.businessethicsresourcecenter.org/),
the Ethics Compliance Initiative (https://www.ethics.org/), and the
Ethics and Compliance Officers Association (https://ecoass.org/).

38

AVOIDING EMAIL NIGHTMARES AND OTHER CRITICAL DOCUMENTATION MISSTEPS

WANT TO IMAGINE A CRISIS crashing over your head like a wave? Imagine discussing something with your boss, in-house counsel, or outside labor attorney only to realize that you put something in writing in an email that could absolutely devastate your case in the litigation arena. It sounds something like this: "Paul, don't worry. As long as you didn't reference his age in that email communication or refer to him as a dinosaur or anything similar, we'll be fine. . . . Wait, you *didn't* commit that to an email, did you?" (Gulp!)

Time to fess up. If you did it, own it. But now, of course, it's too late to undo your actions. Instead, you'll have to find that email, prepare a defense around why you may have written it that way, or simply fall on your sword and confirm that you were mistaken at the time to reference an ex-employee's age in the context of a performance review. Either way, your company will have to dig itself out of a hole and overcome a setback that will clearly be exploited by a plaintiff's attorney: "Mr. Falcone, I see that in your email from December 11, you referenced my client as a *dinosaur*—someone from the prehistoric days before computers. You appeared to be making a joke about it in your exchange to Sara Velasquez.

Did you find it funny at the time? Was your intention to get a laugh at my client's expense? Maybe you were looking to denigrate and humiliate him in the eyes of your peers. Could that have been the case?"

If only you had known at the time that this particular email—one piece of electronic communication that could be taken out of context nine months later to demonstrate the alleged animus that you harbored against this individual due to the protected characteristic of his age—could come back to haunt you while you were being deposed in a law office or in front of a jury on a witness stand. Such are the makings of careless mistakes that first-time managers can potentially engage in without thinking of the ramifications of their actions should a case proceed to litigation.

First, understand that the "E" in email stands for "evidence." Email has become to civil law what DNA has become to criminal law: a rich source of indisputable evidence that can change case outcomes on a dime. Managers arguably write an average of a hundred emails per day, and as a result, email has become an almost casual means of communicating quick thoughts and ideas. Same goes for instant messages and other forms of electronic chatting. And it's just this casual informality that makes it all so deadly: every electronic communication you write as a manager has the potential of being blown up on a large video screen and placed in front of a jury as evidence of your state of mind at the time you wrote it—a state of mind that may reveal some form of ill intent that you allegedly harbored against a plaintiff/ex-employee of yours based on that individual's age, race, disability, or other protected status.

As a result, most defense lawyers will tell you not to commit anything to email that you wouldn't otherwise post on the cover page of the *New York Times*. Ditto for instant messaging and text messaging: all forms of electronic messaging are fairly easily obtained from forensic IT consultants who are trained to scour systems for written communications about a particular topic or person. And all it takes is one or several off-color remarks or exchanges about the individual's background, slowness relating to age, or other protected characteristic to sink your legal defense strategy. Of course, the comment may be taken totally out of context, but all's fair in love and war (and in the world of employment litigation).

Further, never attempt to destroy email evidence, because electronic communication can almost always be traced to its metadata source. Read that: it's practically impossible to destroy electronic communication records. For example, if a manager were to delete an email, empty the trash folder, and somehow reach into the bowels of the hard drive to attempt to delete the deleted trash folder contents, she wouldn't be successful in eradicating the message from the system or from the discerning eyes of a forensic IT specialist. Worse, that manager will potentially have created an electronic record of attempting to destroy evidence, which could arguably lead to a claim of "obstruction of justice" or "spoliation of evidence." You don't want to inadvertently add criminal sanctions to a civil case, so beware of attempting to destroy electronic evidence under any and all circumstances.

Finally, be aware of "codifying the damage" that may have occurred in your writing. For example, "sexual harassment" is generally considered a "legal conclusion." If you write that "Connor harassed Emma" in your documentation, it would likely be exploited by a plaintiff attorney to demonstrate that the company recognized that the harassment indeed occurred. Rather than making such a firm statement, write something more "specifically vague" like "Connor's actions *appear to* violate our company policy on creating and sustaining a friendly and inclusive work environment" or "Connor's actions *suggest that* he didn't take Emma's prior warnings to keep a safe distance from her seriously." Always buy yourself the discretion to argue that what you wrote did not codify any damage done to a member of the staff.

Same thing for systems: if you discipline an employee and state, "Your actions compromised an entire pool of loans," such documentation—if discovered by shareholders or investors—could result in challenges to your organization's fiduciary stewardship. On the other hand, if the disciplinary documentation states, "Your actions *suggest that* you *may have* compromised an entire pool of loans" or "Your actions could have compromised an entire pool of loans," then you will provide the organization with a greater sense of protection and security by not codifying any damage done. (True, damage may have been done, but your internal documentation should not help plaintiff attorneys make their case for them.)

Finally, as a rule of thumb, avoid adverbs (for example, words ending in *ly*) in your formal business writing. Sometimes, managers employ words like *purposefully, willfully, intentionally,* and *deliberately* to their messages or progressive disciplinary documentation to really send home a message that the employee did something seriously wrong. True, adverbs may indeed enforce your message, but the truth is that you really don't know what the individual's state of mind was at the time of the problematic incident. And if you attempt to add those adverbs to your documentation, a plaintiff attorney will likely turn the tables on you and ask, "Mr. Falcone, how did you know my client's state of mind at that time? How were you so sure that he did what he did *deliberately* and *purposely,* as you allege in the disciplinary warning that you issued him?" You can see where you'd likely need to back off those state-of-mind assumptions. A plaintiff attorney would likely engage again in undermining your credibility at the time you disciplined the plaintiff, tying your assumptions about that individual's state of mind to the person's age, race, gender, or other protected category.

I know, I know . . . this sounds like a lot to have to remember. Just keep the *New York Times* rule as well as the "avoid adverbs" rule in mind when you commit anything to writing— electronically or on paper. As casual and familiar as email and instant messaging have become, they are prime hunting grounds for plaintiffs' attorneys these days. Forewarned is forearmed. These documentation tips will always help you steer clear of the snare that potentially awaits in the litigation arena.

39

DEMANDS FOR REMOTE OR HYBRID WORK
Not Going Away Any Time Soon

THE COVID PANDEMIC IN THE early 2020s was an eye opener for many unexpected reasons. But certain patterns and trends were already underway, and remote work was one of them. Remember, as we've made the case elsewhere, demographics is destiny, and the Gen Y millennials and Gen Z Zoomers are the most studied generational cohorts in history. We know what they want more than we've ever known about any generations that preceded them, and work-family balance, control, and equilibrium were at the top of their priority list well before COVID ever entered the scene.

First, sociologists generally consider Gen Z to be the most isolated and lonely generation on the planet today—even more so than retirees in retirement homes. They grew up on technology to the point where, some would argue, the technology displaced human connection. Cell phones became human extensions of their bodies—another hand or arm—and texting and instant messaging became for many the communication medium of choice. This, however, precluded human connection and fostered a sense of isolation. Further, cell phones were on all the time—including during sleeping hours at night—creating a reliance (some might call it an "addiction") to electronic stimulation, whether they were texts from friends, social media alerts, or even breaking news announcements. As such, it became difficult for certain members of this generation to "unplug." Going to work—with its ongoing access to email and other systems—likely perpetuated this inability to disconnect. And quite naturally, this younger cohort is looking to employers to help them differentiate work from their personal lives and "disconnect" safely from work stimulation. COVID and remote work simply sped up these trends, which were already in place and gaining momentum.

For many organizations, intergenerational, geographically dispersed hybrid/remote teams are now the norm. But not for all. One fundamental question for organizations and the C-suite will remain, should remote work be permitted or encouraged to continue in light of the changes made possible (or forced upon us) by COVID? For some companies, the studies showing the productivity increased during COVID's remote working requirement period were enough to convince progressive employers that this new model might kill two birds with one stone—enhancing employee engagement while spiking human performance.

For other organizations, the realization that business could continue and improve without brick-and-mortar office space pointed to incredible cost savings without a lot of downside risk. Still, certain CEOs and business owners suffered under what's known as "productivity paranoia" and wanted everyone back to work as if COVID never existed and put a quick stop to remote working. Those organizations might have come across as tone deaf and experienced challenging talent acquisition and retention trends during the Great Resignation, but only time will tell how the business world recalibrates and rebalances itself in a post-pandemic reintegration phase (which, due to demographic shifts and communication technology upgrades, may last decades).

Assuming your organization continues to permit remote work, what's critical is improving remote individual and team effectiveness. True, operational leaders will worry to a degree about remote employees' engagement levels—specifically about people's accountability, lack of communication, idiosyncrasies, or quirks. But there's a lot that can be done to improve the remote versus on-site balance. The same guidelines about great leadership remain as relevant in a remote relationship as in an on-site one: trust, respect, and honesty; communication, teamwork, and self-less leadership should be the norm. The difference, however, lies in the fact that remote leadership must be more focused, intentional, and purposeful. Less can be left to chance (assuming you'll see everyone in the lunchroom or hanging around the proverbial water cooler) to catch any frustrations, distractions, or tensions. The following tips and strategies may go a long way in addressing the biggest obstacles and strengthening ties to and with remote workers, whether they are fully remote or hybrid remote:

1. Hold regular one-on-one weekly meetings with your direct reports. Assuming a span of control of four to eight team members, this can be broken down over a two-week period. But dedicated one-on-one time is critical to ensure full accountability, project management, goal alignment, and the need to pivot. Discuss if work ever feels like it's becoming overly depersonalized and what can be done about it.

2. Hold regular weekly staff meetings with your direct reports and/or extended team to ensure that everyone feels aligned and in sync. True, staff meetings take time and can sometimes be seen as a "necessary evil," but they're needed more in remote-working relationships than ever before, both to build teamwork and camaraderie but also to keep everyone informed of critical changes and feeling less lonely and isolated.

3. Hold quarterly professional development meetings with your direct reports and ask them to do so with their direct reports (your extended reports). Goal attainment can change quickly in a world with competing priorities, and "annual" goals and performance review meetings are

clearly not enough to get you where you want to go. Make
your team remembers responsible for scheduling those
meetings on your calendar and give them full control of
the content that they'd like to discuss. Further, keep this
all about goal attainment and professional and career
development—not about day-to-day operations. You can
talk about the latter any time: this meeting is for building
talent and leadership muscle, codifying achievements, and
discussing the individual's needs.

4. Schedule occasional ad hoc meetings to conduct
    "postmortem" reviews of what's working well and what
    needs to be improved. You won't know unless you ask. For
    example, one way your team can reinvent itself is by
    holding a Stop-Start-Continue workshop, soliciting honest
    feedback regarding what you and your team need more of,
    less of, or to stop all together.

5. Rely on informal check-ins to calm employee anxiety.
    SHRM conducted a study in 2022 that found that
    50 percent of workers suffered from "Sunday Scaries"
    about returning to work on Monday morning. Walking
    around to check in and see if anyone needs anything is
    easy enough in person; however, reaching out via short
    touch-base phone calls has a similar effect—stemming
    anxiety. Virtual assistants and "chatbots" can also be
    programmed to do the same thing. While lacking a human
    touch, technology outreach can still pose important
    questions like, "Do you have sufficient resources to do your
    job?" or "Is there anything you feel is important to share
    with your manager?" People are getting more comfortable
    with automation, and this virtual assistant option may
    work better than you think, especially for larger teams
    where personal outreach is more challenging.

6. Make professional networks and mentoring relationships
    part of your hybrid or fully remote success strategy. After
    all, career and professional development remains at the top

of the list in terms of Millennial and Gen Z priorities. Building on people's strengths is a core focus of every mentoring program available today, whether the organization employs full-time external executive coaches, appoints internal management mentors, assigns buddies or ambassadors to support new hires, or relies on apps to help workers better themselves. Do this especially with an emphasis on women and minorities as part of your organization's DEI&B initiative.

7. Choose the right technology tools to foster greater communication and teamwork. Most managers are unaware of the full menu of options available in workspace technology platforms. For example, the right technology not only ensures excellent communication but can likewise show leaders that employees are really working by creating a virtual infrastructure that maps to physical infrastructure. This way, managers can see where everyone is, what they're working on, and who they're working with. It eliminates the need for monitoring because you can see from an employee's avatar exactly where they are and what they are doing. It can offer the benefits of in-person work without the commute and of course to permit you to hire the most qualified talent without geographical restrictions. Cool stuff!

8. Consider creating "Personal Preference Worksheets" to allow everyone to express what works best for team members in a remote environment. Such team-building tools help staff members explicitly communicate how to best work with them, who they are as a human being (that is, what they value most), and provide others with advice and a framework on how to best communicate with them. For example, some employees who see themselves as introverted may feel at a disadvantage (relative to their more outgoing peers) in terms of expressing themselves freely over videoconference calls. This type of tool helps

make others aware of their communication and collaboration preferences in an attempt to level the playing field and spike feelings of inclusion and psychological safety. Templates are available online under "Personal User Manuals" and might look like this:

PERSONAL PREFERENCE WORKSHEET (SAMPLE)
What's one "fun fact" (personal or business) that you'd like to share that others probably don't know about you?
How would you define your core values? In terms of values-based leadership, what are your top three priorities (for example, having one another's back, creating a friendly and inclusive work environment, avoiding drama, and the like)?
Where do you have the least amount of patience? What should we be aware of in terms of potential hot buttons that we should try to avoid?
How do you collaborate best and what's your ideal mode of communication—phone, email, or chat?
What gives you energy at work? What still makes you smile about your job? What might drain your energy reserve the most?
Where do you sometimes feel misunderstood? What might people misunderstand about you that you'd like to clear up?
How do you like to give and receive constructive feedback? (Do you pride yourself on your thick skin, or can your feelings sometimes be hurt?)
Do you have any idiosyncrasies in your work style that you're comfortable sharing with the rest of the team? (It's okay if it's funny; laughter is a healing art!)
What subjects do you like to talk about most that don't have anything to do with work (for example, sports, the stock market, travel, and so on)?
What do we do in case of emergency? Is there an emergency shutoff valve? What will SOS look like and how can we survive?

Special note: This exercise lends itself well to pairing with personality or work preferences self-assessments, which can go deeper into these various preferences and be used as a team-building exercise.

The hybrid world will continue to present myriad challenges, but Martine Haas, professor of management at the Wharton School, summed them up nicely for *Harvard Business Review* in 2022 as the "5C Challenges" of communication, coordination, connection, creativity, and culture. There will always be extra effort required to loop in remote workers when others are on-site. Clearly, social connections and the "psychic income" derived from work can be compromised when a mix of in-person and remote work is at hand, for no other reason than certain employees may not feel as comfortable speaking up in a remote landscape or may resent feeling left out of even small decisions. But discussing these 5Cs or any other concerns becomes key in surmounting them. Open communication and information sharing take on a new meaning in the remote-work world because everyone generally enjoys getting to know their peers better. Find your five key concerns and communicate them broadly, asking team members to proffer solutions that will address these potential land mines and avoid potential crises. Make time to address improvements; give your team members the space and encouragement to find creative solutions. Sure, you'll have additional challenges managing remote staff, but think of the critical muscle you'll build in this new and hot area of professional expertise!

40

EMPLOYEE THREATS TO ORGANIZE AND FORM A UNION

ANTICIPATING A UNION ORGANIZING CAMPAIGN is sure to fan the flames of fear in even the boldest business leaders. This isn't meant to be a put-down of unions or your belief that unions may be the solution to many of today's workplace problems. But leaving the political, moral, or social issues aside, most companies will work tirelessly to remain union free. And there's a very logical reason for that: operating a union shop typically costs about one-third more than a nonunion one. And no, that's not because unions are necessarily negotiating higher wages and benefits for their members: it's because unions can potentially slow down decision-making, impede efficiencies, and limit the spirit of innovation. Grievance and arbitration challenges, bumping rights during layoffs, and insistence on hiring more workers (that is, union members) rather than assigning additional responsibilities to existing staff members are part of the union business model. That's not to say this is a "bad" model—it's just a different one. But the differences tend to pit employees against management, which often has the negative side effect of splitting alliances and encouraging a spirit of entitlement. Then again, you may feel that companies constantly exploit workers and sacrifice people for profits or that the "union premium" of higher wage potential may not only justify unions but make them the preferred way forward.

However you personally feel about the matter, it's likely safe to assume that your organization's senior leadership will not want to be unionized. Besides the business interruption of the union organizing campaign itself, the ongoing loss of management flexibility and response time often results in increased labor costs. Being union free may not be an end in and of itself, but it's certainly a beneficial by-product of a healthy workplace culture and day-to-day working environment. Where employees feel that they are treated with dignity and respect and can make meaningful contributions to the organization's success, unions are unnecessary because workers recognize that their legitimate needs and concerns are being met without the need of third-party representation to speak on their behalf.

While union membership has generally fallen to its lowest level since the original passage of the National Labor Relations Act in 1935, there is a new activism surrounding workplace issues that squares with Millennial and Gen Z expectations for greater work-life-family flexibility, stronger childcare and family benefits, a more secure retirement, and more assured job security from technological and globalization disruption. Further, unions are expanding the reach of their organizing efforts, moving beyond the traditional manufacturing trades and targeting new markets in the services sector, especially in areas of once public now private jobs, including educators, health-care workers, security guards, airport screeners, bus drivers, parking attendants, and hotel, restaurant, and casino employees, and the like. There have even been successful and ongoing organizing efforts in the hi-tech Silicon Valley space. So yes, to write off the possibility of unionization is likely shortsighted and somewhat naive on the employer's part. It's always better to keep this possibility on your radar screen and remember that a progressive, positive, and healthy work climate is the first and best preventive measure for union avoidance.

THE PREVENTIVE AUDIT AND
VULNERABILITY ANALYSIS

When the possibility of a union-organizing threat comes your way, first look to conduct a preventive audit. (Even better: conduct periodic, preventive audits, before there's ever a whiff of union organizing.) What is the general tone and tenor of your hourly workforce? What ongoing complaints do they believe have gone on unaddressed for far too long? What did your last climate survey reveal in terms of the specific levels of employee dissatisfaction with pay, benefits, shift availability, leadership accountability, or overall communication and recognition for a job well done? Do your workers have a voice in operations, and do they use it? Where are the largest pockets of dissatisfaction in your office or on your shop floor? Where do employees rank your organization in the key following areas:

- corporate culture with clearly defined goals and values
- safe, healthy, flexible, and nurturing work-life environment
- opportunities for personal and professional growth along with meaningful work
- competitive and equitable compensation and benefits
- fair, consistent, and caring frontline operational management

Here's an important point to keep in mind about periodic, preventive audits: you have every right to conduct climate surveys and hold small focus group meetings with employees to gauge their level of satisfaction with the organization, their immediate supervisor, and their particular job. You likewise have the right to ask what the organization could do differently, especially in terms of today's urgent needs, including staffing shortfalls, work-life balance, scheduling demands, and anything else that may be top of mind. True, you shouldn't ask unless you're willing to make and invest in the appropriate changes, but at best, such exercises open the lines of communication between management and staff. At worst, the management listens but fails to enact any changes based on employees' suggestions, potentially and unwittingly supporting and justifying union involvement. Here's the catch and the bottom line, however: once an organizing effort commences, an employer cannot "solicit grievances" with the promise or implied promise of remedying those grievances. By then, it's too late. It's smart business, therefore, to use periodic, preventive audits to engage your staff members before a union organizing attempt ever comes your way!

Seen another way, periodic, preventive audits permit you to gauge workplace sentiment and feelings about the organization so that you know where you stand and can make small (if financially minor) changes initially, with the hopes of making larger-scale investments and changes down the road. The key, of course, lies in communicating what you learned back to your employees so they're aware that you're taking their concerns seriously. You likewise need to communicate planned changes coming your way in light of what you heard in your assessment meetings. Open communication and recognition of employees' concerns—that you're *hearing* them in the truest sense and making space for their priorities to become your priorities—are the wisest (and least costly) places to begin. The opposite would be to sweep such concerns under the rug and hope they go away. Beware, however, that such a "head in the sand" approach to employee disgruntlement is typically the swiftest path to union organization.

FOE RIGHTS FOR MANAGERS

There are certain things managers and supervisors can communicate during an organizing campaign. Follow the "FOE" rules—Facts, Opinions, and Examples, such as the following:

FACTS

It is legal to share publicly available facts from the National Labor Relations Act, the website unionfacts.com, and other reputable sources.

OPINIONS

It is legal to share why you feel a union is not needed for employees at your worksite.

EXAMPLES

It is legal to share real examples and stories of others to highlight why a union is not necessarily in the employees' best interests.

Following are some practical examples of statements that managers can typically make during a union-organizing campaign:

- Tell employees that the managers and the company are opposed to unionization.
- Review with employees what benefits the company provides and what positive changes the company has recently made.
- Point out that a union can always out-promise an employer, but the union cannot guarantee or make good on any of its promises.
- Remind employees that there is risk involved: they can potentially do better or worse, depending on the union's negotiating abilities, and that current employee benefits may be off the table as a result of the collective bargaining.
- Inform employees that with a union they may have to bring their problems to a shop steward or union representative instead of dealing directly with their supervisor.
- Inform employees that they do not have to speak to union organizers or sign a union authorization card and that the law says that they have the absolute right to refrain from joining a union.

- Point out the costs of belonging to a union, such as the payment of dues and initiation fees and the possibility of fines and assessments.
- Tell employees that if they engage in an economic strike, they may be permanently replaced and will be reinstated only if an opening occurs.
- Advise employees, "Save yourself 2 percent of your salary every year and use it on food for your family or invest it in your 401(k) plan; that's a better use than paying it to a union."

TIPS LIMITATIONS AND PREEMPTING THE UNION'S MESSAGE

Employers actually have the right to express their opposition to being unionized. Management has the right to lawfully explain its position on unions and should exercise that right. The National Labor Relations Act acknowledges that but adds some important caveats. For example, employers cannot undermine workers' free choice by making statements aimed to threaten or intimidate them or make promises that would induce them into voting against the union. Further, there can be no threats of retaliation if the workers unionize. Making a mistake in this area can be costly: unlawful interference during an election campaign is considered an "unfair labor practice," which can carry with it penalties from the National Labor Relations Board (NLRB). In fact, if enough unfair labor practices are committed so that a fair vote cannot be taken, the NLRB can impose the union without the necessity of an election.

While supervisors and managers are not expected to become labor and employment law experts, they must have a general understanding of these issues and how to recognize them so they can escalate matters to senior management, legal, and human resources in a timely manner. That's where you come in as a first-time manager: managers may share facts, opinions, and examples about why employees should not sign a card or join a union. These are basic freedom of speech rights. What you may not do as a first-time manager can be conveniently summed up in the acronym TIPS. Managers may not:

- **T**hreaten,
- **I**nterrogate,
- **P**romise (benefits for voting against the union), or
- **S**urveil or spy.

TIPS are fairly self-explanatory. Logically, you can't threaten to retaliate against anyone who expresses interest in joining a union. You can't grill your employees to find out "who's behind all this, who's driving it, and who's the main voice to the union." While you have the right to speak with your employees about what's ailing them and even attempt to remedy what's broken, you can't promise that you'll fix something "if the employees don't go union." And you can't surveil or spy by looking to see what's going on and where and when. In short, you can't take any adverse action simply because an employee supports a union, votes to join a union, or participates in any activity deemed "concerted and protected" under the National Labor Relations Act without expecting to be charged with "unlawful discrimination." Further questions should be directed to your labor lawyer for more specific information.

Just remember: if an employer gets a report that there is or appears to be union activity, it should move aggressively to start its own countercampaign. But do so carefully: mistakes can be costly. Follow the guidance from your labor attorney very closely, and *when in doubt, don't*. The company is responsible for the acts of its supervisors if committed within the scope of managerial authority. Even the *appearance* of ill will on the employer's part could incentivize unionization or legal challenges. The same goes for restricting the placement of union flyers: if you see them, don't remove them. Simply notify your management team and labor counsel to find out what's contained in the message, where the flyers are placed, and the like. But there are rules and considerations regarding the placement of literature that can be "protected activities" as well, so follow the legal guidance that you receive carefully.

Workers are nervous going through this—having their anger stoked and their vulnerabilities revealed, while worrying about retaliation or losing their jobs. Direct personal communication with specific employees by effective and well-trained managers, combined with insightful communications from senior management, will be the optimal strategy for combating the union narrative and steering your employees in a different direction. But things can turn visceral and personal very quickly, both between management and staff and between staff and staff. Let cooler heads prevail through such trying times. Be sure to "stick closely to the script" and relay management's position that it would prefer to communicate directly with employees rather than through a union.

41

MANEUVERING AROUND STRIKES AND LOCKOUTS
Union Contract Fails That Leave Companies and Workers in Jeopardy

CONTRACT NEGOTIATIONS HAPPEN AT specific windows predetermined by the language in the collective-bargaining agreement. It's not uncommon, for example, for contracts to stipulate that they will remain in place for three years. Then, six months before the three-year expiration date, contract negotiations typically begin. Note that we're usually talking about preparations when we say "begin." It's actually in the union's best interests to delay the start of negotiations so that the contract actually expires at some point during those negotiations. Why? Because once the contract has formally expired, the union then has the right to invoke a strike— that is, an economic weapon used during bargaining to incentivize the company to give into the union's demands. Companies, likewise, have the right to "lock out" union workers in the period after the contract has expired, which means the workers are banned from the company's place of business without pay or benefits for the duration of the lockout period. Sounds pretty intense, doesn't it? Well, it's designed that way.

ECONOMIC WEAPONRY

Strikes typically break out when unions reject a "last, best, and final offer" from the company during collective bargaining. The NLRB stipulates that worker strikes are typically regarded as protected concerted activity as defined under Section 7 of the National Labor Relations Act. "Employees shall have the right . . . to engage in other concerted activities for the purpose of collective bargaining or other mutual aid or protection." Employers and unions each have their own weapons to use when collective bargaining breaks down. For unions, there are strikes, while employers may resort to "permanently replacing" striking employees (in cases of economic strikes only, not ULP, or unfair labor practice strikes—more on that next). This means that after the strike is over, the employees will not return to their jobs but will instead be placed at the top of a rehire list.

Special note: Unions won't want to risk members being "permanently replaced" during an economic strike. Therefore, the company can typically expect a striking union to file a ULP charge to try and get the strike deemed a "ULP strike," which removes the possibility of permanent replacement of workers.

What you need to remember is that labor relations and strike mitigation strategies are complicated and require guidance from qualified legal counsel, which you must follow to the letter. For example, not all strikes are the same and not all strikes are legal. Most strikes fall into one of two categories: economic strikes or unfair labor practice strikes. Depending upon the nature of the strike, and even specific details, a strike may be lawful or unlawful. Workers engaged in unfair labor practice strikes enjoy a higher degree of rights and protection than workers engaged in an economic strike.

Strikes are serious events by nature and can significantly affect both employers and employees. For workers, there is the obvious loss of income and benefits, and in some cases, the possibility of being replaced. For employers, even a one-day event can create serious issues if not handled properly, including disruption of operations, brand damage, loss of customers, and vandalism or violence. Strikes often result in the filing of unfair labor practice charges against the employer, carrying remedies that can include reinstatement and back pay. There are even different guidelines for a company's right to replace workers, depending on whether the strike is deemed to be an economic or an unfair labor practice strike. Specifically, in an unfair labor practice strike, replacement workers can only be temporary until the strike ends; with economic strikes, the strikers may be permanently replaced, though the strikers aren't fired but placed on a preferential rehiring list. Not surprisingly, whether a strike is an economic strike or an unfair labor practice strike can be a hotly debated issue, so once again, defer to senior management under the guidance of qualified legal counsel to determine how to react to such extreme workplace situations.

Expect your organization to provide you with talking points to explain what the company is doing to take countermeasures or to address a lockout. Communications will typically include logistics challenges like:

- Formal responses to picket lines and protests
- Transportation and access for nonstriking workers to be able to move easily and safely to, in, and between facilities
- Human resources planning may include the hiring of temporary workers as strike replacements, protection of nonstriking workers, and redeployment of management into production roles.
- Regulatory compliance is an essential element of a strike response plan, including reporting and documentation. The company will be dealing with many regulatory and government agencies. Police presence is not uncommon on the worksite during a strike or lockout.
- Supply chain issues are a major ongoing concern in any work stoppage, as the purpose of a strike is to stop

production. Contingency plans typically address the processes of taking orders, obtaining raw materials, running production, and shipping. New suppliers may be introduced during an extended strike.

Finally, be sure to ask specific questions of your labor counsel about what, if anything, may be said to nonstriking employees about the strike or picket line, or jeers or threats from coworkers on the other side of the line. True, this is meant to get ugly, but there are few greater opportunities for you to demonstrate exemplary leadership than when under the cloud of a strike or lockout.

42

ENGAGING IN UNION DECERTIFICATION EFFORTS

IT TAKES A LOT TO DECERTIFY A UNION. It's very much like a marriage: extremely easy to get into but horrific to get out of. And unions have been known to quickly turn against their members who were attempting to oust the union. (Think flat tires, keyed cars, and other shenanigans intended to intimidate union members pushing for decertification.) First, unions typically appeal to "restoring the American dream" by bargaining for a paycheck that supports raising a family, quality health care for all, a secure and dignified retirement, and the like. By framing their demands in terms of social and economic justice issues with very broad appeal, special interest groups—the community, political, religious, and civil rights leaders—are engaged to assert tremendous pressure on the targeted employer (or industry). After all, who wouldn't want greater public safety, living wages, and greater health-care access, right? Further, the Service Employees International Union (SEIU) is an aggressive union and in fact the nation's fastest growing union that lobbies for SEIU Kids First, helping families access and improve early care and education options for young children. Again, it would be hard to argue against that, right?

Here's the catch: unions, while organizing, can argue, lobby, appeal to, and demand these programs all day and night. What they shouldn't do is *promise* anything to organizing members since they cannot mandate what an employer is going to do with its money. Yet, it's not uncommon to see such promises being made during organizing campaigns. In fact, if unions lie, there are basically no legal consequences: it's a buyer beware (caveat emptor) situation in the eyes of the law. Workers, as sophisticated consumers, are expected to research what a union can or cannot do for them in exchange for the (roughly) 2 percent of wages that they pay the union for representation. If buyers are shortsighted and don't end up getting what they paid for, that's on them: next time they should be more careful with their money. (That's not the case with employers, however. It is against the law for companies to make promises to vote the union down because companies actually do have the means to make changes to pay, benefits, and other terms and conditions of employment. Therefore, if the employer lies and does not follow through on promises, the employer could be held liable for unlawful activity.)

All that being said, workers sometimes opt to oust the union. Two percent of a worker's pay who earns $50,000 a year is $1,000 right off the top of their gross income—closer to $1,500 before taxes are withheld. That's a lot of money to be pouring into a union's coffers, especially if the workers feel like they're not getting any value for their investment. When rumors begin to swirl that workers are looking to decertify their union, escalate what you've heard to your manager, human resources, and legal affairs. The disgruntlement starts like this: "We pay so much to this union, and it does absolutely nothing for us. In fact, they make things worse. We could do better ourselves by dealing directly with management rather than being forced to go through the union. They're never around and rarely return calls anyway. How do we fire them and begin to represent ourselves?"

WHAT COMPANIES AND MANAGERS MAY NOT SAY UNDER ANY CIRCUMSTANCES

Workers can remove a union through *decertification*: the process by which the NLRB allows workers to call for a special election to remove the union as their exclusive bargaining representative. What's important for you to remember as a first-time manager, though, is that companies or individual managers are not allowed to encourage or assist with decertifying a union. Read that as: stay away and let it play itself out. The effort to decertify must be led entirely by employees. But employees may reach out to other organizations to help, including the National Right to Work Foundation. Likewise, employers may provide "ministerial assistance" (only) to employees for help, meaning they may point out resources where workers can get help. Again, follow the directives of your senior leadership team before attempting to do any of this on your own.

Sample statements that managers, management, and companies may not make under any circumstances during the union decertification process:

"If you don't like paying unions, consider starting a union decertification campaign."

"HR will be distributing a union decertification sign-up sheet."

"If you don't decertify, I'm guessing there will be no merit increases this year."

"If you decertify, they'll be reinstating the tuition reimbursement program that was negotiated away during bargaining."

"I've heard that without a decertification vote, they'll be closing this facility."

Warning: such statements may actually invalidate the decertification process.

The object of decertification is to determine whether a union continues to enjoy "majority status in a bargaining unit." If not, the union's right to represent those workers is terminated. A decertification election is held to test the union's majority status. Once a union is decertified, it no longer has a right to represent workers or to negotiate on their behalf.

Once the petition is properly filed, the NLRB then sets up a secret-ballot election in response to the petition document. The NLRB determines the appropriate group of people to vote in the election. If 50 percent or more of the employees vote against union representation, the union will no longer have representation rights, and the employees will once again be able to deal directly with the company on issues related to pay, benefits, and working conditions. Remember as well that unions cannot prohibit employees from exercising their rights to decertify. If the union tries to pressure employees to stop a decertification effort, it should be reported to the NLRB because such interference is illegal.

There are numerous technical dos and don'ts that go beyond the scope of this book and are better answered by senior management, in-house counsel, or your external labor attorney, including filing period windows, "showing of interest" petitions, secret ballot election rules, and NLRB filings, among other things. What you need to remember is that workers can undertake decertification efforts only during nonwork times and in nonwork areas. They cannot use company equipment or resources. And most important: management cannot be involved in any way.

43

THE NATURE OF WORKPLACE
VIOLENCE AND WHAT YOU CAN
DO TO MINIMIZE IT

UNFORTUNATELY, NO BOOK ON OPERATIONAL MANAGEMENT can avoid covering the topic of workplace violence. The body of knowledge on workplace violence is immense; workplace and school shootings have unfortunately become relatively commonplace in our society relative to other advanced nations. OSHA, the Occupational Safety and Health Administration, is part of the Department of Labor and defines workplace violence as follows:

> Workplace violence is violence or the threat of violence against workers. It can occur at or outside the workplace and can range from threats and verbal abuse to physical assaults and homicide, one of the leading causes of job-related deaths.

However it manifests itself, the hard reality is that some two million American workers are victims of workplace violence each year, and some are at increased risk due to the nature of the work they do. Worker-on-worker violence and violence from personal relationships occurring on the job site remain a critical concern for employers, but many cases likely go unreported, lessening our true understanding of the significance of this threat.

To mitigate such safety risks, employers should establish a zero-tolerance policy toward workplace violence against or by their employees and communicate the message vigorously.

As an immediate second step, employers should establish a workplace violence-prevention program, which complements its safety and accident-prevention program. The violence-prevention program should be communicated via the employee handbook, a manual of standard operating procedures, and posters and other vehicles.

Third, employers are wise to provide safety education and training for workers, so they know what conduct is not acceptable, what to do if they witness or are subjected to workplace violence, and how to protect themselves in emergency situations. For more information on this timely and important subject, please visit OSHA's comprehensive resources at https://www.osha.gov/workplace-violence.

ACTIVE SHOOTER PREPAREDNESS

Of all forms of potential workplace violence, active shooter concerns are most important for most American workers and managers. The "Run/Hide/Fight" approach to defending yourself is worth briefly covering here:

RUN

When in doubt of a potential active shooter on company premises, evacuate as quickly and safely as possible. Identify your escape path in advance. Leave your possessions behind. As you flee the worksite, instruct others to follow you, but do not wait behind for others, even for the wounded. Keep your hands empty and visible to law enforcement so you won't be confused with the assailant. If you have a company badge, wear it so that it is clearly visible to law enforcement.

HIDE

If evacuation is not possible, you should shelter in place. Lock the door. If possible, cover a window opening that makes you visible to an outsider roaming through the hallway. Move furniture behind the door as a blocker or wedge to provide protection should the assailant attempt to break in. Hide under a table or desk or other heavy furniture and turn off anything that can make noise or otherwise indicate that people are present in that location. Be especially careful with cell phones: while they can serve as a communication lifeline to the outside world, an inadvertent incoming call or bling could alert a shooter to your presence.

FIGHT

If all else fails and as a last resort, engage the perpetrator in any way possible, including with makeshift weapons. Scream for help, including instructions to others ("Shooter here in finance!"). Fire extinguisher blasts may temporarily blind an assailant, providing precious seconds to escape. Extinguishers can also be used as blunt objects to strike an assailant's head or upper body area.

When police arrive on the scene, the first officers will not tend to the wounded. (That task will be reserved for the next wave of police support.) Follow police instructions carefully, keep your hands above your head in plain sight so that officers do not mistake you for the offender, and assist the police in tending to the wounded, if possible. For more information, please review the Department of Homeland Security active shooter handbook on the dhs.gov website.

VIOLENT REACTIONS TO BEING TERMINATED OR LAID OFF

What if you suspect that an employee may react violently to being terminated? Despite your best efforts at treating employees with dignity and respect at the termination meeting, some employees may react physically to being terminated. We hear about cases of employees returning to the worksite to exact revenge on their supervisors and coworkers. Bearing that in mind, let's address some important tips for avoiding violence during or after dismissal, a common "triggering event" of workplace violence:

- Conduct termination meetings as early in the day and as early in the week as possible. This allows the terminated employee access to people—even if only remotely—rather than allowing them to stew on their anger over the weekend without any communication. They can likewise get answers to their unemployment and COBRA benefit continuation services, allowing them to focus on their future rather than the past.
- Physically seat yourself between the employee and the door. In other words, you should have access to the door and not be blocked by the employee or your desk should an emergency exit become necessary. (Hint: change your office configuration now if you don't have direct access to the door.)
- Offer to continue an employee's EAP benefits if you expect that he is overly anxious about the loss of his job. This will provide continuing access to a mental health-care provider or resources for mental, financial, or legal help. (You can typically extend the benefit for a terminated worker with your EAP provider by paying an additional monthly fee for the individual for an agreed upon period of time—typically, three months.)

- When necessary, employ the services of a security firm to attend the termination meeting in plain clothes, to wait outside your office door, or to at least be standing nearby in the lobby. (Security firms will provide armed personnel for meetings such as these, but you should have an established relationship before any such meeting occurs. Read that: you might want to establish that relationship with a local security service provider now so that you can rely on them in the future.)

The company also has the advantage of explaining—several times if necessary—its need to separate the individual's employment. Managers can explain that employees terminated for cause typically receive unemployment insurance (that is, the company will not contest the individual's unemployment insurance claim). They can also confirm that no specifics regarding references will be released other than the individual's title and dates of employment. They can offer individuals help with filing for COBRA benefits continuation. And if outplacement services are available, they can introduce terminated workers to the outplacement representative who can help them update their résumés, strengthen their interviewing skills via role-play, introduce them to the firm's job board, and focus their energies on the future rather than ruminating on the past.

All this will usually go a long way in allaying the terminated employee's fears about the immediate future and receiving income while in career transition. More important, this open communication approach could go a long way in aiding an otherwise unbalanced individual trying to come to terms with the reasons for the termination and attempting to find fault with supervisors or coworkers.

44

SURVIVING M&A
Mergers, Acquisitions, and Integrations

NO SELF-RESPECTING BOOK ON management crisis and disruption can look past the eight-hundred-pound gorilla in the room: surviving a merger, acquisition, or divestiture and the subsequent integration that's to follow. Industry giants consolidate for myriad reasons, and we know many household names that have been through this successfully: Disney + Fox, Warner Brothers + Discovery, CVS + Aetna, and Dow Chemical + DuPont, just to name a few. And their reasons vary widely, including industry consolidation, value creation (that is, revenue generation and stock price increase), market share expansion, market diversification, acquisition of particular intellectual property, and tax advantages. And while all may be noble or critical justifications for M&A, the workers of those organizations—whether on the purchasing or acquired side of the equation—undergo tremendous amounts of stress, uncertainty, and concern about job elimination, and so much more.

One definite and often-cited benefit of a merger or acquisition lies in streamlining costs by eliminating duplicative staff functions (think HR, finance, IT, distribution, security, and other areas that can serve more in a "shared services" type of structure). But many M&A transactions are risky ventures that do not end well. In fact, according to most studies, between 70 and 90 percent of acquisitions fail. Most explanations for this depressing statistic emphasize problems with integrating the two parties involved, cultural mismatch, due diligence or deal structure error, external market factors, or failed post-merger integration. Whatever the reason, layoffs are often a natural outcome of merger and acquisition activity. In fact, some industry experts estimate that roughly 30 percent of employees are deemed redundant when firms in the same industry merge.

As such, M&A represents a unique opportunity in your career. The core question is, what do you and how do you approach your career when you learn of potential M&A activity coming your company's way? Following are certain approaches and considerations you might want to keep in mind when you learn of a potential threat posed by mergers, acquisitions, strategic alliances, joint ventures, and other changes.

STEP 1: Don't panic. Instead, take a collective breath to assess the situation by gathering as much information as you can.

M&A represents significant change and crisis. But crisis carries not only tremendous risk but opportunity as well. Besides, adding M&A post-merger integration experience to your résumé can give you a significant leg up on your competition as you move forward in your career because most employers consider it tremendously valuable experience. So, while bailing as soon as you hear about a potential M&A coming your way and getting your résumé out may be your gut reaction, it might be best to assess the situation objectively first. And besides the résumé value alone, significant changes in the corporate structure may create opportunities for voluntary leadership, cross-collaboration, greater responsibility, and potentially promotions.

STEP 2: Conduct a personal SWOT analysis.

SWOT stands for Strengths, Weaknesses, Opportunities, and Threats. A SWOT analysis is an excellent way to assess where you might fall on the spectrum of "keepers" versus those who are more inclined to be made redundant and laid off. Licenses, certifications, specialty knowledge of mission critical systems, and tenure might all work in your favor. Of course, you cannot know for sure how you'll fair because you won't know what talent exists at your level at the other organization. What makes this particularly difficult is:

- You won't know which merged department "wins out" in the end run. For example, it may be the acquiring company's or the acquired company's HR team that remains when all is said and done. Just because you're officially a member of the acquiring company (versus the acquired target company) doesn't mean that your department will be the one that remains.

- Your boss might not be your greatest resource for support. Of course, you should always speak with your boss for guidance if you have a strong working relationship, but mergers can do weird things to good people when they're afraid of losing their jobs and consumed with their own survival. For example, if an opportunity for you might become available in the merged organization, your boss might not embrace the notion of losing a solid contributor at a time when their team's output might be scrutinized. (Your solution: speak with HR or some other trusted resource for objective guidance and input in addition to or rather than your immediate supervisor.)

Whatever the case, make as an objective and fair analysis of your status as you can. Consider this an opportunity for career assessment on steroids: you'll rarely have a chance to look at your career more critically and objectively than when facing a merger or acquisition, so make the best of this "ancillary benefit" once it presents itself.

STEP 3: Decide where you stand moving forward and focus on what you can control.

There's no judgment (or self-judgment) here. Some people simply put their heads down and hope for the best. Others contact head-hunters immediately and get their résumé out on the street without hesitation. But there's a third option that might benefit your career interests best over the long haul: integrate yourself into the merger process. View this as an opportunity to promote yourself and your capabilities—there are a lot of moving parts involved, and you may need to turn up the volume to get noticed. First, the integration process itself is a dynamic, intense opportunity for career introspection and professional growth. Second, mergers typically take between six months and several years to complete, so there may be ample time for you to catch your breath and see where things begin to stack up before deciding to exit.

Third, understand that most people tend to fixate on what they can't control: decisions about who is let go, promoted, reassigned, or relocated can send your imagination into hyperspace mode. Do your best to remain objective and avoid panic thinking of this sort. Fourth, understand that if your position is selected for elimination and you're laid off, you will likely qualify for both a severance package and unemployment, giving you some breathing room to launch an effective job search.

STEP 4: Ask appropriate questions.

Companies that lead M&A activities undergo a "due diligence" process in which they inspect the target company's books. "Buyer beware" is indeed a core mantra and risk of merger activities, and if the acquiring company misses anything significant—underfunded pension liabilities, massive regulatory irregularities, or significant pending litigation—they inadvertently buy that liability at the time the purchase is complete. You should do the same thing. Ask your boss, your HR team, or a representative of the acquiring company any of the following questions:

- What is the reason for the merger?
- Do we know if our department is unique or if we'll be compared to and matched against a similar team in the other company?
- Will my position be eliminated?
- If I lose my job, will there be a severance package?
- Will my compensation or benefits change?
- Who will I report to in the restructured organization?
- Will my responsibilities change?
- Will I need to relocate?

STEP 5: Follow the following survival tips.
The following strategies will likely serve you well when in the midst of a merger or acquisition:

- Always be positive.
- Don't hide. Make yourself part of the renewed organizational structure, to the point you feel comfortable and as appropriate.
- Leave the past in the past. Accept that your "normal" is over and it's time for a new beginning.
- Don't speak negatively about the merger to anyone.
- Give up your turf. Attempting to control what you had or appearing to be territorial likely will not serve you well in a changing environment.
- Find ways to lead the change. Volunteer to support the change effort in whatever capacity you can.
- Be aware of aspects of corporate culture (yours, theirs, or the new company's) that form barriers to change.
- Practice resilience. Reconfigure what you do with what is needed.
- Remain cognizant of signs of being encouraged to quit. A "head in the sand" approach may not serve you well if you refuse to acknowledge a new reality that the organization has no place for you.

Following these tips and strategies might not result in your remaining with the newly integrated organization, either in your current or in a different capacity. But if done right, you can emerge from the process as a winner, no matter what the outcome. After all, if you walk away feeling equipped with greater self-knowledge, heightened visibility, and new skills, you'll have made lemonade out of lemons.

Likewise, even if you don't see a future for yourself in the post-transition organization, you'll have contributed to the integration process and made yourself more valuable to the organization throughout its transition. Finally, you'll have a valid reason for leaving the organization ("post-merger layoff") that you can share with a prospective employer, along with new interview discussion points about how you approached the merger, attempted to contribute to the post-merger integration, and how you handled a seamless and cooperative transition as you left the organization— all positives that prospective employers will see as huge pluses in your candidacy.

45

WHEN GLOBAL CRISES AND NATURAL DISASTERS AFFECT YOUR COMPANY AND ROCK YOUR WORLD

WE'VE DEFINITELY SAVED THE BEST for last in terms of the challenges and crises that you and your organization might face from time to time. Think about it: pandemics, social unrest, economic crashes, or natural disasters can become reality at any time for any of us. What's your role when disruption creates a "new normal" in the workplace? More important, how do you develop a reputation for successful leadership when exceptionally stressful conditions beyond your control leave your employees lacking information, afraid for their or their families' health and safety, or worried about supply chain issues and other practical outcomes of severe disruption?

At the time of this writing alone in early 2023, the following trends were in play in organizations worldwide:

- Inflationary trends and a lingering possibility of recession.
- Mass layoffs affecting the tech, media and entertainment, banking, and other sectors.

- Supply chain problems, which the World Economic Forum said are being spurred by rising costs, labor unrest, energy shortages, geopolitical uncertainty, and extreme weather.
- Worker burnout. (Think of health-care workers working double shifts, sixth and seventh consecutive days, and excessive overtime.)
- The Great Resignation—the pandemic triggered a record-high exit of Americans from the workforce.
- Quiet quitting, which, according to the Gallup polling organization, affected almost half of American workers who drew "mental lines in the sand" in terms of what they were willing or not willing to do for their employer.

While we can't address every type of global event or natural disaster that can come your way, we can work together to build a leadership framework to formulate your response based on human emotional needs. And I do mean "work together" in this instance: every situation will be different, but the suggestions that follow can serve as a helpful baseline to customize solutions and move through the macro changes that come your way.

This isn't meant to be easy, but facing severe struggle helps you grow and evolve as a leader faster than just about anything else. And in that growth, you hone your character, your leadership mettle, and your definition of self. Is it a selfish or a selfless image that you want to portray? Do you see yourself putting others' needs ahead of your own or putting your own needs first? Are you a calming influence helping others focus on their priorities, or do you turn a blind eye to this new reality that's upended everything in your current line of sight? There's no judgment here. But it's important to give thought to who you are and who you choose to be relative to the overwhelming changes that may come your way in an instant and affect your organization, employees, family, or general sense of well-being.

First things first: when catastrophe strikes, tend to the health and safety of your team members immediately, including finding a proper safe zone or shelter to shield yourselves from further harm. Second, listen to your senior management team and inform yourself of current priorities and resources, including the key message points that your organization wants all employees to follow and be aware of. Third, as the situation begins to normalize, ensure that employees and their families have access to food, water, and medical care, as needed. Fourth, as a stabilization phase comes into play, determine where work falls on the spectrum of family-safety-company and ensure that your employees understand that we're all in this together and that in times of crisis, we are all friends and neighbors in addition to coworkers. Put the human element first and keep a healthy perspective of the priorities that your staff members are likely concerned about.

"Getting through the storm together" and "not leaving anyone behind" become critical messages at times of extreme unrest. Exchange your "boss hat" for friend, neighbor, and helper hat and know that people will remember your kindness and feel more loyal to you if you're there to support them when they feel truly vulnerable. Disasters can leave employees anxious, displaced, and unable to work. Compassion and clear communication help restore productivity and a sense of normalcy over time. Be there for them as you would like the ideal boss to be there for you. Keeping this broader perspective in mind, let's develop a template to provide optimal leadership support through any type of crisis that may come your way.

Step 1: Go into immediate "crisis management mode."	• Inform senior leadership and authorities of injuries and significant property damage. • Tend to the wounded/minimize hazards. • Set up an incident command center where centralized decision-making can occur.
Step 2: Communicate, communicate, and then overcommunicate.	• Use email, posters, robocalls, texts, and any other communications means at your disposal. • Provide updates frequently to all stakeholders. • Create a public question and answer forum. • Remember, it is far better to say, "We don't know" and "We'll look into it and get back to you," rather than leave a matter unaddressed.
Step 3: Be clear about roles and next steps.	• Assign those willing to volunteer to help others in specific areas or with specific tasks. • Disseminate updates regarding on-site work expectations, amended hours of operation, or restricted locations. • Begin discussions about next steps, including cleanup and restoration.
Step 4: Remember that normalcy and healing begin as a marathon, not as a sprint.	• Demonstrate empathy, goodwill, and selflessness. • Recognize that humans heal at different speeds and in different ways; patience and flexibility are key. • Check in on your team's well-being and provide resources to help them and their families navigate through significant change.

STEP 1: Go into Immediate "Crisis Management Mode."

In a disaster, activate proper evacuation and safety procedures first. Likewise, remove or reduce hazards and tend to victims. Activate the emergency alarm and notify emergency services and senior management of injuries or severe property damage that poses safety risks. Gather your employees together in a physically safe space to ensure that everyone is accounted for. At that point, create an emergency plan (if your department doesn't have one already). Communicate with your executive leadership team to formulate a plan for handling the crisis. Coordination across the enterprise is key, especially at the onset of a disaster.

Share your plan. Your next step is to tell the entire team about your crisis management plan. Share what you know in real time. Ask for suggestions and feedback and make this all about "we" since no one—regardless of CEO or other title—will be a master of knowledge or wisdom under emergency circumstances. Provide resources that you may have available as an employer that workers can benefit from at home. (Think personal protective equipment, paper towels, disinfectant, masks, or any other supplies that your company has on hand and can distribute.) Demonstrate compassionate leadership. Be compassionate and empathetic, remembering that this goes well beyond the world of work and potentially affects workers' families and friends, financial well-being, or the house they live in.

STEP 2: Communicate, Communicate, and Then Overcommunicate. Remember that during a disaster, our fight-or-flight reactions kick in. People act on pure adrenaline. That means that emotions will be on overdrive, while cognition and logic may initially take a backseat. Under such circumstances, people tend to hear things out of context, misunderstand even the simplest instructions, and sometimes overlay their own fears into messages that distort reality. Therefore, it's critical that messages get repeated multiple times in various ways. Use all the tools you can muster in a short period of time, including company-wide and department-level emails, messages posted on your company intranet and internet sites, communication apps, texts, social media accounts, and even robocalls (automated telephone calls initiated by a computer program to deliver prerecorded messages).

Use every channel available. Using multiple channels simultaneously helps you reach people wherever they are, which can vary in a disaster, depending on the availability of power and cell towers and access to desktops and mobile devices. Check in regularly with your employees and encourage them to do the same. Keep in mind that power shortages and outages are common during disasters, so make your messages as brief as possible.

But don't forget the human touch: ask employee-volunteers to stand at various locations and communicate updates and instructions in real time (especially if you have a specific location where you'd like all employees to gather). Likewise, post bold written updates on poster boards or paper, especially marking unsafe areas with limited or no access or pointing employees to the gathering area. Assign a "runner" from your team to float back and forth between the incident command center (wherever the key decisions and updates are coming from) and your office or building. And try and gather questions from employees and disseminate responses to the most often asked queries that come your way. Note as well that it's always a good idea to send messages on a regular and predictable schedule (such as every morning at 8:00 a.m. and every evening at 5:00 p.m.).

STEP 3: Be Clear About Roles and Next Steps.
Everyone in "shock mode" clearly experiences trauma to some degree. Some naturally handle it better than others, including first-time managers. Simply rest assured that people will have questions beyond the current crisis in short order, so it's important that you're clear about next steps. Once the initial impact and shock of a devastating event have passed, everyone's attention will begin to turn toward cleanup and restoration efforts. As this phase gets underway, assume that your team members will not know what you or the company expects of them. Your communication, therefore, should spell out everything very clearly and in literal terms, including:

- office hours for the days/weeks ahead (including modified or regular schedules)
- flexibility to work remotely or part-time (if that's an option)
- how to log time off work due to a disaster (for example, "excused time off")

- whether it's okay to bring children into the office if school is out
- how often staff members need to update their supervisor on their availability
- which parts of the building or complex are unsafe or not functional
- dress codes, if relaxed from your usual protocol
- customer and vendor updates, especially if any are temporarily closed
- road conditions and traffic workarounds
- ongoing support from the authorities (such as, fire, police, National Guard)

In short, all employees on your team should know what they are expected to do, where they are expected to report, and when they should be present at work versus remote. Keep this communication flowing through the first days of a crisis to create a sense of security and confidence in your team members. And if you haven't done so already, be sure to create a sheet with employees' personal contact information (including personal cell and home phone) so that everyone on your team knows how to get a hold of everyone else.

STEP 4: Remember That Normalcy and Healing Begin as a Marathon, Not as a Sprint.

Disaster resiliency depends on open communication, goodwill, and empathy above all else. Crises jolt our physical and emotional systems, requiring on-the-spot solutions that include emergency response plans, incident command centers, communications measures, and so much more. And that's the way it will always be. We can't prepare for everything, and certain people may panic and lose their sense of self during an emergency. That's where role-model leadership comes in. Holistic disaster management looks not only at economic, operational, and environmental factors but most importantly at the human side of impact.

No one can experience a magnitude of destruction or disaster and not be changed by it, and it will take time for everyone to work through it. There's no rule book or set timeline for getting back to normal, or even establishing a "new normal." Everyone processes change differently. Check on your team's well-being throughout the weeks following a disaster or disruptive event. Recognize that recovery may take weeks or months, and sometimes even years, depending on the level of loss that people may have suffered. That's why it's important that you provide your team members with resources to help them and their families navigate through this.

Share freely information that you become aware of, point employees in the direction of your employee assistance program provider if they need additional mental, financial, or legal help, and practice the adage "Each to their own without judgment." Healing begins when acceptance of this new normal begins. You can't necessarily control when that's going to happen for each of your team members, but you can create the right and certain conditions for healing to begin through your leadership. Above all, show appreciation and gratitude, recognize team members who go out of their way to help others, entrust employees with new responsibilities, and provide individualized support to the extent you can.

Finally, keep things simple. Make it easy for employees to give back to the community by volunteering and donating goods and services. There's a universal message that says "You cannot give away that which you don't already have," so allowing employees to help others in need creates a sense of healing and peace of mind better than just about anything else. Never underestimate the power of even the simplest acts of kindness. Lead by example, and practice selfless leadership by putting others' needs before your own. Rarely will selfless leadership be more needed than during the time of disaster or its aftermath. You may just find that compassion, empathy, goodwill, and clear communication will foster long-lasting results, such as increased camaraderie among employees and loyalty that transcends your organization.

As Winston Churchill once said, "Never let a good crisis go to waste," meaning that dramatic change creates the opportunity for people to reinvent themselves and grow exponentially, including professionally, personally, and spiritually. Be that gift to your team members—especially during times of anxiety, confusion, and chaos—and know in your heart that you have the ability to lead through whatever challenges may come your way, making your team stronger and the world a better place.

CONCLUSION

The First-Time Manager: Leading Through Crisis is a timely book because of the intense changes we face in the new millennium. And the pace of change will only increase as we continue into the second half of the twenty-first century: technology, globalization, and demographics will cause tectonic shifts in our understanding and capabilities in every element of the human spectrum. What won't change, however, is the ability to relate to one another, to socialize, to give back, and to serve as role models in the business world and beyond.

When the authors of the original *First-Time Manager*—Loren B. Belker, Jim McCormick, and Gary S. Topchik—concluded their seventh edition of the book in 2021, they wrote:

> Although events beyond your control do have an impact on your life, you can control how and what you think. That in turn controls your reaction to these events. . . . We must grow. This book is devoted to exploring how you manage your people, but equally important is seeing you grow as a total person. . . . The system itself isn't the payoff; the product isn't the payoff; your impact on the people whose lives you touch is what is important.

And so too we find ourselves at this wisdom point of reflection: a greater awareness that we're all in this together, that life is too short to waste energy on unnecessary drama, and that developing a greater sense of empathy for those around us bears the mark of an enlightened leader. Leadership is the greatest gift the workplace offers because it permits you to influence others to follow your lead, to find their own traction in a world filled with significant challenge as well as tremendous potential. We work best *through* others, not *despite* them. We inherently understand that the greatest leaders are not the ones with the most followers but the ones who create the greatest number of leaders in turn. Make of your life a gift. Yes, even in the big bad business world, selfless leadership defines our way. Even despite our fears that others may take advantage of our goodness, the arc and trajectory of outstanding leadership bends toward people we like, admire, and respect.

So much is written on employee engagement and satisfaction and spiking performance and productivity. But seen through a different lens, it's simply a matter of becoming someone's favorite boss. A "favorite boss" is a prism through which engagement, satisfaction, and productivity flow. After all, who wouldn't give discretionary effort in support of a boss who always has your back? Ask someone about the best boss they've ever had, and you'll hear that she:

Provided us a safe place to grow	Developed us as leaders
Opened career doors	Inspired us to stretch higher
Defended us when we needed it	Led by example
Recognized us and told us our work mattered	Forgave us when we made mistakes and helped us learn from them

And the list goes on, of course. But when people can say, "Nina seemed to have more faith in me than I had in myself" or "Sam almost made me feel like I could never do anything wrong," you'll have created the foundation for people to soar.

Crisis leadership may be our new normal, but little has changed in terms of the basic formula of human connection: those of us fortunate enough to grow and develop talent do so through relationship. Pay it forward. Teach what you choose to learn. And remember that, when in doubt, you should err on the side of compassion. From this peace of mind and wisdom may you create opportunities for people to do their very best work every day and reflect on your contribution to their careers for the rest of their lives.

ACKNOWLEDGMENTS

My very special thanks to a team of subject matter experts that helped with select portions of this manuscript as it made its way through the various stages of editing—all dear friends and exceptionally successful business associates whom I admire more than they know. . . .

- Jacqueline Cookerly Aguilera, partner in the labor and employment practice group at Morgan, Lewis & Bockius LLP in Los Angeles
- Christopher Olmsted, managing shareholder at Ogletree Deakins in San Diego, California
- Henry E. Farber, mediator at RainierADR PLLC and thirty-five-plus-year labor and employment attorney in Washington and California
- Elizabeth Holman, mindful mental health leader and president of The Holman Group, a mental health specialty plan in Los Angeles
- Eve Nasby, president of Band of Hands, a San Diego gig-economy platform and workforce mechanics solution for small businesses looking to leverage great W-2 talent

Thank you all for your time and effort in bringing this manuscript to life and my deepest appreciation for all you do.

APPENDIX 1

Recognizing and Responding to a Person in Crisis

Emotions can often run high in the workplace. Sometimes, they can cause you to say or do things that you may later regret. But the only person responsible for your emotions is you; you own them. That's why developing emotional intelligence is so crucial in protecting your professional reputation. This naturally extends to the people you manage. They look to you and take notice of the behavioral cues that you emote—both in word and via body language—to determine what is acceptable behavior and what crosses the proverbial line of inappropriateness.

Further, recognizing and responding to a person in crisis is a core responsibility and opportunity to help others when you become a first-time manager. It may be a person crying in their office; it could be someone appearing to hyperventilate and need to sit with their head between their knees. Note, however, that the general discussion that follows does not attempt to address formal "behavioral health crises," which can escalate to behavioral health emergencies when a person makes a threat of violence. This can involve the threat of suicide or threat of harm to others. Behavioral health emergencies are life-threatening situations (for example, suicide attempts, psychosis/hallucinations, threats to kill oneself or others, or loss of consciousness due to alcohol or drugs), which go beyond the scope of this book. In such cases, contact your supervisor, reach out to your employee assistance program provider, and/or call 911 for help.

That being said, you're required to identify crucial situations and engage in leadership interventions that help all people in the situation feel heard and respected. Likewise, you need to know how to professionally remove yourself from a situation at times and, when necessary, escalate the matter to someone else's attention (typically your boss or human resources). Outside of being there for one of your staff members or permitting them to vent, know when to escalate a situation for additional help. You're not in this alone as a first-time manager, nor are you the person's best resource for resolving problems that go beyond "basic first aid," which this appendix is all about. Therefore, when in doubt, err on the side of escalating the matter to your boss and to human resources for support.

RECOGNIZING A PERSON IN CRISIS

A person in crisis may exhibit any of the following warning signs and more:

- Abrupt changes in personality or "normal" behavior (that is, out-of-character conduct)
- Excessive worrying or fear
- Feelings of sadness, depression, or lack of motivation
- Ongoing anger or hostile or aggressive behavior toward peers, supervisors, or the organization as a whole
- Overreaction or defensiveness to even the slightest corrective feedback
- Withdrawal from social situations and self-imposed isolation
- Extreme mood changes, including uncontrollable highs or feelings of euphoria and uncontrollable lows, including crying
- Confused thinking or difficulty concentrating

- A "time-clock mentality" where the individual simply goes through the motions of doing work without engaging with others or ensuring completion of tasks or assignments
- Multiple physical ailments without obvious causes (such as headaches, stomachaches, and vague and ongoing "aches and pains")

These mini workplace crises may appear to "come out of nowhere" and can throw you and your other team members into a reactive state, especially if these challenges go on for longer periods of time.

SIGNS OF ESCALATION

Employees in crisis mode tend to reveal the following progressive indicators:

- Early warning signs—mild irritation
- Irritation develops into anger; accusations and blaming starts.
- Issues multiply: one problem turns into several.
- Generalizations: issues become clouded so that "nothing" is right, and "everything" feels wrong (that is, generalized, exaggerated language tends to come into play).
- Goals shift: the goal changes from resolving the conflict to winning an argument.
- Impasse: a refusal to cooperate or communicate takes hold.

When left unaddressed, these errant behaviors can exacerbate a workplace crisis. How you address the matter is important. But sweeping the matter under the rug and turning a blind eye is not fair to the individual or to the rest of the team. Remember again, however, that leadership is a team sport. When you feel a natural concern about someone's odd behavior or how it affects the rest of the team, escalate the matter to your boss and possibly human resources for guidance and to align the leadership team around your plan. After all, you're not expected to read minds, look into people's hearts, or understand the difference between a "minor crisis" and a "major reaction" in a particular situation.

RESPONDING TO A PERSON IN CRISIS

When it comes to intervening when workers experience a crisis of some sort, pay attention to the early warning signs of escalation and address them quickly. The sooner the person gets help, the better. Remember that tense situations can be diffused with active listening and problem solving. And again, if situations escalate beyond your control, get immediate help. Under all circumstances, engage in practices that help all people in the situation feel heard and respected.

- Keep your voice calm and talk slowly.
- Listen to the person with your heart and your eyes in addition to your ears.
- Express support and concern. Human empathy goes a long way when people fall into crisis mode.
- Ask how you can help. Deep breathing enhances oxygenation, and drinking water can help calm nerves.
- Encourage the person to seek treatment or contact their health professional, if appropriate. Remind them of the EAP or other resources that may be available.
- Give the person space. Calmness and peace of mind need to be restored as quickly as possible but not at the expense of the individual's natural timing.

When stress is equal to an individual's coping resources, a healthy balance will be maintained. When anxiety exceeds an individual's coping mechanisms, a crisis may ensue. Helping your team member keep stress levels manageable and making coping resources readily available will help everyone maintain that healthy balance. And no, you don't need to be a psychologist to know when to intervene. But always be the type of boss you'd like to have yourself: one that's concerned about staff members' well-being, one who will make it safe for staffers to make themselves "vulnerable" (in a healthy sense) when they need a guiding hand, and one willing to help others when they're generally feeling down. Finally, when in doubt, escalate. Use your own internal and external (EAP) resources wisely so that you don't inadvertently end up sharing non–work-related advice with employees who may be challenged by factors or feelings outside their control. Enlightened leadership is selfless leadership that knows its limits. Responding carefully and purposefully means that you care. Escalating when matters exceed your ability to help demonstrates wisdom and compassion.

APPENDIX 2

Navigating Your Own Emotions Through Crisis

No one else is responsible for our emotions; we own them, and we must know how to handle them. Anxiety, fear, apprehension, uncertainty, and stress are natural outcomes when experiencing crisis. But improving your emotional self-awareness and responding in a more positive and constructive manner is within our control. Learning how to manage and strengthen your EQ, or "emotional quotient," is akin to building new muscle. And unlike your IQ ("intelligence quotient"), which is pretty much fixed by the age of twenty, provides you the opportunity to understand, use, and manage your own emotions in positive ways to relieve stress, communicate effectively, empathize with others, overcome challenges, and defuse conflict. That's why leadership books abound: building stronger EQ increases your sense of empathy, self-awareness, and understanding of others, which are some of the most important ingredients for successful managers.

Recognize that feelings and emotions go hand in hand. What's critical is your awareness of when you're being dragged down into a rabbit hole of emotional distress. It's helpful to understand that linear progression of how and when this can happen:

Step 1: The initial event occurs, and your immediate interpretation (or possible misinterpretation) is triggered.

Step 2: The *feelings* you experience stem from automatic responses in your brain.

Step 3: The triggering of your *emotion* occurs, which is a state of mind that results from your body's physiological sensation.

Step 4: Your reaction or overreaction to the event dictates your response and sends a message to those around you as to whether you are in control, confident, or self-assured about a new way forward or in a more reactive state of panic, worry, or fright.

So how should you attempt to navigate your emotions through crisis? Said another way, how do you develop stronger emotional intelligence to lead more effectively through the sudden changes that crises often sweep in? The science behind emotion tells us that self-management techniques can be learned and strengthened to handle stressful situations more effectively. There are methods for preempting emotional flare-ups as well as recovering from emotional hijacking, which might look like this:

Step 1: Slow down.	Pay attention to your physical body and self-talk. Emotions are hardwired but not something we can't overcome with the appropriate level of self-awareness and self-discipline.
Step 2: Avoid negative self-judgment.	Recognize the emotion. Monitor your mental chatter for stressful thoughts. Acknowledge how you're feeling without judging yourself. Ask yourself why you may be feeling a certain way. (Internal honesty requires a high level of self-awareness.)
Step 3: Recast initial negative thoughts.	Pay attention to your inner dialogue, which tells you how you feel. Listen specifically for negativity in your self-talk. You can change negative self-talk into more positive thought, which leads to more productive and positive actions. Becoming more self-aware is about acknowledging and controlling your negative thoughts while focusing on solutions within your control.

Step 4: Focus on solutions that are within your control.	Use logic to reframe your emotions to neutralize negative emotions; shift your emotional state to think positive, not negative. Small wins are wins, nevertheless. In times of crises, focus on putting one foot in front of the other is about as much as you need to redirect energy in a new and more positive direction.
Step 5: See yourself in the eyes of others.	Emotions strike hard and fast. You suddenly feel different. Leaving emotions unchecked can negatively affect your relations with others. Remember that self-management is self-control. Mindfulness stems from managing your emotions while showing empathy for others. Judge no one. When in doubt, err on the side of compassion. But help others find and restore their peace of mind to the extent possible. Follow the adage "What you want for yourself give to another."

Self-awareness is the cornerstone of building emotional intelligence. Emotional ownership is a way of caring for yourself and noticing what's happening in your mind and body so you can remain healthy. There are additional techniques you can use to build self-awareness over time so that you are better prepared in an emotionally charged crisis to move from knee-jerk reactions to more thoughtful, deliberate, and confident responses:

- Eliminate all-or-nothing thinking (by avoiding "always/never" mental constructs).
- Be honest about your weaknesses: do you tend to overreact and become overly defensive? Do you avoid situations that you know you should address?
- Learn how to master deep breathing (slow, deep breathing and visualization exercises calm the mind). Practice the 4×4 method used by Navy SEALs before engaging in military action: breathe deeply for four seconds through the nose; release the air for four seconds through the mouth. Repeat for four cycles to oxygenate your blood and clear your head.

- Master meditation: tense and then relax all the muscles in your body, starting at your feet and moving up to your head.
- Begin journaling: writing things down makes it safe to express your feelings and quiet your mind by gaining a different perspective. More important, it eliminates the need to keep thinking about something.
- Look to professional mentors for guidance. Where mentors might not be available, mentor yourself by asking:

> The best advice I could give myself is . . .
> I'm grateful for . . .
> The biggest change I want to make is . . .

- Incorporate exercise and personal hobbies into your life to decrease stress. Drinking water helps calm nerves in emotionally intense situations by decreasing stress hormones.

Taking ownership of your emotions, becoming emotionally self-aware, and identifying your emotional triggers will go a long way in building your emotional intelligence muscle, especially during crisis situations. Adopting useful behaviors to help you more effectively manage disruptive emotions during crises is an excellent way to lead through current crises and better prepare for future ones.

APPENDIX 3
Leading Effectively Through Change

Change is the only constant in life. In a very real sense, life is change. But rapid change involving fundamental beliefs and assumptions about who we are and what we do and stand for can have a significant impact on the decisions we make and the way we communicate them. How do we define change? Change is an event or process that causes something to alter or become different than it was as it passes from one phase to another. It represents a break in our normal routine or a challenge to our status quo. The challenge of change grows stronger, however, when dealing with cataclysmic events like global crises and natural disasters. Likewise, whiplash reactions to changing rules (remember how quickly masking and testing mandates changed during COVID?) and company, team, and individual events can have a similar disquieting effect on ourselves and those we lead: introduction of new management, restructuring the workforce, implementing new technology, introducing new performance standards, adapting to new regulatory requirements, or extreme financial market conditions can leave employees feeling overwhelmed, exhausted, and angst ridden.

THE DYNAMICS OF CHANGE

It's important that we take time to understand our own feelings regarding the change we're experiencing before we react. We will not be as effective in managing change unless we explore and understand the dynamics of change and our own responses. Typical reasons for resistance to change include: "I have no idea what to expect," "How do we know what impact this will have on our jobs?" and "I wonder if the company will survive." Fear is the foundational element of resistance to change: fear of the unknown, uncertainty about the future, fear of loss of control, and fear of being changed. Author, professor, and founder of the Society for Organizational Learning, Peter Senge, famously wrote, "People don't resist change; they resist being changed." As such, people may not be resisting the actual change itself, as much as the feeling that they may have to change who they are. They might perceive that they are being asked to change their core values or personalities, rather than behaviors or habits. This fear includes responses like: "I already have a set way of things that works" and "I can't be expected to be someone I'm not."

Often, the change itself is not negative; it is our perception and attitude about the change that make it seem negative. Fear of loss creates a sense of losing something: for example, control, autonomy, competence, money, or freedom. Typical human responses to change include "I like things just the way they are" and "Why do we have to do this anyway?" Sometimes this stems from a fear of more work: typical internal resistance responses include: "I already have too much work to do," "How long is it going to take to get up to speed on this?" and "I'm already underpaid for what I do." Likewise, fear of a negative outcome may be the key driver behind the resistance: "I could fail in my new job," "These things never work out the way they should," and "This new system isn't going to be effective."

On the other hand, change can also be viewed as a positive, exciting, and even enjoyable experience that creates new opportunities. For example, self-imposed change (for example, a promotion or transfer to a new part of the company) typically creates a positive, uplifting experience rather than a sense of immediate resistance. The key, then, lies in perception. Change your perspective and you'll change your perception. In other words, consider altering the way you regard something, and you will likely experience it differently. No, changing your perspective will not change the external effects of the situation: there may still be layoffs, for example. But coming from the thirty-thousand-foot view (rather than in the weeds) provides a healthy sense of distance that allows for career introspection. For example, "Even if I were to lose my job or if I had to lay off members of my team, I'll be okay. Layoffs are a rite of passage in corporate America: companies expect you to have weathered a storm or two during your career. They're more interested in seeing how I bounce back and recover from a corporate downsizing. So, if it happens to me, I'll be okay and see it as a learning experience and opportunity to prove my agility and resourcefulness. And if it doesn't happen to me, I'll be grateful but mindful of how I can help others weather the storm." As always, selfless leadership and career introspection provide an inner peace of mind that help us through the crises and challenges that come our way throughout our careers.

BECOMING A HEALTHY AGENT OF CHANGE

A change agent is someone who leads, guides, and supports change. There are certain characteristics, behaviors, and actions required to be an effective change agent, and as you'd expect, communication is key. As a rule, what we tell ourselves about the change strongly influences the degree to which we embrace or resist change. Identifying our own emotions and then gathering factual information about the change will help us neutralize the resistance in ourselves and others. The following tips and guidelines help successful change agents lead through the unexpected:

- Allow for feelings of anxiety, worry, or anger. (Remember, feelings aren't right or wrong; they just are.)

- Communicate the "whys" and the positives of the change (that is, personal benefits). Again, perspective and perception go hand in hand.
- Make it safe to let go of the past. In other words, look to the future with eager anticipation, to the extent possible. (Layoffs, on the other hand, may make it hard to do so.)
- Develop and articulate a clear plan for the future. Clear direction and well-defined goals and roles help allay fear and anxiety.
- Provide sufficient training and coaching. Help your staff members appreciate the opportunity to increase their relevance by acquiring new skills and systems mastery.
- Boost morale through team building. People will resist change less if they feel they're part of a strong, cohesive team and not in it alone.
- Practice patience. Each hurdle is a step closer to the ultimate goals of the change, yet people process feelings at very different speeds and in different ways. Allow people an appropriate amount of time to come to terms with their "new normal."

Likewise, make it safe for people to express their concerns. No, you won't want to inadvertently create a crying towel that perpetuates feelings of loss or resentment. But if you don't encourage people to share their feelings, their negative emotions could affect their work. Help guide them through these feelings in a healthy and constructive way. Going through change together can help bond a team of employees. Core fears are usually associated with resistance to change; recognizing them in yourself and others is key to moving forward constructively. What do effective and successful change agents have in common in assisting others in understanding the needs for change? Typically, you'll find the following characteristics and skills present:

CHARACTERISTIC	WHAT IT LOOKS LIKE	WHAT IT FEELS LIKE
VISIONARY THINKING	The ability to see beyond what is going on in the present and demonstrate a broader vision of what is possible (that is, not getting lost in the weeds)	"How do we change this narrative from 'Why is that happening to us?' to 'Why is this happening for us?' What are we meant to learn. How will this make us stronger?"
RESILIENCY	The ability to absorb high levels of disruptive change while displaying minimal emotional stress because of their flexibility and high capacity to rebound	"Resiliency and change are the most important skills that anyone can have these days. This is a chance for us to prove our mettle and build muscle around change leadership."
COMMUNICATION AND INTERPERSONAL SKILLS	The ability to engage others in dialogue, make others feel "safe in their skin," and encourage others that they're capable of success in the new environment	"I want to hear what you have to say, so we're going to talk through your concerns. I want to make it safe for you to go through this successfully by focusing on the positive and leaving behind any sense of guilt or anger."
COACHING SKILLS	The ability to encourage open, honest feedback and earn the trust of others by addressing perception challenges and potentially negative feedback in a constructive way with respect and candor	"I know we're capable of making this happen. What can I help with and what do you need from one another?"
FACILITATION SKILLS	The ability to help team members work together in a collaborative manner, especially in larger group meetings where many of the change discussions take place	"How are we going to agree as a group what our objectives are? How do we ensure that we have enough structure and clarity in place to move forward on a positive footing?"

CHARACTERISTIC (CONT.)	WHAT IT LOOKS LIKE (CONT.)	WHAT IT FEELS LIKE (CONT.)
EMOTIONAL INTELLIGENCE	Ability to practice self-awareness and self-regulation in managing your own emotions and eliciting a similar effect on others, especially in terms of incorporating diversity of thoughts, ideas, and voices	"I'm sensing that employees are feeling a lot of stress right now. That's understandable—I do too. What can we do to support one another through this and make sure we're all successful?"
CONFLICT MANAGEMENT SKILLS	Ability to recognize when stress is elevating to the conflict level; an ability to remain calm and objective in helping others work out their differences	"I know we have different views of the situation. Let's take an objective look at what's happening and how we can address this issue. Better yet, let's do so by supporting one another through this and giving everyone time to process these changes in their minds."
SELF-MOTIVATION	When the going gets tough, the change agents get going! High capacity to stay focused on and passionate about their own work while motivating others	"How do we demonstrate our ability to master the changes coming our way? What do we want other departments to say about our ability to lead through this and become early adopters?"
SELFLESS LEADERSHIP	A heightened awareness of others' needs and placing others' needs ahead of your own and expecting them to respond in kind	"How do we apply the adage 'What you want for yourself, give to another' to this new change? How can we have one another's backs and make sure that no one gets left behind."
SELF-AWARENESS AND EMPATHY	Listening with your eyes and heart in addition to your ears, and sharing a common bond with someone experiencing pain or loss	"Empathy sounds like you truly care. It doesn't sound like you're trying to solve the problem, and you're not dismissing the issue. You're simply being present for someone else in their time of need."

Not only can supervisors and managers help lessen their employee's potential resistance to change, they can also boost morale, confidence, and a sense of team unity throughout the change. Where do you stand relative to these ten characteristics and skills? What are your top three strengths? Which three do you recognize that you need to develop? This particular list of characteristics will better define your leadership brand and abilities better than just about anything else. As we end this book, take these ten skill sets with you and hone them over the course of your career. You will become a more effective, compassionate, and resilient leader as a result.

INDEX

ABOUT THE AUTHOR

PAUL FALCONE (WWW.PAULFALCONEHR.COM) is principal of Paul Falcone Workplace Leadership Consulting, LLC, specializing in management and leadership training, executive coaching, international keynote speaking, and corporate offsite retreats. He's the former chief human resources officer (CHRO) of Nickelodeon Animation Studios and former head of international human resources for Paramount Pictures in Hollywood. Paul served as head of HR for the TV production unit of NBCUniversal, where he oversaw HR operations for NBC's late night and primetime programming lineup, including *The Tonight Show*, *Saturday Night Live*, and *The Office*. Paul is a renowned expert on effective interviewing and hiring, performance management, and leadership development, especially in terms of helping companies build higher-performing leadership teams. He also has extensive experience in healthcare/ biotech and financial services across international, nonprofit, and union environments.

Paul is the author of a number of HarperCollins Leadership, AMACOM, and SHRM books, many of which have been ranked on Amazon as #1 bestsellers in the areas of human resources management, labor and employment law, business mentoring and coaching, communication in management, and business decision-making and problem-solving. Bestselling books like *101 Tough Conversations to Have with Employees*, *101 Sample Write-Ups for Documenting Employee Performance Problems*, and *96 Great Interview Questions to Ask Before You Hire* have been translated into Chinese, Vietnamese, Korean, Indonesian, and Turkish.

Paul is a certified executive coach through the Marshall Goldsmith Stakeholder Centered Coaching program, a long-term contributor to SHRM.org and *HR Magazine*, and an adjunct faculty member in UCLA Extension's School of Business and Management, where he's taught courses on workplace ethics, recruitment and selection, legal aspects of human resources management, and international human resources. He is an accomplished keynote presenter, inhouse trainer, and webinar facilitator in the areas of talent management and effective leadership communication.